The Charter Revolution
and the Court Party

The Charter Revolution
and the Court Party

F.L. Morton & Rainer Knopff

broadview press

Canadian Cataloguing in Publication Data

Main entry under title:

The Charter revolution and the Court party

Includes bibliographical references and index.

ISBN 1-55111-089-X

1. Canada. Canadian Charter of Rights and Freedoms. 2. Canada. Supreme Court. 3. Political questions and judicial power – Canada. 4. Civil rights – Canada. I. Knopff, Rainer, 1948- . II. Morton, F. L. (Frederick Lee), 1949- .

KE4381.5.Z85C533 2000   342.71'085   C00-930213-1
KF4483.C519C42 2000

Broadview Press Ltd., is an independent, international publishing house, incorporated in 1985.

North America:
P.O. Box 1243, Peterborough, Ontario, Canada K9J 7H5
3576 California Road, Orchard Park, NY 14127
TEL: (705) 743-8990; FAX: (705) 743-8353;
E-MAIL: customerservice@broadviewpress.com

United Kingdom:
Turpin Distribution Services Ltd.,
Blackhorse Rd., Letchworth, Hertfordshire SG6 1HN
TEL: (1462) 672555; FAX (1462) 480947; E-MAIL: turpin@rsc.org

Australia:
St. Clair Press, P.O. Box 287, Rozelle, NSW 2039
TEL: (02) 818-1942; FAX: (02) 418-1923

www.broadviewpress.com

Broadview Press gratefully acknowledges the financial support of the Ministry of Canadian Heritage through the Book Publishing Industry Development Program.

Design and composition by George Kirkpatrick
Cover photo by Peter Christopher

PRINTED IN CANADA

for Walter Berns

CONTENTS

PREFACE

As recently as 1966 the Supreme Court of Canada was described as "the quiet court in the unquiet country." Today this same Court often takes centre stage in Canada's political drama. Scarcely a week goes by without a front-page story reporting yet another controversial court ruling. The Court is now as unquiet as the country.

How did this happen? How did an institution that for more than a century occupied an important but secondary role in our political system suddenly become such a pivotal player? Most commentators attribute this institutional and political revolution to the 1982 entrenchment of the Canadian Charter of Rights and Freedoms. While there is more than a grain of truth to this explanation, it is, on its own, overly legalistic. Parchment barriers do not cause revolutions; leaders, elite cadres, and their supporters do.

Judges themselves are the most prominent leaders of the Charter revolution. The judges deny this, claiming that they do only what they are mandated to do by the constitutional documents. Nonsense! More often than not, they make up the law as they go along. In our 1992 book, *Charter Politics*, we described and analyzed the new judicial self-understanding that underlies the Charter revolution.

Judges did not – could not – make the Charter revolution alone. At every turn their innovations have been promoted and supported by a coalition of societal interests that strategically straddle the state-society divide. Despite important differences, these groups share a common interest in enhancing judicial power. Accordingly, we call this coalition the Court Party, and it is the subject of the present book.

This book culminates a decade's work, and we have accumulated many debts along the way. We presented the first version of the Court Party thesis in 1989 at the urging of our former colleague Professor Leslie Pal, now at Carleton University. In the interim, Pal's own work, especially his 1992 book, *Interests of State*, has greatly influenced our thinking. Professor Chris Manfredi of McGill University is a valued co-worker in the vineyard of Charter politics, and we have benefitted from his commentary. Over the past three summers, we have been ably assisted by several talented graduate students – most recently and importantly, Kelly Morrison, and before her, Kim Groenendyk and Noelle Chorney. In addition, Troy Riddell, Brenda Long, Shawn Ho, Lori Hausegger, Matthew Hennigar, Sam Bottomley and David Greener wrote excellent MA theses that have contributed to this work. Similarly, Gregory Hein and James Kelly generously made available to us their doctoral studies as well as their subsequent research findings. Finally, we have drawn freely and shamelessly from Ian Brodie's 1997 Ph.D. thesis, "Interest Groups and the Charter of Rights"; he taught us at least as much as we taught him.

Separate grants to each author from the Social Sciences and Humanities Research Council (SSHRC) helped to support much of the research that produced this book. In addition, F.L. Morton wishes to acknowledge the special contribution of the Calgary Institute for the Humanities, where he was able to work as a resident scholar in 1995-96; the Bora Laskin National Fellowship in Human Rights Research in 1995; and a research grant from the Earhart Foundation. Rainer Knopff thanks the Donner Canadian Foundation for its generous support in recent years.

The Charter Revolution and the Court Party incorporates and builds on a number of previously published studies: Rainer Knopff and F. L. Morton, "Does the Charter Hinder Canadians from Becoming a Sovereign People?" *Ideas into Action: Essays in Honour of Peter Russell* ed. J. Fletcher (Toronto: University of Toronto Press, 1999); F.L. Morton, "Dialogue or Monologue," *Policy Options* 20:3 (April, 1999), 23-26; Rainer Knopff and F. L. Morton, "Canada's Court Party," *Rethinking the Constitution* ed. Anthony Peacock (Toronto: Oxford University Press, 1996); F.L. Morton and Rainer Knopff, "The Supreme Court as the Vanguard of the Intelligentsia: The Charter Movement as Post Materialist Politics," *Canadian Constitutionalism: 1791-1991* ed. Janet Ajzenstat (Ottawa: Canadian Study of Parliament Group, 1992); and F.L. Morton, "The Charter Revolution and the Court Party," *The Impact of the Charter on the Public Policy Process*, ed. Patrick Monahan and Marie Finkelstein (North York, ON: York University Centre for Law and Public Policy, 1993). We are grateful for permission to draw on this material.

LIST OF ABBREVIATIONS

AFN	Assembly of First Nations
BWS	Battered Wife Syndrome
CACSW	Canadian Advisory Council on the Status of Women
CBA	Canadian Bar Association
CCLA	Canadian Civil Liberties Association
CCLO	Canadian Congress for Learning Opportunities for Women
CCP	Court Challenges Program
CDCAA	Canadian Day Care Advocacy Association
CEC	Canadian Ethno-cultural Council
CHRC	Canadian Human Rights Commission
CIAJ	Canadian Institute for the Administration of Justice
CJC	Canadian Judicial Council
CJWL	*Canadian Journal of Women and the Law*
CLS	Critical Legal Studies
CNEO	Council of National Ethnic-cultural Organizations
COPOH	Coalition of Provincial Organizations of the Handicapped
CPF	Canadian Parents for French
CPRN	Canadian Prisoners' Rights Network
CRIAW	Canadian Research Institute for the Advancement of Women
CUPE	Canadian Union of Public Employees
DIAND	Department of Indian Affairs and Northern Development
EGALE	Equality for Gays and Lesbians Everywhere
FFHQ	Fédération des francophones hors Québec
FLA	Family Law Act
HRA	Human Rights Act
HRC	Human Rights Commission
ITA	Income Tax Act
LAPO	Legal Aid Plan of Ontario
LEAF	Women's Legal Education and Action Fund
LRC	Law Reform Commission of Canada

NAC	National Action Committee on the Status of Women
NACOI	National Association of Canadians of Origins in India
NAWL	National Association of Women and the Law
NCC	National Citizens' Coalition
NGO	Non-Governmental Organization
NIB	National Indian Brotherhood
NJI	National Judicial Institute
OLA	Official Languages Act
OLMG	Official Language Minority Group
OPSEU	Ontario Public Service Employees' Union
PCO	Privy Council Office
PMO	Prime Minister's Office
PSQ	Policy Status Quo
RCMP	Royal Canadian Mounted Police
REAL	REAL Women
ROC	Rest of Canada (outside Quebec)
SOS	Secretary of State
SSHRC	Social Sciences and Humanities Research Council
TCF	Test Case Funding Program
WJEC	Western Judicial Education Centre

ONE

INTRODUCTION

[The Charter represents] a revolution on the scale of the introduction of the metric system, the great medical discoveries of Louis Pasteur, and the invention of penicillin and the laser.

Chief Justice Antonio Lamer
on the tenth anniversary of the Charter of Rights, April 1992.

Just as the 1960s are remembered by Canadian historians as the decade of Quebec's "Quiet Revolution," so the 1980s and 1990s will be remembered as the period of Canada's "Charter Revolution." Since the adoption of the Charter of Rights and Freedoms in 1982, Canadian politics has been transformed. A long tradition of parliamentary supremacy has been replaced by a regime of constitutional supremacy verging on judicial supremacy. On rights issues, judges have abandoned the deference and self-restraint that characterized their pre-Charter jurisprudence and become more active players in the political process. As Chief Justice Lamer observed in 1998, "There is no doubt that [with the adoption of the Charter] the judiciary was drawn into the political arena to a degree unknown prior to 1982."[1]

Encouraged by the judiciary's more active policymaking role, interest groups – many funded by the very governments whose laws they challenge – have increasingly turned to the courts to advance their policy objectives. As a result, policymakers are ever watchful for what a justice department lawyer describes as judicial "bombshells" which "shock ... the system."[2] In addition to making the courtroom a new arena for the pursuit of interest-group politics, in other words, Charter litigation – or its threat – also casts its shadow over the more traditional arenas of electoral, legislative, and administrative politics. Not only are judges now influencing public policy to a previously unheard-of degree, but lawyers and legal arguments are increasingly shaping political discourse and policy formation.[3] According to a cabinet-level policy professional from Ontario, "Charter awareness permeates the corporate consciousness of government policymakers."[4]

The contrary fates of the 1960 Bill of Rights and 1982 Charter illustrate the magnitude of the Charter Revolution. The Bill of Rights was an ordinary statute, which applied only within areas of federal jurisdiction. Despite these limitations, rights advocates at the time of the Bill's passage hoped it would have a significant legal impact. They were to be disappointed. Between 1960 to 1982, only five of 35 rights claimants under the Bill of Rights won their cases before the Supreme Court, and in only one instance did the Court actually declare a federal statute invalid.[5] By contrast, the first 16 years of Charter-of-Rights jurisprudence (1982-1998) saw the Court ruling in favour of rights claimants in 125 of 373 Charter cases and striking down 58 statutes (31 federal and 27 provincial).[6] The Court's 1999 decision in *M. v. H.* (prohibiting government use of the traditional definition of spouse as "a member of the opposite sex") potentially affects more laws than all its previous Charter rulings combined — 58 federal statutes and hundreds of provincial statutes.[7] Hopes dashed under the Bill were revived and met under the Charter.

~ In the area of criminal procedure, the Court found that the Bill of Rights contained neither a right-to-counsel warning nor an "exclusionary rule" that would prohibit the use of otherwise reliable evidence that had been obtained in a manner that violated the rights of the accused. The Charter contains both, and the Court has not been reluctant to apply them stringently. It has interpreted the exclusionary rule in a manner that is at least as rigorous as the American practice. Similarly, the Charter version of the right to counsel has been interpreted to discourage any police questioning of suspects in the absence of counsel and to preclude judicial use of almost any form of self-incrimination at any stage in the investigative process. According to a comparative study, the accused in Canadian courts now enjoy more due process rights than their American counterparts when it comes to using evidence such as involuntary blood samples and police line-ups.[8]

In the field of abortion rights, the Court found no conflict between the Bill of Rights and the Criminal Code restrictions on abortion. In 1976, the Court sent abortion-rights crusader Henry Morgentaler to prison for ten months. When Morgentaler returned to challenge the same law under the Charter of Rights and Freedoms, the Court struck it down. In five subsequent cases, courts have rejected legal claims on behalf of the unborn, struck down provincial restrictions on access to abortion services, and overruled attempts by welfare agencies to provide protection for the unborn.[9]

With respect to issues of racial and sexual discrimination, the Court said that the right to "equality before the law" in the Bill of Rights required only equal application and administration of laws, not equal laws, and upheld a law that clearly discriminated against Native women. The Charter's equality rights, by contrast, have been read to prohibit not just clearly discriminatory laws, but also laws that, precisely because they treat everyone the same, have a disparate impact on some groups, an interpretation whose breadth again surpasses that of its American counterpart. Equality rights have even been invoked to prevent the repeal of legislation. When the government of Ontario fulfilled a campaign promise and repealed portions of the preceding government's pay equity law, the repealing legislation was deemed to infringe the Charter's equality rights.[10]

Paralleling the dramatic shift from Bill-of-Rights to Charter jurisprudence has been a new approach to remedying constitutional infirmities. Historically, Canadian courts have limited themselves to negative remedies: declarations that a government statute is invalid or that a government must cease behaviour found unconstitutional; to do more was considered undue judicial encroachment on legislative and executive functions. Under the Charter, the Supreme Court has sanctioned judicially ordered affirmative remedies. That is, they no longer just tell policymakers what they may not do but also what they must do. Courts now order legislatures to spend money on matters that would otherwise not receive any. They determine when, and to what extent, minority language school boards must be established. They have ordered provincial governments to create judicial compensation committees to determine salary increases for judges. Courts have even bypassed the legislative process altogether and rewritten legislation themselves to expand the scope of social benefit programs.[11] In its 1998 *Vriend* ruling, for example, the Supreme Court read "sexual orientation" into the list of prohibited grounds of discrimination in Alberta's Human Rights Act.

In a word, the courts became much more activist after the Charter's advent in 1982. Judicial activism, it is true, has become a loaded and hotly disputed term, with almost as many meanings as there are people who use it. But labels are needed for the judicial "readiness to veto the policies of other branches of government" that, after 1982, replaced the contrary inclination to defer to the other branches.[12] Whatever other meanings they may have acquired, activism and self-restraint are admirably suited to designate these contrary judicial dispositions and have long been used in that way. We are not inclined to invent new (and inevitably more awkward) labels.

In addition to being more activist, in the sense of squarely opposing the other branches of government, the courts have also been innovative in interpreting laws they uphold. In *Butler*, for example, the Court rejected freedom of expression claims and upheld the censorship of obscenity; it did so, however, on the basis of what everyone acknowledges was a novel, feminist understanding of the censorship law in question. No longer would the law be interpreted as a bulwark of public morality against sexual depravity; it would now be seen primarily as a way of protecting women and children against male oppression. Consensual erotica would thus be distinguished from the objectification of women for the pleasure of men. Catherine Mackinnon, a leading US feminist, characterized *Butler* as "a stunning victory for women ... [making] Canada the first place in the world that says what is obscene is what harms women, not what offends our values."[13] Similarly, in its 1995 *Egan* decision, the Court upheld the challenged legislation even as it added sexual orientation to the list of prohibited grounds of discrimination in section 15 of the Charter.[14] The Court thereby laid the groundwork for its subsequent activism on behalf of gay rights in *Vriend* (1998) and *M. v. H.* (1999). Thus, even when courts uphold legislation, they can have significant policy influence.

Until recently, many well-placed observers, including both Charter enthusiasts and Charter sceptics, confirmed the revolutionary character of Charter-inspired change, including increased judicial activism. On the tenth anniversary of the Charter, Chief Justice Lamer described its adoption as "a revolution on the scale of the introduction of the metric system, the great medical discoveries of Louis Pasteur, and the invention of penicillin and the laser."[15] Five years later, on the Charter's fifteenth anniversary, he was similarly effusive. "Thank God for the Charter," he proclaimed. "[People] just don't realize what it would be like if we didn't have these rights."[16] Similarly, constitutional scholar Patrick Monahan observed that in 1982 the focus of debate was whether the Charter transferred too much power to the courts, while in the early 1990s with the call for a charter of social rights the debate became whether to transfer still more power. The same conference at which Monahan made these remarks saw Peter Hogg, one of Canada's foremost constitutional experts, referring to the "tidal wave of rights consciousness that is engulfing the country," which "has permeated the consciousness of the current Supreme Court justices." Cataloguing the convulsions in recent Canadian politics – the failed Meech Lake Accord and the emergence of the Reform Party and the Bloc Québécois as political forces – Jeffrey Simpson suggested that they could not be understood without reference to the Charter.[17]

The inevitable cost of political prominence is, of course, becoming the object of political attack. The courts are not immune to this iron law of political life. If, to repeat Chief Justice Lamer's formulation, the courts have been "drawn into the political arena to a degree unknown prior to 1982," we should expect to see accompanying challenges to their policy influence. And, in fact, there has been a considerable rise of court bashing. Several news magazines have run feature stories castigating the Supreme Court for excessive activism.[18] Critics have urged the use of the Charter's section 33 "notwithstanding clause" to override controversial court decisions dealing with gay rights and child pornography.[19] Two of the premiers who helped write the Charter in 1981, Peter Lougheed and Allan Blakeney, have similarly endorsed utilizing section 33.[20] One province, Alberta, has pledged to use the notwithstanding power in response to any attempt by the courts to impose same-sex marriage and has introduced legislation to hold a referendum on any other use of section 33.[21] Alberta has also joined the Reform Party, *The Globe and Mail*, the *National Post*, several academics and one retired Supreme Court justice in calling for a more public and accountable appointment process for Supreme Court justices.[22] These challenges to the courts are themselves a sure sign of the judges' more influential policy role.

It would be a mistake to exaggerate the political opposition to judicial power. In the abstract, the Charter remains immensely popular with the Canadian public. In 1987 and again in 1999, national surveys found that 82 per cent of Canadians thought that the Charter was a "good thing."[23] In the same surveys, 62 per cent expressed greater confidence in courts and judges than in legislatures and politicians when it came to having the final say on rights issues.

Still, the growth of court bashing appears to have had some effect. In a 1999 survey, Canadians divided evenly (42 per cent to 42 per cent) on the proposition that "the right of the Supreme Court to decide certain controversial issues should be reduced." More dramatically, only 8 per cent of the respondents supported the status quo of unilateral prime ministerial appointment of Supreme Court Judges.[24]

These developments have caught the concerned attention of judges. Based on interviews with 101 appellate court judges between 1991 and 1995, Greene *et al.* reported that all but two "now admit to having at least some lawmaking role," but that half "were clearly uncomfortable with this newly visible role, as reflected by their responses to the 'crisis of legitimacy' question." This concern did not affect the Supreme Court, however. All five of the Supreme Court justices interviewed in the study "disagreed with the proposition that the Charter had created a crisis of legitimacy for the court."[25]

Since Greene's interviews, the Supreme Court has woken up. If Chief Justice Lamer thanked God for the Charter in 1997, a year later he worried that such Charter piety was not widespread enough. Addressing the 1998 annual meeting of the Canadian Bar Association, Lamer noted the Court's rights decisions have become "a matter of considerable public debate and controversy" and complained that "the tradition of judicial silence" forbids judges to reply to their critics. Worried that "the judiciary has no voice and no champion," he wondered "whether judges ... should be rolling up their sleeves ... and involving themselves in these public discussions more directly."[26]

Where Justice Lamer got the idea that the judiciary lacked champions is difficult to imagine. Defenders of judicial power in recent years have always outnumbered critics. Moreover, even the most controversial decisions regularly attract positive as well as negative reactions. Anyone who canvasses the commentary on the 1998 Quebec secession case, for example, would conclude that the Court's judgment received more praise than blame. Or consider *Vriend*, the Court's controversial 1998 gay-rights decision, which was as strongly defended in some quarters as it was criticized in others. The same is true of almost any case one cares to mention. To say that judges should be free to speak out publicly because they lack defenders is nonsense.

It is equally nonsensical to suggest that the tradition of judicial silence prevents judges themselves from replying to their critics. Judges may not engage in public controversy outside their courtroom, but they are far from silent public figures. They speak through their judgments, and those judgments provide ample opportunity to reply to critics.[27]

In any case, there has been no lack of response to the challenges brought by Charter sceptics. For example, Lorraine Weinrib, a University of Toronto law professor, insists that the Court's policymaking is mandated by the Charter itself. In an article aptly titled "The Activist Charter," Weinrib writes that, "The Charter is unequivocal in departing from the values of a stable, hierarchical, paternalistic and patriarchal society." "The Charter," she continues, "thus transformed the values and institutional responsibilities at the core of Canadian constitutionalism."[28] By Weinrib's account, the Supreme Court has only been doing what the Charter requires it to do.

Elaborating on this theme, Supreme Court Justice McLachlin, in a speech in April, 1999, suggested that legislatures were perfectly free to implement the new Charter values, and that judicial activism would be necessary only if they failed to do so. Experience shows, she argued, that when legislatures duck serious issues, courts "move in to fill the vacuum." A couple of months later, Justice Lamer made the same point. "If legislators choose not to legislate [on divisive issues]," he said, "that's their doing. If they prefer to leave it up to the court that's their choice." Noting that "a problem is not going to go away because legislators aren't dealing with it," Lamer thanked God (yet again) that the Court was there to step into the breech. "People say we're activist," he concluded, "but we're doing our job." But just why must judges act when legislatures fail to do so? As a *National Post* editorial put it, when politicians "avoid controversial issues, such as homosexual rights or doctor-assisted suicide, or child pornography," they "*are* taking a stand – for the status quo."[29] Justices Lamer and McLachlin do not explain why a legislative stand supporting the policy status quo is *ipso facto* an impermissible option.

A somewhat different approach is to deny that the courts have in fact been activist in their Charter decisions. Citing a 1999 statistical study of Supreme Court Charter decisions, Patrick Monahan observed that "when you look at the overall record, it's difficult to see where the court is usurping the role of the legislature.... If anything, they could be faulted in some cases for not being active enough."[30] For example, of the 98 Charter decisions handed down by the Court between 1996 and 1998, 12 invalidated statutes. Nor is the longer-term view much different: over the Charter's first 16 years, only 58 of 373 Supreme Court Charter decisions (16 per cent) struck down statutes. For Monahan, this does not amount to undue judicial activism. Likewise, Mary Eberts, a prominent feminist litigator, told a Toronto conference in April 1999 that, prior to the 1998 *Vriend* ruling, the Court's "policy of judicial deference to the legislature had become so pronounced that it almost seemed to make the Charter disappear." She went on to praise the *Vriend* judgment for bringing us "back from the brink of a potentially disastrous policy of undue judicial deference to legislative action."[31]

In this view, even if Justice Lamer was right in saying that the courts have been "drawn into the political arena to a degree unknown prior to 1982," they still haven't been drawn in very far. In effect, if the baseline for political involvement is almost zero – as it was during the Bill-of-Rights era – an increase that is huge in proportional terms may nevertheless be quite small in absolute terms. Fifty-eight statutory nullifications by the Supreme Court in the first 16 years under the Charter sounds immense in comparison to 1 such nullification in 22 years under the Bill of Rights, but it is still only 16 per cent of 373 Charter cases. In other words, whatever increase in activism there has been is not nearly enough.

Upon closer inspection, however, Monahan's analysis understates the Court's activism by counting only cases in which the courts struck down laws. If, as we have argued, judicial activism designates opposition to the policies and actions of the other branches of government, it includes more than the nullification of statutes. For example, approximately 54 per cent of the Supreme Court's caseload is drawn from the area of criminal law enforcement. Here, the Court's search-and-seizure and right-to-counsel rulings have transformed pre-trial investigative procedures, to the chagrin of the police and to the delight of criminal lawyers and their clients. Although this jurisprudence is clearly activist, many of the relevant cases overrule police practices rather than laws, and are thus not counted in Monahan's activism statistics. Had Monahan counted them, his activism figures would have been higher. Similarly, granting Monahan's definition of activism, the rate at which statutes are nullified should be based not on all Charter challenges but only on those actually involving challenges to legislation. Counting just Charter challenges to statutes over 16 years, the nullification rate is 32 per cent (58/183), not 16 per cent (58/373).[32] In addition, Monahan's concentration on the nullification of statutes fails to account for cases like *Butler* and *Egan*, which, as we have seen, involve considerable policy innovation in the very course of upholding a statute. Finally, global assessments of activism and innovation mask concentrations of judicial policy-making in certain areas. For example, a study of 47 cases involving feminist issues found a success rate of 70 per cent. Similarly, pockets of activism and innovation exist in litigation involving aboriginal rights, language rights, and gay rights. Indeed, as we noted above, the Court's gay-rights ruling in *M. v. H.*, a same-sex-spouse decision, lays the groundwork for invalidating hundreds of federal and provincial laws.[33] A single blockbuster case like this renders denials of judicial activism problematic.

With these qualifications in mind, let us for the sake of argument concede the claim that judicial activism and innovation represent only a small proportion of the courts' work. It is nevertheless a proportion significant enough to attract political interests to the courtroom much more often than in the past. It doesn't take a bonfire to attract moths; a small flame will do. The few sparks of activism and innovation generated by the Bill of Rights never ignited a flame of any size, and those interested in litigating policy change under that document soon gave up. The fact that the first 16 years of the Charter saw roughly ten times as many cases go to the Supreme Court as went there under the Bill of Rights shows that the current flame of judicial policymaking is bright enough to make the courtroom an attractive political arena. As Peter Russell has demonstrated in the case of federalism litigation, one doesn't have to be certain of victory to be attracted to the courtroom; to the contrary, legal uncertainty tends to fuel litigation more than legal certainty. A reasonable prospect that the Court will significantly influence an important policy decision in either direction on the partisan continuum is enough to fill the courtroom. And that prospect certainly exists under the Charter in a way that it didn't under the Bill of Rights.[34]

It is extensive recourse to the courtroom as a policymaking arena, not necessarily the particular outcomes of litigation, that constitutes the heart of the Charter revolution. Must interpreters for deaf patients be funded as a public health care benefit? Should spousal benefits be extended to gay and lesbian couples? May women go topless on city streets? Is euthanasia permissible? Do we have the right to possess kiddie porn?[35] To these and a host of similar questions, the judiciary is now certain to supply at least part of the answer. Sometimes rights claimants win in court; sometimes they lose; sometimes they do a little of both. Sometimes the judiciary has the predominant influence in a litigated policy area; sometimes legislatures do; sometimes both have some influence. Regardless, policymaking is judicialized, legalized, and conducted in the vernacular of rights talk to a greater extent than ever before. Therein lies the Charter revolution.

The Charter revolution has unfolded so quickly that it is hard to gain perspective on it. So much is so new that we still do not have the concepts to describe what is happening. As usual, understanding and vocabulary lag behind action. This book analyzes an important facet of the Charter revolution that remains inadequately understood: its social underpinnings. The Charter revolution is driven only partly by the constitutional document itself. More important are its judicial interpreters; more important still is a coalition of social interests — what we call the Court Party — that has promoted the growth of judicial power.

The Role of Judges

The Charter itself is not so much the cause of the revolution as the means through which it is carried out. The Declaration of Independence did not "cause" the American Revolution, nor the Declaration of the Rights of Man the French Revolution. A revolution cannot occur without leaders and the support of interested classes. Judges are professionally obliged to declare that the Charter requires their decisions, but this kind of formal legalism is hardly persuasive outside the courtroom. As we shall see in detail in the next chapter, the Charter rarely required the full extent of legal transformation undertaken in its name. Something in addition to the document is at work.

Judges themselves are at work, of course. Precisely because their decisions are generally not required by the Charter, judges are more important to explaining the Charter revolution than is the document itself. In 1983 at the

dawn of the Charter era, the late Eugene Forsey, the pre-eminent constitutional scholar of an earlier generation, predicted that the Charter would be
"a field-day for crackpots ... a headache for judges ... [and] a goldmine for
lawyers."[36] Forsey was certainly right about crackpots and lawyers, but he
was wrong about judges. Far from giving judges a headache, the Charter has
given them a second opportunity – the Bill of Rights was the first – to suc-
cumb to the seduction of power. It is the different responses of two generations of judges, especially Supreme Court judges, to this seduction that
explain the very different fates of the 1960 Bill of Rights and the 1982 Charter
of Rights and Freedoms.

The seduction of power certainly gave a headache to an earlier, more self-
disciplined generation of judges, a generation steeped in the doctrine of parliamentary supremacy. That generation, with only an occasional slip,
resolutely resisted the temptation. The judges' interpretation of the 1960 Bill
of Rights deprived it, and thus the judges themselves, of any real influence
on public policy.

Judicial restraint under the Bill of Rights was consistent with Ronald
Cheffins's 1966 description of the Supreme Court as "the quiet court in the
unquiet country." Similarly, in 1975, on the one-hundredth anniversary of
the Supreme Court of Canada, the historian Kenneth McNaught wrote that
"Our judges and lawyers, supported by the press and public opinion, reject
any concept of the courts as a positive instrument in the political process."
Also in 1975, the late Chief Justice Bora Laskin, one of the more activist
judges of his time, came to the same conclusion. "How foreign to our constitutional traditions, to our constitutional law, and to our concept of judicial review," he wrote, "was any interference by a court with the substantive
content of legislation." A decade later, just as the Supreme Court was about
to take an activist turn, Dalhousie law professor Wayne Mackay similarly
observed that "the Canadian judiciary has historically been quite different
from its counterpart in the United States [in that] Canada's judges do not
have an activist tradition."[37]

On this basis, J.R. Mallory confidently predicted that Canadian courts
"will be fairly circumspect in using the Charter to nullify the acts of governments and legislatures."[38] Law professors Berend Hovius and Robert Martin
also predicted that the Charter "would not transform the Canadian system
of government." They pointed out that "the approach of the court to the
Canadian Bill of Rights was characterized by restraint, a restraint which was
demanded by neither the status nor the wording of the Bill." Believing that
there was "nothing in the Charter which requires the abandoning of this

tradition," they predicted that the Supreme Court, would "strive to ensure that the legislatures continue to bear the ultimate responsibility for determining social policy...."[39]

We have seen how wrong such predictions were. By 1982 a new generation of lawyers had entered the legal profession. While still a minority, they were strategically situated in the law schools, and, through their academic commentary, enjoyed a privileged position for influencing judges, especially appeal court judges. Having carefully observed the development of judicial power south of the border, they saw in the Charter an opportunity for empowering Canadian courts as an agency of political reform. After some initial hesitation by lower-court judges, the Supreme Court, led by recent Trudeau appointees, followed the commentators' advice and seized the opportunity.

Judges often insist that their new activism is required by the Charter itself.[40] In 1985, for example, Justice LeDain proclaimed that the Charter's constitutional status as compared to the purely statutory Bill of Rights made it "a new affirmation of rights and freedoms and of judicial power and responsibility in relation to their protection." In 1997, Chief Justice Lamer conceded that under the Charter "very fundamental issues of great importance to the kind of society we want are being made by unelected persons." But, he asked, "that's a command that came from where? It came from the elected [Parliament]. We're heeding the command of the elected ... that's their doing, that's not ours."[41]

As a justification of judicial activism and innovation, this line of thought is persuasive only to an audience suffering from historical amnesia. There are numerous historical and contemporary examples of judicial self-restraint in the face of constitutionally entrenched rights. The Swedish constitution explicitly authorizes its Supreme Court to declare legislation invalid, but the Court has resolutely refused to do so.[42] Even in the United States, the birthplace of judicial review, the Supreme Court declared only two federal laws invalid during its first 75 years. Indeed, under Chief Justice Rehnquist, the contemporary American Court initiated a new period of judicial self-restraint, just as the Canadian Court took off in the opposite direction. Clearly, the activist or restrained exercise of judicial review under an entrenched constitution is more an attribute of the judges than of the document being interpreted.

The reverse is also true: if constitutional documents do not inevitably generate activism, neither is activism precluded by the absence of such documents. For example, high courts in France, Israel, and most recently Australia have engaged in considerable judicial activism in defense of rights without any explicit constitutional document.[43] Closer to home, the Canadian Supreme Court was more activist in its defense freedom of speech and religion during the 1950s, when we had no explicit rights-protecting document, than it was under the 1960 Diefenbaker Bill of Rights.[44] In sum, an explicit bill of rights is neither a necessary nor a sufficient condition for judicial activism. Where they exist, moreover, constitutional documents are generally vague enough to allow both activist and restrained interpretations; the Charter is no exception.

We do not mean to suggest that the absence or presence of constitutional documents make no difference at all. As Samuel Bottomley has demonstrated, although innovative judges can be very creative even without a constitutional bill of rights, they remain somewhat more cautious than their activist counterparts under an entrenched bill.[45] Similarly, where a constitutional document exists, groups without an explicit foothold among its provisions may have less legal leverage. In Canada, for example, environmentalists and property rights enthusiasts do not have the kind of constitutional platform that, say, feminists or ethnic groups enjoy under the Charter. Gregory Hein's finding that feminists have indeed enjoyed more litigation success than have environmental groups in the post-Charter era thus comes as no surprise. Hein is quite right in attributing the feminist litigation advantage to "the benefits of fully entrenched constitutional guarantees." Giving innovative judges more confidence, explicit constitutional provisions do tend to extend the scope and range of their policy involvement. Still, as we have just noted, entrenched documents do not guarantee judicial activism. The Charter may enhance the policy involvement of activist judges, but it rarely requires their policy innovations. Judges drive the Charter, not vice-versa.[46]

The Court Party

It would be as absurd to say that Canadian judges are alone responsible for the Charter revolution as it is to say that the Charter is itself the sole cause. Left to its own devices, the judiciary is hardly inclined to be a hotbed of political ferment. Like the Charter itself, judges are as much a means as a cause of the rights revolution in Canada. While they are in the vanguard of the revolution, they are being pushed as much as they lead: pushed by what we call the "Court Party." The Charter revolution, in other words, is characterized by the rising prominence in Canadian public life of both a policy-making institution (the judiciary) and its partisans (the Court Party). As

Mark Silverstein has noted "Political power [including judicial power] is inevitably a function of constituency."[47]

Using a different label, Charles Epp comes to a similar conclusion. A rights instrument by itself, Epp argues, is not likely to have much practical effect. Rights become practically powerful only where there exists a "support structure for legal mobilization" with at least three components: rights-advocacy organizations, government or foundation funding of test cases, and the availability of sympathetic and competent lawyers.[48] While Epp is more sanguine about the consequences than we are, we share his view that a rights-litigation infrastructure has been the necessary precondition of the surge in judicial power since the adoption of the Charter. Indeed, we argue that Epp has not gone far enough in identifying the actors and institutions that have contributed to the growth of judicial power in Canada.

Alan Cairns has coined the term "Charter Canadians" to describe many of the groups that form part of the Court Party coalition. Some of these groups were active in shaping the Charter's content in 1980-81 and then contributing the support necessary for its adoption; others sprang up in response to the Charter. They all seek to constitutionalize policy preferences that could not easily be achieved through the legislative process.

The Canadian Civil Liberties Association (CCLA) is one of the key interest-group members of the Court Party. At the stage of Charter-drafting, CCLA representatives lobbied hard to change the wording of certain key passages in its legal rights sections. They recommended that the right against illegal search and seizure be re-written as the right against unreasonable search and seizure. They urged the government to broaden the right to counsel to include the right to be informed of this right. The government's original version of the Charter preserved the Canadian (and British) practice of allowing illegally obtained evidence to be used at trial. The CCLA wanted this rewritten to exclude such evidence. The CCLA joined feminists and other rights-advocacy groups in calling for the rewording of section 1 of the Charter, which permits reasonable limits on rights, so as to place a greater burden of proof on governments. When the Trudeau government unveiled amendments to the draft version of the Charter in January 1981, Walter Tarnopolsky, the President of the CCLA, exulted: "It's incredible.... [I]t appears that they have given us just about exactly what we asked for." The CCLA has gone on to become one of the most frequent interveners in Charter cases before the Supreme Court of Canada.[49]

The CCLA is not the most frequent intervener, however. It ranks second to The Women's Legal Education and Action Fund (LEAF). Like the CCLA, feminists heavily influenced the wording of key Charter sections. Representatives from the National Action Committee on the Status of Women (NAC) derided the original version of section 1 of the Charter as the "Mac truck clause," alleging that it created such a large loophole that any exception could be "driven through it."[50] Like the CCLA, feminists successfully urged the rewording of their favourite Charter provision – section 15. Moreover, when the section 33 override clause was added to the Charter, feminists mounted a furious and successful campaign to add section 28, exempting the principle of the equality of the sexes from the override.[51]

Feminist groups then sought ways to take advantage of the Charter's broad wording. In 1984 the Canadian Advisory Council on the Status of Women published a study calling for the creation of a single, nationwide legal action fund to coordinate and pay for a policy of systematic litigation of strategic test cases. The study reported that, with the adoption of the Charter, "we find ourselves at the opportune moment to stress litigation as a vehicle for social change." A year later LEAF was launched, and it has gone on to become not only the most frequent but also the most successful non-government intervener in cases before the Supreme Court.[52]

What is true of LEAF is true of a rapidly growing list of organizations with a similar political genesis: the Charter Committee on Poverty Issues, Equality for Gays and Lesbians Everywhere (EGALE), the Canadian Prisoners' Rights Network, Canadian Committee on Refugees, and the Equality Rights Committee of the Canadian Ethnocultural Council, to name just some. These groups have been organized in response to the adoption of the Charter, and they all litigate or intervene in Charter cases, usually with the financial support of sympathetic public bureaucracies.[53]

Such interest-group litigation differs from that of the individual litigant who employs constitutional arguments primarily as a means to protect his own liberty or other interests and for whom the broader policy consequences of a judicial opinion are unimportant. For systematic litigation groups, the reverse is true: the primary focus of their interventions is to change the meaning of constitutional rules and the policy outcomes shaped by these rules. The actual dispute becomes just a vehicle for pursuing the policy objective. For example, one of LEAF's early Charter triumphs was *Andrews v. Law Society of British Columbia*.[54] Yet when LEAF intervened in this landmark section 15 case, it did not even take a position on the outcome of Andrews' dispute with the Law Society. Andrews, a male non-citizen, claimed that the law permitting only citizens to become lawyers in British Columbia was unconstitutionally discriminatory. LEAF cared not a whit about Andrews' fate. It was concerned only to ensure that the Supreme

Court adopt a definition of equality rights and discrimination that would best support LEAF's own policy agenda in future litigation. While Canadian interest groups occasionally used the courts prior to 1982, systematic political litigation has increased dramatically under the Charter, and systematic litigation groups lie at the heart of the Court Party.

In addition to litigating on behalf of their respective policy agendas, Court Party groups use the Charter in a variety of other ways. They employ the Charter and its judicial glosses as symbolic resources in the normal course of political lobbying. In an ongoing campaign of influencing the influencers, they attempt to affect Charter interpretation through Charter scholarship, the politics of judicial appointment, and judicial education seminars after appointment.[55] A well-organized group pursues the judicial protection and expansion of its Charter turf on all of these fronts simultaneously. This is the process aptly described by Alan Cairns as "Charter imperialism," whereby the Charter's "various clientele seek to extend its jurisdiction."[56] What we call the Court Party is the agency of this "Charter imperialism."

Needless to say, the Court Party is not a party organized to compete for elected office, like the Liberals or the Reform Party. It is more a loose coalition of interests than a disciplined political machine. Indeed, Court Party interest groups are sometimes policy enemies rather than allies. Feminists and civil libertarians, for example, have found themselves on opposite sides of such issues as rape shield laws and censorship of pornography. Similarly, feminists and aboriginal groups have crossed swords on the question of whether the Charter should apply to aboriginal forms of self-government.[57]

The Court Party coalition is not so fragmented, however, that its coherence or identity exists mainly in the mind of the analyst; when galvanized into action, it can pull together as a self-conscious and highly effective political force. During the debates over the Meech Lake Accord (1987-90), for example, a variety of Charter groups formed the Canadian Coalition on the Constitution to oppose the accord. At the time, Deborah Coyne, chairperson of the Coalition, provided an apt (self) definition of what we are calling the Court Party. She went so far as to describe it as a new "power structure" in Canadian society.

> The Charter's appeal to our non-territorial identities — shared characteristics such as gender, ethnicity and disability — is finding concrete expression in an emerging new power structure in society.... This power structure involves new networks and coalitions among

women, the disabled, aboriginal groups, social reform activists, church groups, environmentalists, ethnocultural organizations, just to name a few. All these new groups have mobilized a broad range of interests that draw their inspiration from the Charter and the Constitution....[58]

The efficacy of this "emerging power structure" cannot be doubted, for it achieved what was unimaginable only a decade earlier: the defeat of a constitutional amendment that enjoyed the support of all 11 first ministers and of the leaders of both opposition parties.[59] While the coalition of Charter groups may initially have been an alliance of convenience and circumstance, it is now as entrenched in Canada's ("small c") constitution as the Charter is in the ("large C") Constitution.

The involvement of Charter Canadians in the politics of formal constitutional amendment is paralleled by their enthusiastic participation in the less obvious but generally more significant process of informal constitutional amendment that goes on every day in the appeal courts of this country. While formal constitutional change is purposely made difficult to achieve and is thus rare, real change can and does occur in an incremental fashion through judicial interpretation. This is especially true for a new constitutional text like the Charter, where each judicial interpretation is analogous to a mini-amendment.[60] The reasoning of judges adds new constitutional meaning that can expand or contract the rights, and thus the policy influence, of the groups involved. Since it is the courts that most directly influence the content and scope of their Charter provisions, the Charter groups have a vested interest in judicial power. As self-described outsiders who believe that the traditional institutions of parliamentary democracy and federalism have failed them, they look to the courts for more favourable policy outcomes. Certainly, these groups and their academic supporters have become the chief exponents of judicial power in Canada, though not at the cost of abandoning more traditional political strategies.

In sum, part of what unites the various elements of Coyne's "new power structure" – and what leads us to call it the "Court Party" – is an interest in the judicialization of politics. Parties are partisan, and the Court Party is a partisan of the courts.

To speak of the partisans of the judiciary may seem a little strange at first, but only because we have become accustomed to thinking of the courts as non-political bodies. With respect to other governmental institutions there is nothing at all remarkable in speaking of their partisans and of the resulting inter-institutional politics. The federal and provincial governments in Canada, for example, certainly have their respective partisans, and the politics of centralization versus provincial rights has been a perennial feature of Canadian public life. The same is true in other federal systems.

The executive and legislative branches of government also attract partisans in battles against each other. Violent rebellions broke out in nineteenth century Canada over the question of whether to make the executive responsible to the legislature by requiring it to maintain the confidence of a majority of legislators. Today the tables have turned: worrying about the overly disciplined parties and cabinet-dominated legislatures produced by responsible government, we now wonder whether it might be better to stop treating every major legislative vote as a test of confidence. Similarly, in the United States, while it was once common to celebrate or lament an imperial presidency, observers later became more likely to debate the merits of an imperial judiciary or an imperial Congress.[61]

The different political institutions in any regime attract partisans because institutions are not neutral arenas in which substantive political battles are fought. Different institutions privilege different types of political resources, which are not equally distributed among social interests. Moving responsibility for a policy decision from legislatures to courts, for example, hurts interests with superior electoral clout but helps interests with better legal resources (e.g., sympathetic judges, skilled lawyers). Because institutions shape the political process in ways that enhance the prospects of certain outcomes and diminish the prospects of others, political partisans will gravitate to institutions that appear most open to their policy preferences or most closed to the preferences of their opponents. "Far from being external to the substance of politics, institutions are often the very things at stake in political struggles; politics is as much about institutions as it is constrained and channelled by them."[62]

To repeat, the notion that institutions attract political partisans is commonplace with respect to all governmental institutions but the courts. The idea of a Court Party seems outlandish to the extent that courts are perceived as non-political institutions, but as the courts have never, in fact, been entirely non-political,[63] this is hardly the first time that their association with partisan factions has been noticed.

In the decades preceding the Great Depression, business elites in both Canada and the US successfully used litigation to slow the advent of the emergent welfare state. The proponents of laissez-faire economics turned to the courts to argue that many of the new regulatory and redistributive policies violated their freedom of contract or exceeded the legislative jurisdictions assigned by the federal division of powers. In short, business interests successfully defended their policy interests by cloaking them in legal garb. It turns out that the modern court parties in both Canada and the United States had earlier predecessors.

Sceptics on the left were quick to dispatch the veil of legalism cast over public policy by the earlier court parties of the right. The sceptics argued persuasively that it was not law but judicial sympathy with business interests that fuelled anti-welfare state judgments. In the US, the leftist opponents of judicial power brought right-wing judicial activism to heel in the famous court-packing crises of 1937. President Roosevelt threatened to expand the size of the Supreme Court from 9 to 15 and to fill the new vacancies with pro-New Deal judges. This threat was never carried out, partly because the Supreme Court quickly backed down. For the next decade and a half, the Supreme Court, gradually filled with hand picked Roosevelt confidants and New Deal loyalists, practiced the newfound virtue of judicial self-restraint. Abandoning a century's worth of constitutional law, the Roosevelt Court allowed Democratic presidents and congresses to build the American welfare state. In Canada, leftist criticism of judicial opposition to the welfare state contributed to the 1949 abolition of appeals to the British Judicial Committee of the Privy Council. Again, the result was greater judicial openness to the modern interventionist and regulatory state. Between 1950 and 1972, for example, the Supreme Court of Canada did not strike down a single federal law.[64]

In time, however, those who criticized judicial power have become its partisans. By the 1980s, the US Democratic Party, which during its Roosevelt heyday had been vociferous in its criticism of judicial power, "became the advocate and champion of a liberal agenda institutionalized by the Warren Court,"[65] while Republicans, who had earlier sided with the courts, took over Roosevelt's court curbing agenda. According to Silverstein, the weaker the Democrats became politically, the more they relied on the Supreme Court. "To an extraordinary degree," he writes, "the judiciary has [permitted] the New Progressives [within the Democratic Party] to substitute court victories for electoral failures."[66] This analysis is echoed by Lowi and Ginsberg:

During the 1960s and 1970s, the power of the federal courts expanded in the same way that the power of the executive expanded during the 1930s — through links with constituencies, such as civil rights, consumer, environmental, and feminist groups, that staunchly defended the Supreme Court in its battle with Congress, the executive, or other interest groups.[67]

This, in turn, is why Republican presidents nominated "conservative" judges such as William Rehnquist, Antonin Scalia, Robert Bork, and Clarence Thomas for appointment to the Supreme Court after 1980, and why liberal Democrats fought so fiercely to defeat those nominations (successfully in the case of Bork).

Again, a similar pattern is evident in Canada. Here, too, the systematic defence of judicial power under the Charter now comes mainly from the left – though, to be sure (and as one would expect), those of all political persuasions seek to harness judicial power to their purposes when the opportunity presents itself. Here, too, "court curbing" tendencies are found most prominently on the right. True, there are important critics of judicial power on the left, but they have had little influence on recent partisan politics. Outside of Quebec, court-curbing tendencies are found chiefly in the Reform Party and among conservative provincial politicians, journalists, and academics.[68]

The current debate about judicial power, in short, is largely a reprise of the similar debate that occurred in the 1930s, with only the partisan positions reversed. We believe that the sceptics, both then and now, have a point. Indeed, scepticism of judicial power may be even more appropriate now, when prominent contemporary legal theory, drawing inspiration from postmodernism, insists that the legal rationales of judges are little more than rationalizations of the power of particular interests. What interests and whose power are served by the newly reinvigorated judiciary? This should be the first question of analysis. If, to use our term, there was a "court party" backing the Depression-era assertion of judicial power, chances are that a court party also underlies the current outbreak of that power.

The political interests and dispositions at the heart of the Court Party, we contend, fall into five distinct (albeit overlapping) categories: national unity advocates, civil libertarians, equality-seekers, social engineers, and postmaterialists. We analyse these Court Party constituencies in chapter 3.

In chapters 4 and 5 we show that the strength of the Court Party cannot be understood independently of its state connections. The Canadian state has conferred three types of resources on the Court Party: legislative, financial, and bureaucratic. Chapter four elaborates the first two, while chapter 5 explores the third.

Ideas drive the Charter revolution even more than do laws, dollars, or state officials. In postmaterialist societies, knowledge is power. Chapter 6 thus examines the central role of university-based intellectuals in the Court Party. In the seventh and concluding chapter, we explain our critical assessment of both the Charter Revolution and the Court Party.

Before proceeding to our analysis of the Court Party, we devote the next chapter to the judges whose policymaking discretion the Court Party seeks to influence.

TWO

JUDGES AND THE CHARTER REVOLUTION

People have been taught to believe that when the Supreme Court speaks it is not they who speak but the Constitution, whereas, of course, in so many vital cases, it is they who speak and not the Constitution.

US Supreme Court Justice Felix Frankfurter
in a letter to President Franklin D. Roosevelt.[1]

The Charter does not so much guarantee rights as give judges the power to make policy by choosing among competing interpretations of broadly worded provisions. Judges often deny that they make policy, insisting that they are simply applying the Charter, and thus implementing established legal policy. In *Vriend*, for example, the Supreme Court spoke of judges as "trustees" of the Charter whose job it was to scrutinize the work of the other branches of government in the name of the "new social contract" it represented.[2] The hollowness of these denials is evident whenever some of the trustees disagree with others about how to interpret the Charter, as members of appeal court panels regularly do. During the Charter's first decade, for example, fewer than 60 per cent of the Supreme Court's Charter decisions were unanimous, compared with an average of over 80 per cent for its non-Charter rulings. From 1991 to 1998 the rate of unanimous Supreme Court Charter decisions dropped further, to less than 50 per cent – to the dismay of lower court judges, who are supposed to follow Supreme Court precedents.[3]

When judges disagree, each one indulges in the legal fiction that his understanding of the Charter is correct and that his colleagues are mistaken. In fact, there are usually several plausible interpretations and no obviously correct answer. The Charter, in short, is largely indeterminate with respect to the questions that arise under it. Does the section 2 guarantee of freedom of expression prevent the censorship of pornography or hate literature, or do the section 15 equality rights justify – perhaps even require – such censorship? Does section 7, which guarantees "everyone's" right to "life, liberty, and security of the person," protect the life of a fetus or the liberty of a woman to have an abortion? No clear answer to these questions can be found in the broadly worded text of the Charter, and judges are thus free to choose.

Judicial policymaking requires more than interpretive discretion, however. The traditional barriers that restrict access to the courts, and thus limit the scope of the courts' policy review powers, must also be removed. The classic adjudication-of-disputes function of courts places many such restrictions on both litigants and courts: the rules of standing, mootness, intervener (third-party) participation, and others. Step by step, these have been removed by the Supreme Court. The result is that many policy decisions that offend well organized interest groups can now be directly challenged. In a dazzling exercise of self-empowerment, the Supreme Court has transformed itself from an adjudicator of disputes to a constitutional oracle that is able and willing to pronounce on the validity of a broad range of public policies. Interpretive discretion and an oracular courtroom – these are two of the chief building blocks of Canada's Charter revolution, and the focus of this chapter.

Judicial Discretion

Judicial discretion tends to be most vigorously denied when it is most flagrantly employed. In a democratic age, those who use or benefit from the power of appointed and unaccountable offices typically deny the reality of that power lest they undermine its legitimacy. In the case of judges, the denials will not withstand scrutiny.

There are three main ways in which judges might deny the claim that the Charter revolution is caused chiefly by judicial discretion: (1) that the Charter gives effect to certain obvious or core values that are beyond the discretion of judges to transform; (2) that some parts of the Charter revolution are clearly required by the Charter's text; and (3) that where the text is unclear, judges can find objective guidance for their decisions in such non-textual sources as the original intent, traditional understanding, or essential purpose of Charter rights.

Upon inspection, none of these constraints on judicial discretion turns out to be significant. Some of them, especially the claims of original intent or traditional understanding, might indeed tie judicial hands. However, they have been rejected by the interpretive community of judges and Charter experts. The other constraints either impose no limits of practical significance or actually enhance judicial discretion.

Core Values Do Not Constrain Judicial Discretion

The Charter is not completely malleable; it is not a blank cheque made out to judicial power. On the contrary, its provisions clearly give effect to a number of unchallenged and uncontested core values. Virtually everyone in contemporary Canada would agree, for example, that a theocratic religious establishment would violate freedom of religion; that prohibiting the political participation of women or racial minorities would infringe equality and democratic rights; and that hanging pickpockets would constitute cruel and unusual punishment.

The Charter is perfectly clear about such questions. And perfectly useless. The core values guaranteed by the Charter were already legally established in common law and statutory form well before its entrenchment in 1982. More importantly, they were solidly embedded in the beliefs and habits of Canadian citizens. Precisely because there *is* a consensus about the core values of the Charter, however, they will not arise as questions for judicial determination.

There are, of course, plenty of questions that do arise for judicial determination, which is to say that there is widespread, and often passionate, disagreement about the meaning of the Charter. But do these disagreements really go to the core of Charter values? How could it be that "we find ourselves arguing, so vehemently and so often, about the very core of what we have, as participants in a democratic polity, long since presumably agreed upon?"[4] How can a society simultaneously agree upon and endlessly dispute its foundational norms?

The answer is that our disagreements about the Charter – the questions we actually litigate – involve not the well established core but the indeterminate peripheral meaning of Charter rights. While the core meaning of a right may be widely agreed upon, its outer-limits are inherently contestable.[5] Religious freedom is certainly infringed by theocratic establishments, but what about laws that criminalize the use of certain drugs? Do religions that make sacramental use of those drugs have a fundamental right to an exemption not available to others? Some claim such a right to be exempted on religious grounds from otherwise valid laws, but John Locke, universally recognized as a friend of religious freedom, argued against it.[6] This is not a disagreement that pits tyrants against the true friends of liberty; it is a disagreement that divides liberal democrats of good standing.

Similarly, we would surely agree that a confession obtained under torture is not admissible as evidence in a criminal trial. But what if the discovery of the "smoking gun," covered with fingerprints, was not legitimized by a proper search warrant? Should that evidence also be excluded, or are there ways of punishing police misbehaviour (or misjudgment) without jeopardizing the search for truth in the trial itself?[7] Here again we confront a question that is subject to reasonable disagreement.

Canada, in short, would remain a member in good standing of the liberal democracies of the world regardless of the outcome of such Charter issues as whether Sikhs in the RCMP are allowed to wear turbans or the legal definition of spouse is read to include homosexuals.[8] The "wrong" answer to such questions does not turn the country into a tyranny, though that is precisely what rights claimants tend to argue. Rights claiming under the Charter, in other words, often represents the attempt to enhance the normative appeal of a debatable policy claim by casting the other side in the debate as evil and tyrannical. Exaggerating policy claims is, of course, a natural and ineradicable feature of political life, but healthy polities seek ways of moderating the bellicose tendency to exaggerate. Charter-based rights talk fuels this dangerous tendency rather than checking it.[9]

None of this is to suggest that real tyranny is impossible. Legislation establishing a particular church and threatening to jail heretics would certainly be tyrannical, and history is littered with examples of such policies. But we don't have any theocratic governments in modern Canada about to pass this kind of legislation, and if we did — if governments really were prepared to violate the core of a fundamental right — judges would be able to do nothing about it. Armed with neither "the sword [nor] the purse,"[10] courts are normally too weak to oppose either the tyranny of the majority or that of a single despot. In Uganda, when the Supreme Court tried to stop Idi Amin's persecution of his political opponents, he had his secret police shoot the judges.

This is what the American founder James Madison meant when he wrote, "experience proves the inefficacy of a bill of rights on those occasions when its control is most needed."[11] Two hundred years later, Canadian legal scholar Michael Mandel described the same phenomenon as the "when push comes to shove" principle of constitutional law. Mandel was referring to Russian President Boris Yeltsin's suspension of the new Russian constitution after the Russian Supreme Court had declared his suspension of parliament illegal. For good measure, Yeltsin also forced the chief justice to resign.[12]

Nor is judicial impotence in the face of determined governments limited to third-world dictatorships. Writing about the American Supreme Court's refusal to strike down restrictions on the freedom speech and association of

Communists after World War II, McCloskey observed that "[a]t no time in its history had the Court been able to maintain a position squarely opposed to a strong popular majority. There was no reason to expect it could do so now." McCloskey had in mind incidents such as President Andrew Jackson's response to Chief Justice John Marshall's 1832 ruling that the state of Georgia's treatment of the Cherokee Indians was unconstitutional. Jackson is said to have remarked: "Well, John Marshall has made his decision, now let him enforce it." More recently, the American Supreme Court was unwilling or unable to oppose the wartime relocation of Japanese Americans or McCarthyism during the 1950s.[13]

To summarize, legal indeterminacy and judicial discretion emerge not with respect to core values, about which consensus exists, but with respect to second-order questions, about which dissensus prevails. Canadians may agree that the Charter prohibits theocracy or grossly discriminatory laws, but they certainly do not agree about what it implies for mandatory retirement or the public funding of religious schools. No one nowadays advocates the hanging of pickpockets, but many people support capital punishment for the most heinous crimes. The Charter supplies few obvious answers to the second order questions that actually come before the courts. The text rarely settles such issues of reasonable disagreement; judges do. The Charter's core values – those matters that the text *does* settle – are not responsible for the Charter revolution.

Textual Innovation Has Not Constrained Judicial Discretion

While the text of the Charter rarely mandates significant policy change in areas of reasonable disagreement, it does so in a few instances. A second line of defense against the charge of unbridled judicial law-reform is thus to point to those sections of the Charter which clearly do effect legal change. For example, section 24(2) of the Charter creates an exclusionary rule where none had existed before. Whether or not to exclude perfectly reliable evidence because of improprieties in the way it was collected remains much more controversial than the hanging of pickpockets, yet the Charter unmistakably mandates such exclusion in certain circumstances.

Similarly, whereas the equality provision in the 1960 Bill of Rights guaranteed only "equality before the law," section 15 of the Charter contains the additional guarantees of "equality under the law" and "equal benefit of the law." The history of section 15 shows that these phrases were added, at the behest of feminist lobbying, to overrule the *Lavell* and *Bliss* decisions, two Bill of Rights decisions from the 1970s. In *Lavell*, the Supreme Court held that "equality before the law" required only equal application of the laws, not equal laws; it thus upheld a provision of the Indian Act that blatantly discriminated against Native women because it discriminated against all of them in the same way. In *Bliss*, the Court suggested that government benefit programs, such as unemployment insurance, were exempt from equality requirements.[14] The new wording of section 15 directed the courts to give a more substantive meaning to equality under the Charter.

Another example is section 10(b) of the Charter, which not only replicates the Bill-of-Rights guarantee of a right to counsel upon detention or arrest, but adds an American-style requirement for police to inform detainees of this right. In its 1964 *Miranda* decision, the American Supreme Court added such a requirement to the pre-existing right to counsel in the US Constitution. The Canadian Supreme Court refused to add a similar requirement to the 1960 Bill of Rights in the 1978 case, *Hogan v. The Queen*.[15] In effect, section 10(b) of the Charter overrules *Hogan*.

Section 23 of the Charter provides yet another example. It imposes on provincial governments new obligations to provide primary and secondary education to official language minorities in their own language.

Such exceptions notwithstanding, relatively little of the Charter revolution can be explained by textually mandated change. Despite a few textual innovations in the Charter, Canadians did not go to bed on April 17, 1982 with a substantially new set of rights and freedoms. For the most part, the Charter simply constitutionalized concepts − religious freedom, freedom of expression, fair trial, the right against self-incrimination, etc. − that had a long history of legal protection in this country. Common law and statute, including the 1960 statutory Bill of Rights, had protected them. Although the legal *status* of many of these concepts changed through constitutional entrenchment in 1982, there was generally no textual indication that their *content* was also to change. The fact that the Charter revolution is more a judicial than a legal revolution is evident in the many cases that brought about dramatic legal change without any textual warrant for such change.

For example, nowhere does the Charter explicitly give suspects the right to remain silent during pre-trial investigation. Indeed, civil libertarians' requests to place this right in the Charter were rejected by the framers.[16] This did not stop the Supreme Court from reading in such a right as a necessary corollary of both the Charter's right to counsel and its requirement of "fundamental justice." Nor did it stop the Court from extending the Canadian version of this right to blood-sample and lineup evidence gathered in the absence of counsel, something that not even the American version requires.[17]

The fate of many Bill-of-Rights precedents provides a particularly dramatic example of legal transformation without textual warrant. While the Charter clearly overruled a few Bill-of-Rights precedents, such as *Hogan* and *Lavell*, in most cases it did not. While the Charter adds freedom of conscience to the Bill of Rights guarantee of freedom of religion, there is no indication that this change was intended to alter the judicial approach to Sunday-closing legislation.[18] Yet in one of its earliest Charter decisions, the Supreme Court declared the Lord's Day Act unconstitutional, notwithstanding its own Bill-of-Rights precedent that this law did not violate religious freedom.[19] Similarly, the right-to-counsel provisions in both documents are identical except for the Charter's addition of the requirement to be informed of that right. This addition surely does not explain why in 1980 the Supreme Court ruled that the right to counsel did not apply to breathalyzer stops under the Bill but in 1985 ruled that it does under the Charter.[20]

Even where clear textual changes exist, the legal transformations undertaken in their name are often anything but obvious. As noted earlier, the Charter does explicitly provide for the exclusion of evidence if it has been "obtained in a manner that infringed or denied" Charter rights. However, unlike the American rule, which tended toward automatic exclusion, the new Canadian exclusionary rule was explicitly conditional. Only if a judge deemed that "its admission would bring the administration of justice into disrepute" was evidence to be excluded. During the framing process, the government defended this new wording on the grounds that it would allow exclusion only in extreme, and therefore rare, circumstances.[21]

In the hands of the Supreme Court, however, exclusion has become anything but rare. In a series of rulings, the most important of which is *R. v. Collins*, the Supreme Court has progressively lowered the threshold for exclusion of evidence. Given this low threshold, the Court has chosen to exclude evidence 45 per cent of the time; when the evidence takes the form of confessions or other incriminating statements, the exclusion rate jumps to 60 per cent.[22]

Critics claim that the Court has "produced [an exclusionary] rule which bears little resemblance to the text of the section."[23] Even those who applaud this development concede that "neither the rigour of the exclusionary rule nor its extension … were anticipated by the framers of the Charter. Both are due to the Court's willingness to give its provisions a purposive interpretation."[24] By 1996 Crown prosecutors had become so frustrated with the judges' frequent exclusion of reliable evidence, including involuntary police line-up identification and blood samples, that the attorney-general of Canada asked the Supreme Court to formally overrule the *Collins* precedent. The Court not only refused, but extended the list of prohibited forms of self-incrimination to include involuntary DNA samples.[25]

The equality rights provision of the Charter — section 15 — provides a second example of how judicial innovations have gone well beyond those mandated by the text. As noted above, the framers expanded the traditional wording of the right to force judges to scrutinize the substance of laws as well as their application and administration. However, the opening words of section 15 refer to these expanded rights as belonging to "every individual." Despite such textual clarity, the Supreme Court has interpreted equality rights in a manner that extends them mainly to members of so-called disadvantaged groups. As Anthony Peacock has observed, the Court's interpretation of section 15 has transformed the Charter from a "citizens' constitution" to a "victims' constitution."[26]

In sum, while the Charter does include some textual innovation, this innovation explains relatively little of the Charter revolution. Most of the important questions arising under the Charter have been settled by judges exercising policymaking discretion, not by its text.

Original Intent, Traditional Understanding, and Purposive Analysis Do Not Constrain Judicial Discretion

Does the inability of the naked text to settle the kinds of questions typically raised under the Charter necessarily mean that they are settled by judicial discretion? When laws fail to settle questions arising under them, it used to be common to look behind the unclear text and consult the intention of the law's framers. And when the original intent was unclear or ambiguous, judges often fell back on the well-established or traditional understanding of the relevant legal language. Reliance on either original intent or traditional understanding provides a strong *prima facie* answer to the charge of judicial policymaking. Judges who can plausibly claim to be giving effect to the framers' intent or to longstanding understandings are indeed applying the law, not their personal policy predilections. A currently popular alternative to original intent and traditional understanding is "purposive analysis," which seeks to deduce answers to interpretive questions from the broader purposes of the legal provision. Can Canada's judges rely on original intent, traditional understanding, or purposive analysis to avoid the charge that they, more than the Charter itself, are responsible for the Charter revolution?

They certainly can't rely on the concept of traditional understanding, which can act only as a brake on policy innovation; it cannot be the basis of the kinds of policy innovations undertaken in the name of the Charter. Indeed, an emphasis on traditional understanding reflects the classical view that the very purpose of constitutionally entrenching certain rights is to protect established principles against corruption by future democratic majorities. This premise of distrust distinguishes the written from the unwritten approach to constitutionalism, with the former purposely being more difficult to amend or update. Under a written constitution, the judge's mandate is to protect existing rights, which may entail striking down new legislation supported by democratic majorities. At bottom, this doctrine is conservative, in the sense that it seeks to preserve past practices. But, while the courts have occasionally used the Charter to protect existing practice against legislative innovation, they have often used it to initiate new policy themselves.[27] In effect, the Supreme Court, inspired by its academic chroniclers, has inverted the traditional understanding of constitutionalism and judicial review as conserving forces, and transformed them into instruments of social reform. Rather than serving as a prudent brake on political change, the judiciary has become a catalyst for change.

If traditional understanding cannot explain the Charter revolution, can original intent do so? Where the text does not clearly require a policy innovation, in other words, might the framers nevertheless have intended that innovation? It seems improbable. Because the questions that arise under the Charter are contentious, second-level questions, about which no consensus exists, it is unlikely that the framers would have come down clearly on one side or the other.[28] To have done so, moreover, would arguably have been inappropriate. The relative permanence and loftiness of constitutional law, one might think, should be used to enshrine principles of deep consensus, not to settle ongoing matters of reasonable disagreement. If the framers had nevertheless intended to settle a highly contested issue, wouldn't they have been absolutely clear about it in the text, rather than leaving it to the discretion of judges? One cannot escape the conclusion that when the text is unclear, judicial policy innovation undertaken in its name cannot be justified in terms of the original intent of the framers.

This conclusion is borne out when one actually looks for evidence of original intent on some of the more contentious questions that have been answered by the courts. Original intent is admittedly a slippery concept. For instance, different framers might intend to achieve very different things with precisely the same legal wording. Still, the evidence we do have makes it difficult for the Supreme Court to claim that its substantive policy innovations are grounded in original intention rather than judicial discretion.

We have already noted, for example, that the Court ran counter to the expectations of many of the framers when it created a pre-trial right to silence for criminal suspects and operated the exclusionary rule in a manner that makes exclusion of evidence the rule rather than the exception. The same is true of Henry Morgentaler's successful Charter challenge to the abortion provisions of the Criminal Code. During the framing process, the Trudeau government rejected numerous petitions from both pro-choice and pro-life groups to entrench their respective positions in the Charter. There was strong evidence that influential framers intended to leave abortion entirely to the regular political process, beyond the scope of judicial review. This evidence was cited by the two dissenting judges in *Morgentaler*, who argued vigorously in favour of a hands-off approach by the Court.[29] Not surprisingly, the five-judge majority in *Morgentaler* did not appeal to original intent to justify their activism; indeed, they ignored the issue of original intent altogether.

Neither can the Court invoke the intention of the framers to support its policy innovations in the area of aboriginal rights. In the 1982 Constitution Act, section 35 declares that "The existing aboriginal and treaty rights of the aboriginal peoples of Canada are hereby recognized and confirmed." (Section 35 is technically "outside" of the Charter, but as a declaration of the special rights of Canada's most salient racial minority – rights that are enforceable in the courts – it has become an important part of the Charter revolution.) In 1981 there was no consensus on what practical meaning "aboriginal rights" might have. Provincial premiers, led by Peter Lougheed of Alberta (himself part Native), prudently wished to limit the recognition of aboriginal and treaty rights to those in effect at the time. They demanded that the Government amend the wording by adding the qualifier "existing." The prevailing understanding of this wording affirmed previously enacted extinguishments of aboriginal rights but protected against any future attempts to extinguish such rights by ordinary legislation.[30] The restrictive intent of this qualification was so clear that three of the four major Canadian aboriginal groups opposed it. Indeed, the National Indian Brotherhood declared April 17 (the day the Constitution Act was proclaimed) "a day of mourning" and said that any Indian participating in the celebration would be committing a "treasonous act against the Indian nations and their citizens."[31]

Nevertheless, the Supreme Court effectively removed this explicit limitation by announcing an unprecedented and generous definition of "existing" in its 1990 *Sparrow* decision.[32] According to the Court, any aboriginal right, such as fishing for food, that has not been legally "extinguished" is deemed to still be "an existing aboriginal right." So far, so good. But the Court then set out such strict rules for determining the extinguishment of an aboriginal right that it found that the aboriginal right to fish for food in the Fraser River was not nullified despite almost 100 years of government regulation. The judges justified their new invention by declaring that section 35 invokes "the honour of the Crown" and thus imposes a "fiduciary obligation" on all government dealing with natives with the courts to judge whether this duty has been met.

Sparrow is to the aboriginal rights movement what *Morgentaler* is to the pro-choice movement. The effect of *Sparrow* has been described as "a virtual revolution in consciousness ... a sea change in Canadian law ... kick-started to a large degree by the courts."[33] With allies like this in the courts, it is hardly surprising that Native leaders demanded that the so-called "inherent right to aboriginal self-government" in the 1992 Charlottetown Accord be justiciable; that is, that it be ultimately enforced by the courts.[34]

The issue of gay rights provides another example of the disjunction between framers' intent and judicial policymaking. During the period of Chartermaking, the Trudeau government and the Parliamentary Committee on the Constitution rejected repeated requests by gay rights activists to insert protection for sexual orientation in the Charter. As with the abortion issue, the lack of any societal consensus on these issues counselled against addressing them in the Charter. Trudeau's advisors feared that anticipated public controversy might swamp their entire package of constitutional reform. As recently as 1992, sexual orientation was not included in the Charlottetown Accord, despite symbolic mention of all the other Charter groups. Nevertheless, in its 1995 *Egan* ruling the Supreme Court added sexual orientation to the list of prohibited grounds of discrimination in section 15.[35]

True, there is evidence that some framers, such as Jean Chrétien (then the justice minister), were prepared to leave the matter of gay rights to future judicial discretion. Indeed, Patrick Monahan contends that Chrétien's view was common among the framers. "They had," says Monahan, "a relatively sophisticated and realistic view of the nature of the adjudication process," one that recognized "the significant degree of discretion available to courts interpreting constitutional texts." The framers, in this view, undoubtedly had "substantive intent" about particular policy issues, but they did not necessarily regard "those substantive views as conclusive." If one wants to be "really serious about fidelity to the intention of the drafters," argues Monahan, one must acknowledge their intent to hand over considerable policymaking discretion to the judiciary. The drafters, he contends, "saw their task as making educated guesses as to how the courts might interpret particular constitutional language, and choosing the language which was most likely to secure for them the results they desired," while accepting that their expectations might be upset by "inevitable" judicial originality.[36] In other words, what might be called the framers' general intent to confer broad policy discretion on the courts takes precedence over their specific or substantive intent about particular policy questions that might arise for judicial determination.

This kind of claim has become a regular feature in judicial defences of the Charter revolution. In the 1985 *British Columbia Motor Vehicle Reference*, for example, Justice Lamer confronted the charge that the Charter had created a "judicial 'super-legislature' beyond the reach of parliament, the provincial legislatures and the electorate." To the extent that this is true, Lamer reminded his readers, critics should blame not the courts but "the elected representatives of the people of Canada. It was those representatives who extended the scope of constitutional adjudication and entrusted the courts with this new and onerous responsibility."[37] As noted in the previous chapter, Lamer expanded on this theme in 1997, arguing that judges were "heeding the command" of legislators, that it was "their doing ... not ours."[38] In 1998 the Court said in *Vriend* that "it was the deliberate choice of our provincial and federal legislatures in adopting the Charter to assign an interpretive role to the courts and to command them under s. 52 to declare unconstitutional legislation invalid."[39] And in 1999, retired Supreme Court Justice Wilson wrote that judges "did not volunteer" for "the onerous responsibility of reviewing legislative and executive action for compliance with the constitution." To the contrary, the Canadian public, acting through "a widely accepted constitution process," intentionally gave the courts wide policy discretion.[40]

Surely a general intent to permit judicial discretion cannot be used to escape the charge that it is precisely this discretion, not the intent of the framers, that accounts for particular, substantive policy innovations undertaken in the name of the Charter. Framers who intend judicial *discretion* necessarily leave judges free to take different paths on controversial policy questions. If the general intent underlying the Charter truly gives judges policy discretion, then they can just as plausibly defer to the other branches of government as oppose them. Commentators who claim that deferential judgments themselves violate the Charter by ignoring "the values of the

Charter text, its political history and its stated institutional roles"[41] cannot simultaneously embrace a general intent of judicial *discretion*; they must be claiming an activist substantive intent to transform particular policies. One cannot have it both ways.

In fact, as we have seen, it is exceedingly difficult to explain judicial policy innovations in terms of the substantive intent of the framers. Understanding this difficulty, the Supreme Court itself rejected substantive intent as a significant standard of interpretation early in its Charter jurisprudence in the *British Columbia Motor Vehicle Reference*, the very case in which Justice Lamer embraced the general intent to confer policymaking power on the courts. *BC Motor Vehicles* confronted the Court with the question of whether section 7 of the Charter – the right not to be deprived of life, liberty or security of the person except in accordance with the principles of fundamental justice – was to be given a substantive or procedural meaning. On a procedural reading, governments could infringe the rights to life, liberty, and security of the person, as long as they did so in a manner that was procedurally fair. On a substantive reading, even procedural fairness could not justify some violations of the section 7 rights. There was ample documentary evidence that many of the most influential framers intended the narrower, procedural reading.[42]

Such evidence did not deter Justice Lamer. Characterizing indications of substantive intent as "inherently unreliable" and "nearly impossible of proof," Lamer declared that, "it would be erroneous to give these materials anything but minimal weight." If the Court bound itself to substantive intent, he warned, the Charter's rights and freedoms would "in effect become frozen in time to the moment of adoption, with little or no possibility of growth and adjustment to changing societal needs." The preferred alternative, Lamer concluded, is to approach the Charter as "a living tree ... [capable] of growth and adjustment over time."[43]

Not only did Justice Lamer reject substantive intent as a constraint on judicial discretion, he relied, as we have seen, on a general intent to legitimize that discretion. In addition, he used the living tree metaphor in a manner calculated to maximize discretion. Notice that Justice Lamer associates original intent with frozen concepts and treats both as hostile to the flexibility of a living tree. In fact, constitutionalism only makes sense if frozen concepts can somehow coexist with flexibility and adaptability. Certainly, the whole point of writing a constitution is to freeze certain concepts for the long-term future, to entrench them, and thus make them hard to change. At the same time, no constitution can actually govern the future except as a living tree that is capable of growth and adjustment over time.

For example, when the eighteenth-century framers of the American Constitution included a guarantee against unreasonable search and seizure, they knew nothing of twentieth-century techniques of electronic surveillance. Does this mean that the search-and-seizure provision of the US Constitution does not apply to modern electronic surveillance, that it is frozen in its application to the search-and-seizure technologies prevalent in the eighteenth century, that every new technology can be subjected to constitutional standards only through formal amendment? Surely not. On any sensible reading, the search-and-seizure provision can readily accommodate unforeseen technologies; it is indeed a living tree.

To complete the biological metaphor, however, the search-and-seizure principle remained somehow itself even as it grew to accommodate new technologies. An old idea – that unreasonable searches and seizures be prohibited – was simply applied to new facts. The right itself was unchanged. The elm remained an elm; it grew new branches but did not transform itself into an oak or a willow. For all its flexibility and adaptability, a living tree, in the strict biological sense, *is* a frozen concept, Justice Lamer to the contrary notwithstanding.

A sensible version of the living tree metaphor, in other words, is quite compatible with fidelity to original intent or traditional understanding. Stated differently, a frozen concept is not the foe of appropriate – indeed, inescapable – constitutional flexibility. But modern proponents of the living tree metaphor, such as Justice Lamer, want more than the flexibility of applying existing rights to new facts; they want the freedom to create new rights and then apply them to old facts.

In the US, for example, religious freedom was traditionally understood to prevent government from publicly preferring one religion to others but not to prevent the public preference of religion to irreligion. In other words, nondiscriminatory support of all religions was perfectly constitutional. In the mid-twentieth century, the US Supreme Court suddenly reversed this long-standing interpretation, establishing a strict "wall of separation" that required the state to be neutral not only between religions but between religion and irreligion.[44] Through this judicial about-face, practices that had been treated as constitutional for most of US history suddenly became unconstitutional. There was no adaptation of old rights to new facts here. Old facts were treated differently by a new, judicially created right.

Even more revealing is the (thus far unsuccessful) attempt by living tree enthusiasts in the US to declare capital punishment a violation of the cruel and unusual punishment clause of the Constitution, despite the fact that three other clauses of the Constitution explicitly allow for the death penalty.[45] The framers obviously did not think that capital punishment, subject to due process, was cruel and unusual. But opponents of capital punishment argued that the understanding of what was cruel and unusual had evolved to include the death penalty and that the constitution should be interpreted accordingly. Here again, a new right would be applied to old facts. This was not an elm growing new branches, but an elm transforming itself into a willow under the careful supervision of judicial gardeners. No frozen concepts in sight!

In Canada, the Supreme Court has created a new right against self-incrimination for criminal defendants lucky enough to get a retrial because of procedural irregularities in their first trial. Traditionally, the right against self-incrimination, which had been legislatively protected prior to the Charter, was understood to protect witnesses against self-incriminating statements made in testimony against someone else, but not to protect the accused himself against incriminating statements made under cross examination at a previous trial on the same charge. The Court, however, expanded the right against self-incrimination to cover the latter situation. It did so over the objection of Justice McIntyre, who accused the majority of adopting an interpretation of the Charter that was "not dictated by its language," and that abandoned "long-accepted and sound principles of evidence."[46]

Clearly, the Canadian Supreme Court has adopted the radical version of the living tree metaphor. Although the more modest version allows for flexibility and adaptation over time, it is obviously too restrictive for our judges. They want the flexibility to create new rights, not just the flexibility to adapt existing concepts to new facts.

Proponents of such radical flexibility say that to be constrained by rights as originally or traditionally understood is to be ruled by the dead hand of the past. Why should the views of earlier generations trump those of the present? If we today understand rights differently — indeed, if we want new rights altogether — why should stodgy judges, with their heads buried in yesteryear, deny them to us?

The obvious answer is that judicial fidelity to traditional understanding or substantive original intent rarely prevents the creation of new rights. Although the US Constitution *permits* capital punishment, it clearly does not *require* it; state legislatures remain free to abolish the death penalty, and several have. Similarly, a constitution that *permits* restrictive regulation of abortion may leave legislatures free to relax such restrictions, and legislatures are not prevented from protecting homosexuals against discrimination by a constitution that does not explicitly require such protection.[47] Moreover, if there is a sufficient public consensus in favour of a new right, it can be constitutionalized through a formal constitutional amendment. To the extent that the current generation is free to *legislate* new rights, the judicial creation of new rights does not liberate the living majority from the dead hand of the past. To the contrary, when legislatures are free to act, judicial policymaking is more accurately portrayed as a minority imposing its views on a reluctant majority.

Sometimes, of course, constitutional law does stand in the way of the legislative development of new policies for new circumstances, and in such cases the living tree metaphor *can* liberate the current generation from the constraints of the past. But when this happens, the metaphor supports judicial deference to legislative problem-solving, not judicial activism. For example, when courts in the 1920s and 1930s read both the Canadian and American constitutions as preventing the establishment of the welfare state, the living tree metaphor was invoked to free legislatures from this conservative judicial activism.[48]

Indeed, it was precisely to liberate legislative and governmental policy innovation from judicially imposed constraints that the living tree analogy was first developed. At the outset, in other words, the living tree metaphor was a technique of judicial interpretation that allowed *legislators* to develop new policies to meet new social and economic conditions. As applied to the Charter, however, it encourages *judges* to develop new policies to meet new social and economic conditions.[49] When used in the first sense – to permit legislative innovation – the living tree metaphor does indeed liberate current majorities from the constraints of the past. When used to impose new policies on reluctant legislatures, the metaphor liberates only an appointed minority from these constraints. It is surely ironic that a doctrine that began its career as a justification for legislative discretion has been transformed into a bulwark of judicial discretion.

Interestingly, although the Canadian Supreme Court prefers the discretion-enhancing living tree metaphor, it has not completely scrapped the notion of substantive original intent. Thus, when the Court struck down the education provisions of Quebec's Official Language Act (Bill 101) – the Charter ruling that has most infuriated Quebec nationalists and fuelled our ongoing national unity crisis – the judges did not hesitate to justify their decision with an appeal to original intent. The Court declared that section 23 of the Charter, which it used to invalidate parts of Bill 101, "was not enacted by the legislator in a vacuum. The legislator knew, and clearly had in mind the regimes governing anglophone and francophone linguistic minorities in various provinces in Canada ... and their intention was to remedy the perceived defects of these regimes by uniform corrective measures, namely those contained in s. 23 of the Charter."[50] In other words, the framers enacted s. 23 precisely in order to invalidate the educational provisions of Bill 101.

Similarly, in Chantal Daigle's famous 1989 challenge to an injunction preventing her abortion, the Supreme Court appealed to framers' intent to justify its ruling in favour of Daigle. The Quebec Court of Appeal had ruled that Daigle's unborn child was protected by the Quebec Charter of Human Rights, pointing to that document's declarations that every "human being [has] the right to life," and that "Every human being whose life is in peril has a right to assistance."[51] This did not satisfy the Supreme Court. "The Quebec Charter," the Court wrote, "does not display any clear intention on the part of its framers to consider the status of the fetus.... If the legislature had wished to grant fetuses the right to life, then it seems unlikely that it would have left the protection of this right to such happenstance."[52]

The Court was probably correct on this issue, but the dissenters in the *Morgentaler* case, decided only a year earlier, had made the same point. "The Charter is entirely silent on the point of abortion," Justice McIntyre had written, and the legislative history made it clear that this omission was intentional. In other words, if the framers had intended to set policy for the highly contentious issue of abortion, they would not have left the matter to "happenstance." Yet, as we have seen, the five judges who ruled in favour of Morgentaler were completely silent on the issue of original intent. In effect, the majority in *Daigle* used the interpretive methods of the minority in *Morgentaler*. Why did the Court treat framers' intent as decisive when dealing with the rights of the unborn, but as completely irrelevant when dealing with the rights of the mother?[53]

One cannot escape the conclusion that the Supreme Court has adopted an entirely unprincipled approach to the question of original intent, subordinating it to the question of desired policy result. If the judges can find evidence of original intent that supports their policy predilections, they will embrace it; if original intent would obstruct the desired policy, they ignore or reject it. Far from being a constraint on judicial discretion, original intent has itself become a matter of judicial discretion.

If neither original intent nor traditional understanding provide objective support for the judicial policy innovations undertaken in the name of the Charter, can such support be found in purposive analysis? Can Charter decisions be more objectively rooted in the broader purposes of the Charter's language than in the original intent of its framers? Our judges certainly think so. As the Supreme Court downplayed substantive original intent in its early Charter jurisprudence, it enthusiastically embraced purposive analysis as a way of justifying its policy innovations.[54]

According to purposive analysis, judges should be guided by the essential purpose of a Charter right, or by the set of interests that the right is designed to protect. To discern the relevant purpose, judges are to look not to the intentions (or purposes) of the framers but to the evolving traditions of our society. The emphasis here is not on tradition simply, but on *evolving* tradition. Purposive analysis is forward looking. It draws on the past, but does so selectively, and only to discern a trend whose perfection or end point can be achieved by judicial policymaking. The point is not to maintain tradition against legislative policy innovation, but to justify judicial policy innovation. As we have argued elsewhere, "purposive analysis generally means the selective abstraction of highly general concepts from the tradition of liberal democracy in order to transform actual practice."[55] The problem is that almost anything can be abstracted from the past in this way. In Peter Russell's words, "The history and philosophy of liberal democracy do not exactly form an open book containing clear definitions of the activities and interests" to be protected by the Charter. Russell concludes that purposive analysis "is an approach which may not yield the same results for all who apply it." In purposive analysis we confront yet another recipe for judicial discretion rather than a source of objectivity.[56] Combined with the living tree approach, purposive analysis of rights enhances the ability of courts to act as agents of policy reform. It gives them free rein to discover new meaning in broadly conceived constitutional principles and to establish new rights if societal need, as appointed judges understand it, calls for them.

In sum, none of the defences against the charge of judicial discretion and policymaking work. The truly fundamental issues about which the text is clear simply do not generate court cases, and if they did, judges would be unable to settle them. Of the secondary issues that do arise for judicial determination, a handful is indeed settled by the Charter's text, but they are too few to account for the Charter revolution. As for the extra-textual standards that might be used to justify the interpretation of ambiguous text, the judges themselves have rejected traditional understanding and substantive original intent. Original intent in a more general sense is used to portray the constitution as a living tree of such wondrous power that it can transform itself from one species into another. When called upon to mask the wide open discretion that flows from this radical form of the living tree metaphor, judges resort to a transparent sleight of hand known as purposive analysis. When all is said and done, the reality of judicial discretion cannot be evaded. It is judges who drive the Charter, and not vice-versa.

The attempt to deny or hide this truth can lead to a certain mendacity in judicial decision-making. In other words, to the extent that judges labour to camouflage their discretionary choices as the inescapable commands of the Charter, their overt reasons for deciding as they do may not be their real reasons. Consider the revelations provided in an interview given by Chief Justice Lamer on the fifteenth anniversary of the Charter in 1997. Lamer sought to defend what he admitted was one of the Supreme Court's most controversial Charter decisions, the *Morgentaler* abortion ruling. While claiming that he was "personally" against abortion, he added that he also believed that, "I should not impose upon others my personal beliefs." What then was the basis for his decision? Instead of pointing to a section of the Charter or some other conventional source of legal authority, Lamer invoked public opinion. Arguing that Canadians were split about 50-50 on the issue of abortion, he said "you should not make a crime out of something that does not have the large support of the community.... Who am I to tell 50 per cent of the population that they are criminals?"[57]

For all the talk of living trees and purposive analysis, what Justice Lamer is really up to, it appears, is surveying public opinion and ensuring that public policy has "the large support of the community." Presumably, this is the kind of thing he had in mind when he said in a 1999 interview that in some of its controversial rulings, the Court was "just keeping in sync with society."[58] Even if we accepted this as a legitimate judicial role, we might wish that Lamer would get his facts straight. Canadian public opinion toward abortion had not changed significantly since Parliament's 1969 abortion reform law and a plurality of Canadians have always supported the kind of policy compromise the 1969 law represented.[59]

Even if Lamer had had his facts straight, there would be reason to question this view of the judicial function. Will the Court invalidate all policy that does not enjoy the support of at least 50 per cent of the population? Under an electoral system in which the party that forms the government in Ottawa routinely receives less than 45 per cent of the popular vote (in 1997 the Chrétien Liberals were re-elected with only 38 per cent), this would be a lot of legislation. More to the point, where in the Charter are judges directed to base their decisions on second-hand personal assessments of public opinion? Politicians are entitled to make such assessments – and to get them wrong – because we can "throw the rascals out." Judges are appointed for life precisely in order to insulate them from public opinion. Apparently these problems did not occur to the Chief Justice.

At this point we must take note of a certain schizophrenia among judges on the matter of policymaking discretion. Although judges strive mightily to make their judgments appear to flow inescapably from the Charter, they sometimes admit their discretionary policymaking role in more informal settings off the bench. Thus, the late Justice John Sopinka once admitted to a reporter that "when ... deciding a Charter case, the court is in a sense legislating."[60] Under similar circumstances, Chief Justice Lamer has said that judging laws under the Charter, "especially when one has to look at Section 1 ... is asking us to make essentially what used to be a political call."[61]

A recent study of Canadian appeal court judges by Greene *et al.* uncovered similarly frank acknowledgments by the judges of their new role under the Charter. Four out of five Supreme Court judges interviewed agreed that the Charter *had given* the Court a "greater" law-making role. The comparable figure for other appeal court judges was 50 per cent. The authors concluded:

> It was almost certainly the case prior to the Charter that nearly all Canadian judges resisted a lawmaking role for the courts, and many denied its possibility altogether. Instead they espoused the legal positivist school of thought that good judges merely interpret the law. It is striking how quickly and completely this traditional view has faded: all but two appellate court judges now admit to having at least some lawmaking role.[62]

When thus confronting the reality of judicial discretion, defenders of judicial power shift ground. The discretion conferred on judges by the Charter is really nothing new, they now insist. Judges have always had a similar discretion in developing the common law and interpreting ambiguously worded legislation. At the constitutional level, moreover, Canadian judges have necessarily exercised some discretion in applying the law of federalism. In this view, the Charter simply adds to a long tradition of judicial policymaking. There is nothing particularly new, and certainly nothing revolutionary about it. As Chief Justice Lamer put it in a 1999 interview, the Court "hasn't become activist under my stewardship, it has always been activist."[63]

It is certainly true that policymaking discretion is inherent in the interpretive enterprise. Judicial policymaking, as we have ourselves argued many times, is quite unavoidable. But legislatures can overrule judicial interpretations of the common law or legislation much more easily than they can overrule Charter rulings, the section 33 override clause to the contrary notwithstanding. Although legislative majorities also cannot overrule the jurisprudence of federalism, it is more limited in scope. Deciding under the Charter *whether* government as such may (or must) do something, goes far beyond deciding *which* government may do it.[64] As Ian Hunter has aptly put it, "It may be true that elephants and chipmunks are both mammals, but to fail to acknowledge the difference between them is wilful deception."[65]

While it is true, in other words, that judicial discretion under the Charter is just one example of unavoidable judicial discretion, it is disingenuous to say that there is nothing new or different about it. Recall Chief Justice Lamer's comment that, with the advent of the Charter, the courts have been "drawn into the political arena to a degree unknown prior to 1982." Surely this would not have been the case if there was really nothing new going on. In fact, not only does the Charter provide broader scope for judicial policymaking, but the judges' embrace of the living tree and purposive analysis has significantly enhanced their policymaking potential. The sheer scope of judicial policy involvement under the Charter is certainly new, as are such innovations as judges rewriting legislation themselves rather than simply striking it down and allowing legislatures to decide how (or whether) to rewrite it. Indeed, as the next section shows, the innovations discussed thus far do not exhaust the institutional retooling undertaken by judges in the service of greater policy influence.

Oracularism

If newly created judicial standards are to have widespread effect on public policies, they must apply well beyond the confines of the particular case before the court. Thus, encouraged and applauded by the advocacy scholarship of Court Party academics, the Supreme Court has transformed the judiciary from an adjudicative institution, whose primary purpose is to settle concrete disputes between individuals or between individuals and the state, into an oracle of the constitution, whose primary purpose is to solve social problems by issuing broad declarations of constitutional policy.[66] Accompanying the substantive revolution described above, in other words, has been an equally important procedural revolution. The Court has swept aside traditional common law rules that restricted access to the courts and limited the scope of judicial influence.

Traditionally, the defining characteristic of courts was their dispute adjudication function. Yes, judges also interpret, and thus add to, the law, but such judicial law making was strictly confined by the adjudicative context.

This meant that constitutional rights were understood to be not just "for" but also "by" individuals. Individual litigants raised rights claims in the course of settling legal disputes with the state. Among other things, this meant that the dispute came first, the constitutional issue second. The corollary to this was that the courts might never address many important constitutional questions.[67] This was perfectly acceptable because constitutional interpretation and enforcement was not a monopoly of judges.

The Supreme Court of Canada has abandoned this view. It now sees itself as the authoritative oracle of the constitution, whose main job is to develop constitutional standards for society as a whole, rather than just for the litigants before it. The establishment of constitutional policy now comes first, the concrete dispute second. Indeed, with the important exception of criminal cases involving legal rights, the individual litigant is vanishing in Charter litigation. Corporations bring cases, and for policy charged cases, interest groups are increasingly prominent carriers of Charter litigation, if not as litigants, then as financial backers[68] or interveners.

The Supreme Court has expedited interest group use of litigation, and thus its own policy-review role, by eliminating two of the three most significant barriers to access to the courts: standing and mootness. (The third barrier, costs, has been removed by government subsidies of Charter litigation through the federal Court Challenges Program and provincial legal aid programs.)

The doctrine of standing required the existence of a real-world legal dispute before a court could take jurisdiction. This prevented lawsuits by individuals who objected to a law for policy reasons but were not directly affected by it. As recently as 1981, Chief Justice Laskin articulated the rationale for standing in the first *Borowski* appeal when he wrote that "mere distaste [for a policy] has never been a ground upon which to seek the assistance of a Court."[69] This restriction on citizen access limited the opportunities for judges to review legislation, but protected the courts from constantly being forced into confrontations with Parliament by disgruntled losers in the political arena. But Laskin spoke in dissent. A majority of the Supreme Court voted to grant Joe Borowski standing to challenge Canada's abortion law despite the fact that he was not directly affected by it.[70]

Similarly, the doctrine of mootness restricted access to the courts by requiring that a legal dispute still be a "live" dispute. If the original parties had resolved their differences, gone away or died, judges were barred from pronouncing on the legal questions raised. The Supreme Court began chipping away at this restriction in its very first Charter ruling: it ruled on the validity of Ontario's restriction on non-citizens becoming lawyers even though the original plaintiff had long since become a Canadian citizen and a member of the bar. In 1988, the Court ruled on the validity of Saskatchewan's English-only parking-tickets, even though the offender/challenger, an activist French-Catholic priest, had died. Most recently, the Court ruled that homosexual couples were entitled to spousal-support protections upon the breakup of their relationships despite the fact that the couple who brought the case – known to the public as M. and H. – had reconciled. True, the Court continues to dismiss moot cases on occasion. In 1989, for example, it declared the second *Borowski* case moot because the law challenged by Borowski had already been struck down in *Morgentaler*. Nevertheless, the Court's opinion in *Borowski* underlined what its practice in other cases makes clear – that mootness *per se* is no longer a significant barrier to hearing a case.[71] Like original intent, mootness has become a completely discretionary rule.

The Supreme Court has further facilitated interest group litigation by adopting a new, open-door policy for non-government interveners. Interveners are not parties to the dispute, but may be affected by or have an interest in the resolution of the legal questions raised. They thus seek to intervene in the appeal to signal their interest and present their opinions on the issue to the court. Historically, the Supreme Court had been stingy in granting intervener status to citizens or interest groups, precisely because the latter were not parties to the actual dispute, the Court's primary focus.

Initially the Court was wary about allowing interest groups to intervene in Charter decisions. Groups such as LEAF and the CCLA quickly realized that without access as interveners, they would be deprived of direct participation in the interpretive development of Charter law in the critical early cases. Beginning in 1984, they mounted a furious public relations campaign in law journals, at academic conferences, and by private and public letters to persuade the Court to loosen the rules on intervention. In 1986, the Court relented and adopted what amounts to an open-door policy on interveners. In 1987, it accepted 95 per cent of the intervener applications it received, up from 20 per cent in 1985.[72] The acceptance rate has remained in the 80 to 90 per cent range.

Drawing on the American experience of systematic litigation strategies, a new breed of Canadian interest groups seized the opportunity offered by the Court's change of heart. Applications from non-government interveners tripled from 1986 to 1987. In the first three years of Supreme Court Charter decisions there were only 17 non-government interveners. By 1990, more than 100 interest-group interveners participated in over half of all the Supreme Court's Charter cases.[73] By the end of 1993, the number had risen to 229. In politically charged cases involving abortion (*Daigle*, 1989) and language rights (*Mahé*, 1990), the number of interest-group interveners reached nine. In the landmark aboriginal rights case, *Sparrow*, there were 22 interveners, 16 of them non-government groups.[74]

Interest groups intervene out of policy concerns that may be quite different from the more practical concerns of the immediate parties. In such cases, they have benefited from the Court's willingness to address issues not actually raised by the factual situations of the parties. In *Big M Drug Mart*, the Court struck down the Lord's Day Act as a violation of freedom of conscience despite the fact that the litigant challenging the law, a corporation, could not have a religious conscience.[75] In *Andrews* the Court responded to broad issues of equality jurisprudence raised by LEAF and other interveners, issues that did not address the immediate issue before the Court. In *R. v. Smith*, the Court overturned a mandatory seven-year minimum sentence for importing illegal drugs even though everyone agreed that Smith, the litigant, deserved at least seven years.[76] The Court is quite willing to issue broad declarations of constitutional policy even when there is no bona fide legal dispute before it that clearly implicates the policy questions it wishes to address. Disputes, the traditional stock in trade of courts, are now merely a sufficient and no longer a necessary condition for judicial intervention in public policy. As Lorraine Weinrib approvingly observes, courts in Canada are no longer restricted to addressing "constitutional questions within legal disputes." They now enjoy the power of "abstract constitutional review," which affords "wider opportunities to initiate litigation and greater public involvement."[77] In other words, the Supreme Court is no longer a court, but an overtly political censor, an oracle ready to second-guess disputable political judgments whenever it sees the need.

The Court has further empowered itself by changing the status of its own *obiter dicta*. Literally, "words spoken in passing," *obiter dicta* are those portions of a judgment that are outside the reasons – the *ratio decidendi* – that actually determine the outcome of a case. They are asides, or digressions. In common law jurisdictions, the *obiter dicta* of appeal courts have never been considered binding on lower courts. In Canada, the Supreme Court changed this in a 1980 decision in which it ruled that its own judicially considered *obiter* have the force of law.[78] Baar points out that this is what bound lower courts to apply the Supreme Court's "6 to 8 month *Askov* rule" to all cases. In *Askov*, the Supreme Court had found that nearly two years of delay between committal and trial amounted to a Charter violation, and then, in obiter, opined that anything over six to eight months was similarly unreasonable. When lower courts began applying this standard, over 40,000 cases were stayed, dismissed or withdrawn in Ontario alone, prompting the Supreme Court later to complain that it had been misunderstood. As Baar notes, "The binding force of judicially considered *dicta* in Canada gives its Supreme Court much more leverage than its American counterpart."[79]

Although the Canadian Supreme Court occasionally surpasses its American counterpart, in many respects the high courts of both countries have undertaken the same kind of institutional retooling. Prodded and encouraged by the new generation of Canadian legal academics who had studied American constitutional law – many of them at US law schools – the Canadian Court has gone down much the same path taken by its American counterpart a generation earlier. As a prelude to its own rights revolution of the 1960s, the Warren Court (named after its Chief Justice, Earl Warren) began by sweeping aside the traditional restrictions on access such as mootness and standing.[80] "To the justices of the Warren court," writes Silverstein, "throwing off the shackles of a constricted view of the Court's power simply brought a greater diversity of litigants before the Court and rendered a wider range of issues subject to judicial determination," thus "enhancing the opportunity of the courts to promote a new social and political agenda."[81] If, as Laurence Tribe observes, the approach to such issues as standing and mootness describes "an institutional psychology: an account of how … the Justices of the Supreme Court view their own role,"[82] then the Warren Court clearly viewed its role as "that of an active partner with the executive branch in the transformation of American politics."[83] Our own Supreme Court's institutional retooling under the Charter indicates that it aspires to a similar role.

Conclusion

The Charter provides the occasion for judicial policymaking, but the document itself is not the most important explanation for that policymaking. Judges themselves have chosen to treat the Charter as granting them open-ended policymaking discretion. They do not always admit their discretion; indeed, they often try to camouflage it. But their attempts to do so cannot withstand close inspection and are contradicted by the judges' own, more frank off-the-bench observations.

In addition, the Supreme Court has multiplied the opportunities for judicial policymaking by substantially redesigning itself – changing its rules of evidence, relevance, standing, mootness, and intervener status – from a constitutional adjudicator to a constitutional oracle. This institutional retooling, combined with the new sophistication of Canadian interest groups in using litigation, means that few major government policy initiatives are likely to escape a Charter challenge. Judicial intervention in the policymaking process is no longer *ad hoc* and sporadic, dependent upon the fortuitous collision of individual interests and government policy; it has become systematic and continuous. The Supreme Court now functions more like a *de facto* third chamber of the legislature than a court. The nine Supreme Court justices are now positioned to have more influence on how Canada is governed than are all of the parliamentarians who sit outside of cabinet.

THREE

THE COURT PARTY

The fate of a bill of rights ... depends on forces outside of it.
Charles R. Epp.[1]

If judges are a more important cause of the Charter revolution than the Charter itself, an even more significant cause is the Court Party. The social movements composing the Court Party would have grown in prominence even without the Charter; they would not have gone so far so fast, however. The Charter gave them a new venue, the courtroom, to pursue their agendas and conferred on them the status needed to participate in the arena of constitutional politics. The result has been enhanced legitimacy (and generous state funding) for Court Party efforts in the legal arena.

While many of the Court Party constituencies would have gained prominence in the absence of the Charter, the opposite is not true. Without a Court Party, the Charter and the courts would not have attained their current political significance. It was the underdevelopment of such a constituency that helped stunt the 1960 Diefenbaker Bill of Rights. The Court Party has provided the political buoyancy that gave life and energy to the Charter, lifting it out of the statute books and making it a new force in Canadian politics.

Like the more familiar electoral parties, or political movements generally, the Court Party is a coalition of several overlapping constituencies. We have identified five main strands or dimensions of the Court Party coalition: (1) national unity advocates, (2) civil libertarians, (3) equality seekers, (4) social engineers, and (5) postmaterialists.[2] A variety of overlapping interests and ideological orientations (as well as membership) lead these constituencies to join in promoting judicial power.

Unifiers

Unifiers see the Charter, and the judicial power it fosters, as helping to solve Canada's national unity crisis. Former Prime Minister Pierre Trudeau, the "father" of the Charter, most prominently represents this wing of the Court

Party. From the beginning, Trudeau saw the Charter as much more than a rights-protecting document. Indeed, he saw it mainly as a counterweight to the forces of decentralizing regionalism and provincialism.[3] The Charter, he hoped, would lead Canadians to define themselves more in terms of rights they held in common and less in terms of geographical communities that divided them.[4] As early as 1967, Trudeau described his Charter project as "essentially testing, and hopefully establishing, the unity of Canada." Fifteen years later, in debating the Charter in parliament, Trudeau described it as defining "the common thread that binds us together," overcoming "the forces of self-interest [that threaten to] tear us apart."[5] Peter Russell has described this position as "Charter patriotism."[6]

For Trudeau and the unifiers, the centerpiece of the Charter is language rights. Entrenching language rights in the constitution culminated Trudeau's long-standing strategy to use bilingualism to undercut the appeal of Quebec nationalism and preserve Canadian unity.[7] In 1969, the newly elected Trudeau government enacted the Official Languages Act (OLA), which, however, was restricted to areas of federal jurisdiction. Section 23 of the Charter, which grants minority language education rights, represented an extension of bilingualism into the field of primary and secondary education, hitherto an exclusive provincial jurisdiction.

The importance Trudeau attached to language rights is reflected in its privileged position *vis-à-vis* the rest of the Charter. During the two-year period in which the wording and structure of the Charter was negotiated, Trudeau refused to compromise on the entrenchment of language rights. When the western premiers finally succeeded in their demand for the section 33 override, the language rights provisions (ss.16-23) were exempted. Trudeau was not about to subject compliance with his new policy breakthrough to the consent of traditionally hostile provincial governments.[8]

With the adoption of section 23 of the Charter, Ottawa encouraged francophone and anglophone rights groups to pressure provincial governments to comply with their new obligation to provide minority language education services. If a province refused or dragged its heels, Ottawa made sure the language rights groups could afford to go to court. These official language minority groups (OLMGs) were already receiving annual operating grants from Ottawa, which also established a "Court Challenges Program" to fund the costs of language rights litigation.[9] Predictably, section 23 lawsuits were soon launched in almost every province. As Trudeau had anticipated, this flurry of litigation made the Supreme Court of Canada the *de facto* national school board for bilingual education.[10]

Encouraged by federal funding, OLMGs have become some of the most active and successful litigators under the Charter. OLMGs have won 16 of the 21 language rights cases decided by appeal courts since the Court Challenges Program was established. Thirteen of these decisions resulted in positive policy changes from the OLMG perspective.[11] Outside Quebec, francophone groups have won major section 23 education cases in British Columbia, Alberta, Manitoba, Ontario, Nova Scotia, and PEI. In non-education cases, they have also won major language rights victories in Manitoba and Saskatchewan.[12] Without exception, these cases have been strategic test cases brought by OLMGs such as La Société franco-manitobaine, Société des Acadiens, L'association francophones des conseils scolaires de l'Ontario, and l'Association culturelle franco-canadienne de la Saskatchewan. A frequent interverner is the Fédération des francophones hors Québec (FFHQ), the national umbrella organization for all the provincial groups.

In Quebec, anglophone rights groups – Alliance Quebec or its precursors[13] – have helped bring successful court challenges to three different policy provisions of Bill 101. First, in a pre-Charter case, the Supreme Court prevented the Parti Québécois from making French the only official language of Quebec. Second, it used section 23 of the Charter to strike down the restriction of access to English-language education. Third, it invalidated provisions banning English-language signs in outdoor advertising.[14]

Like other wings of the Court Party, the unifiers straddle the state-society, public sector-private sector divide. While these OLMGs are typically presented as private-sector non-governmental organizations (NGOs) or citizens' groups, their dependence on federal funding has made them a *de facto* instrument of Ottawa's national unity policy. Not only do they litigate the expansion of language rights in their own provinces, but they intervene in one another's cases to encourage the courts to expand the scope of section 23.[15]

In addition, the governments of Ontario and New Brunswick, Trudeau's two original constitutional allies from the 1980-81 Chartermaking process, have frequently intervened in language rights cases *against* other provinces. The federal Commissioner for Official Languages also frequently intervenes on behalf of OLMGs against the provinces.[16] These government allies give OLMG Charter claims added legitimacy before the courts and contribute to their high success rates.

With respect to most of francophone Quebec, Charter patriotism has been a dismal failure.[17] The OLMGs' success has actually intensified, rather than ameliorated, nationalist projects for Quebec's disengagement from

Canada. Because the Charter was constitutionally entrenched without Quebec's consent, it is held up in that province as evidence of English Canada's betrayal of its founding partner and has symbolically fuelled, rather than doused, nationalist fires. In addition, Quebec nationalists see the 1990 defeat of the Meech Lake accord as a second Charter-related betrayal. The accord brought into sharp focus the tension between the Charter patriots' vision of a common pan-Canadian citizenship and the Quebec nationalists' desire for constitutional recognition of Quebec as a distinct society.[18] Once again, the Charter patriots won.

While the Charter has aggravated Canada's deepest national-unity wound, unifiers retain high hopes for the Charter's unifying potential, if not with respect to the forces of Quebec separatism (at least in the short term), then certainly with respect to the forces of regional alienation in the rest of Canada. If one leaves Quebec out of the picture, it turns out that Canadians are as much divided by Charter issues as they are by regionalism, but these Charter-related disagreements cut across regions, thus acting as counterweights to regionalism.[19]

As we have seen, the boundaries of Charter rights are difficult to define with precision, and thus occasion battles over their proper interpretation. For example, the pro-life and pro-choice factions in the abortion controversy have engaged in prolonged and highly charged battles about whether section 7 of the Charter protects the life of the fetus or the liberty of the mother to abort that fetus, a question to which there is no obvious textual answer. Unifiers, however, prefer such cross-cutting cleavages to the regional cleavages at the root of Canada's national unity crisis, and they like the Charter for its tendency to emphasize them. How people view abortion or employment equity, for example, has little to do with what provinces they live in. Surveys of attitudes toward civil liberties issues conducted in 1987 and again in 1999 found no significant variations between regions.[20]

The Charter does not just engender battles about crosscutting issues; it also makes the courtroom the most publicly prominent arena for conducting these battles. The courts now make more policy than they used to in areas that were previously dominated by legislatures. But the legislative branch of government in Canada is federally divided, while the judicial branch is not. The Canadian judiciary constitutes a single hierarchy, culminating in the Supreme Court, whose Charter interpretations are applicable across the country, regardless of federal jurisdiction. Thus a national court can now make major decisions in controversial policy areas, such as minority language education, which otherwise fall under provincial jurisdiction.[21]

In short, the Charter has effected a forum shift. It has transferred authority over language education (and other policy areas) out of provincial legislatures and into the nationally unified court system. By transforming
minority interests into minority rights, the Charter transferred ultimate
responsibility to the Supreme Court of Canada, a much more sympathetic
forum. While OLMGs were the initial beneficiaries of Trudeau's strategy,
other similarly situated groups – politically weak at the provincial level but
with support in Ottawa – soon took advantage of the Charter (and federal
funding) to use the courts to do an end run around unsympathetic provincial governments. In this sense, the Charter represents an empowerment of
social interests (Charter Canadians) favoured by the federal government.
These groups in turn mobilize support for the Charter, the courts, the
Court Challenges Program and the federal government generally.

That the transfer of policymaking power from legislatures to courts
amounts to a centralization of policymaking power is something the pro-
moters of judicial review have always understood. In the US, from the
founding onwards, the partisans of judicial review have often favoured the
national government over the states.[22] In Canada, many of the proponents
and opponents of the first Supreme Court Act saw judicial review as a form of
"disallowance in disguise"; that is, a way for the political centre to control
the periphery regions. The critique of the Court as a covert agency of centralization is still very much alive, especially in Quebec.[23] This is one of the
reasons that the western premiers demanded that Trudeau add the section
33 override if he wanted their support for the Charter. For unifiers, however,
the centralizing tendency of judicial review is a virtue not a vice.

Civil Libertarians

Those who want to protect individual freedom from the potentially oppressive power of the state have also promoted the Charter and judicial power.
As Russell has observed, "The Charter's political sponsors were aided and
abetted by a phalanx of academics and lawyers who believed a Charter was
needed to enhance our freedom and secure our liberty."[24] From this civil libertarian perspective, when the enormous state leviathan turns its baleful
gaze on the puny individual, the latter needs all the help he can get.

Sometimes libertarians speak as though government was the only threat
to individual liberty, but the original formulation of their perspective recognized that equally serious threats could come from other individuals.
Indeed, it is the danger individuals pose to each other that justifies the estab-

lishment of a government strong enough to enforce the peace and security on which liberty depends.[25] The problem is that the governmental strength required to secure individuals against each other is itself a danger to those individuals. John Stuart Mill, the patron saint of libertarianism, expressed the dilemma in colourful terms:

> To prevent the weaker members of the community from being preyed upon by innumerable vultures, it was needful that there should be an animal of prey stronger than the rest, commissioned to keep them down. But as the king of the vultures would be no less bent upon preying on the flock than any of the minor harpies, it was indispensable to be in a perpetual attitude of defense against his beak and claws.

Mill denied that transforming the chief vulture from a king into a representative and responsible parliament made its beak and claws any less dangerous. The advent of democracy, he argued, protected the majority against oppression by minorities but did nothing to protect individuals and minorities against the "tyranny of the majority." Indeed, tyrannical majorities were in some respects more dangerous than individual tyrants. It thus remained necessary to "set limits to the power which the ruler should be suffered to exercise over the community."[26] For modern libertarians, the necessary limits are best set by a constitutionally entrenched bill or charter of rights, enforced by the governmental institution most independent of the dangerous majority; i.e., the judiciary.[27]

In the 1920s and 1930s, libertarians looked to the judiciary mainly to protect economic liberty and property rights against the emerging welfare state. In both Canada and the United States, this economic libertarianism succeeded in having the courts strike down such welfare-state regulation as minimum wage and maximum hour legislation.[28] As Mallory pointed out over a generation ago, in Canada "the force that start[ed] our interpretive machinery in motion" in many constitutional cases was "the reaction of a free economy against regulation."[29] The same was true in the US. The court parties of that era, in other words, were the libertarian partisans of private property and laissez faire, while their opponents, who controlled the legislatures, favoured public regulation and the redistribution of private wealth.

The generation of intellectuals who developed the welfare state — what Doug Owram called the "government generation"[30] — went to war against judicial power and eventually influenced the courts to abandon their opposition to the welfare state. As noted in chapter 1, the conflict between the US Supreme Court and Franklin Roosevelt's New Deal culminated in the Court's capitulation in 1937. Corwin described this capitulation as nothing less than a "constitutional revolution," because it marked the end in practice (if not in popular myth) of the American Founders' ideal of guaranteeing limited government through a written constitution. After the 1937 Court Crisis, the American Court publicly abdicated its traditional constitutional responsibilities (federalism, economic liberty, and property rights) and virtually disappeared from American politics for almost two decades, until its *School Desegregation Decision* in 1954.

In Canada an analogous if less dramatic conflict between the judiciary and the new welfare-state interventionism of the federal government also appeared to spell the end of a significant political role for the courts. In particular, the Judicial Committee of the Privy Council, which had mounted the judicial opposition to the welfare state, was replaced by the Supreme Court as Canada's highest court of appeal, and political negotiation replaced judicial review as the preferred means of managing federal-provincial jurisdictional disputes. The triumphant government generation in both countries, in short, was to a considerable extent an anti-court party. Its perspective lingered on in Canada into the 1960s, helping to swamp Diefenbaker's 1960 Bill of Rights and render it without effect.[31] To liberals on both sides of the border, "whose political truths were formed during the era of the New Deal, judicial activism was simply incompatible with progressive politics."[32]

If the libertarians in the older court party focused on economic liberty, the libertarians in today's Court Party emphasize other liberties. Concerned especially with protecting individual rights of freedom of religion and expression against state restriction, they typically oppose censorship and state-support for religion. They are also concerned with ensuring that individual freedom is not unnecessarily or unjustly infringed by either the state's criminal justice system or its administrative procedures. Criminals should certainly be caught, punished, and deterred, but state enthusiasm to do so effectively and efficiently must not lead to the unnecessary harassment or, much worse, the punishment of innocent individuals. Far better from the libertarian perspective to have the occasional guilty party go free than to interfere with the liberties of the innocent. The power imbalance between the state leviathan and the individual must be similarly redressed in administrative contexts, such as hearings to determine whether an otherwise illegal immigrant should get the benefit of refugee status.[33]

The Canadian Civil Liberties Association (CCLA) is the oldest and most influential representative of the civil libertarian perspective. It has independent affiliates in most provinces, such as the BC and Alberta Civil Liberties Associations. The CCLA pre-dates the Charter. In the 1970s, it was bitterly disappointed with the Supreme Court's failure to adopt libertarian interpretations of the 1960 Bill of Rights in cases involving issues such as abortion, right to counsel, and exclusion of evidence. The CCLA opposed the original version of the Trudeau Charter because it was worded so similarly to the Bill of Rights that they feared it would simply mean more of the same. As noted in chapter 1, however, CCLA criticisms of the early drafts of the Charter produced important changes in that document.

The CCLA has been active in using and developing the Charter. Up to 1997 it intervened in 32 cases and was the primary litigant in two others. It is second only to LEAF in interventions before the Supreme Court of Canada.[34] Most of the CCLA's interventions – 15 – have been to defend freedom of speech. The CCLA has also been involved in six criminal law/legal rights cases and five freedom of religion cases, and has participated in cases involving abortion, privacy, labour law, and equality issues. Overall the CCLA has been successful in 63 per cent of its interventions and changed the policy status quo in the direction it wanted in 16 cases. It successfully challenged the practice of voluntary school prayer in Ontario and directly influenced the Supreme Court's nullification of the rape shield law. On the other hand, it failed in its challenges to censorship of pornography and hate-speech.[35]

Equality Seekers

Peter Russell has described the civil libertarian supporters of the Charter as the "believers" and juxtaposes them to yet another "cluster of interest groups and ideologues ... 'the hopers': the egalitarians on the left who hoped the Charter would be an instrument for reforming society. Whereas the civil libertarians believed the Charter was essential for preserving liberty, the egalitarians hoped it would bring about social equality."[36]

The Charter equality seekers are drawn primarily from the social left, not the older economic left and organized labour. From the start, spokesmen for the economic left have been sceptical, even scornful, of using courts and litigation as an instrument for economic leveling.[37] They associated judges with lawyers and lawyers with the interests of the business class, not an unreasonable deduction given the well-documented antipathy of courts to the creation of the welfare state in Canada, the US and the UK earlier in this century. Former NDP Premier of Saskatchewan, Allan Blakeney, strongly opposed the adoption of the Charter for these very reasons.

While the old left has always sought to reduce or abolish class inequalities, the social left is more concerned with life-style issues and the politics of identity. The former is associated with politically organized labour; the latter with the new social movements: feminism, environmentalism, the anti-nuclear/peace movement, ethnic nationalism, and gay rights. To the extent that the hopers address economic equality, their stated goal is usually not the abolition of class inequality, but rather the proportional representation of their group within each of the different rungs of the economic ladder. As Michael Mandel, a prominent advocate of the economic left perspective, puts it, Charter litigation "take[s] for granted basic power relations." He maintains, for example, that equality-rights cases "are all about equal access to existing institutions while leaving these institutions and especially the employment relationship itself ... untouched. In other words, they lack all class character.... They challenge nothing but the place of [minorities] within an otherwise intact status quo."[38]

Russell, failing to distinguish between the economic and the social left, wrongly concludes that the egalitarian dreams of the hopers have not been fulfilled under the Charter. While this is true for the old left, it is not as true for the social left. Feminists and gay rights advocates have achieved significant victories and policy changes through Charter litigation.[39] The kind of equality they seek is not the same as Mandel's economic leveling.

The social left's idea of equality is also different from the traditional liberal understanding of equality as equal (i.e., the same) treatment. The hopers emphasize group rather than individual equality, equality of results rather than equality of opportunity. Indeed, they insist that the liberal principle of non-discrimination against individuals must be temporarily suspended until the goal of equality of results for specified groups is achieved. They support preferential governmental treatment that either "compensates" group members for past injustices or promotes group equality in the future.[40]

For example, Judge Rosalie Abella, a leading light within the equality-seeking movement, argues that traditional civil liberties are overly individualistic and anchored in a formal account of equality — "treating every one the same." Abella distinguishes between such "civil liberties" and a newer breed of "human rights," which require governments "to treat us differently to redress the abuses our differences have attracted." Abella describes the discovery of such human rights as an epochal moment in human history.

It was as if we had awakened from a 300 year sleep, looked around us and realized how limited our rights vision had become and with stunning energy and enthusiasm, acknowledged more rights and remedies in one generation than we had in all the centuries since the Glorious Revolution in England in 1688.[41]

This kind of evangelical enthusiasm for the new human rights vision has led feminist legal scholars to reject a policy of non-discrimination as inadequate. Instead they have proposed sophisticated jurisprudential theories of disparate impact and systemic discrimination that invite judicial revision of legislative decision-making.[42] Other members of the section 15 club have endorsed this theory of systemic discrimination. At a minimum this interpretation of section 15 challenges otherwise neutral government policies that disproportionately burden women and other "disadvantaged" minorities. At a maximum it sanctions judicially ordered positive remedies to achieve equal results. In the latter instance, Charter experts advocate the use of the structural injunction, a legal instrument pioneered by American activists whereby the courts manage the reconstruction of a social institution such as schools or prisons until they comply with constitutional standards. Failure to use such aggressive, state-extending remedies, says Helena Orton, former litigation director for LEAF, will render "the guarantee of equality ... deceitful and meaningless."[43] In its 1989 *Andrews* decision, and in such subsequent cases as *Vriend*, the Supreme Court embraced much of this revolutionary human rights understanding of the Charter's equality provisions.[44]

The list of equality-seeking groups includes the "charter" members of the section 15 club: women, visible and religious minorities, the mentally and physically disabled, and the elderly. Also included are the so-called "analogous" section 15 groups added by the courts via interpretation: homosexuals and non-citizens.[45] Official language minorities (sections 16-23), the multicultural communities (section 27), and aboriginals (sections 25 and 35) round out the equality-seekers. When Deborah Coyne observed that a "new emerging power structure" has formed around the Charter, these groups were mostly what she had in mind.[46] Since the egalitarian hopers seek to fulfill their hopes through judicial enforcement of their Charter rights, they have a vested interest in judicial power.

Encouraged by funding from the Secretary of State and the Court Challenges Program, each of these groups has formed a litigation organization to press their causes in court. The first, the most influential, and the model for the rest has been the feminist organization, LEAF. As noted in chapter 1, LEAF was formed after the adoption of the Charter for the express purpose of carrying out strategic litigation of test cases. The lead national advocacy group for homosexuals is EGALE (Equality for Gays and Lesbians Everywhere), supported by numerous provincial counterparts such as the Coalition for Lesbian and Gay Rights in Ontario. The disabled are represented by COPOH (Coalition of Provincial Organizations of the Handicapped) and the Disabled Women's Network; non-citizens by the Canadian Council for Refugees; and visible minorities by the Canadian Ethnocultural Council (Equality Committee) and the Minority Advocacy Rights Council. There are also "wannabe" members of the section 15 club who have not yet received the blessing of the Court but do have litigation organizations, thanks to grants from the Court Challenges Program. Prisoners are now represented by the Canadian Prisoners' Rights Network (CPRN) and the poor by the Charter Committee on Poverty Issues and End Legislated Poverty. While the Assembly of First Nations (AFN) has a broader mandate, it has also become a frequent intervener in aboriginal rights cases.[47]

The unifiers and OLMGs also qualify as equality-seekers. The crusade for national bilingualism has always invoked the symbols and rhetoric of equality. For Trudeau and his disciples, achieving the symbolic and practical equality of French with English was to be the antidote to Quebec separatism. When the Canadian Coalition on the Constitution formed to protect the Charter against the 1987 Meech Lake Accord, Alliance Quebec, the FFHQ, and its various provincial affiliates were all counted as members.

While these groups all march under the banner of equality, there are important differences among them. The tension between bilingualism and multiculturalism is longstanding. The logic of two founding nations is not particularly flattering to those Canadians, now a majority, whose ancestry is neither French nor English. Not unreasonably, aboriginals take some offense at the concept of two founding nations when it ignores first nations. Aboriginal self-government, an idea that often rejects review of rights claims by outsiders (i.e., white judges), has prompted strong criticism from feminists.[48]

There are also tensions between the libertarian and egalitarian wings of the Court Party. Both economic and social libertarians wish to protect their favoured liberties against overweening government. By contrast, the hopers' equality-of-results agenda generally means more government, not less. This is clearly true of the section 23 minority language education rights, which often expand educational bureaucracy.[49] It is also often the object of feminists and other equality seekers, whose policy agendas reject formal equality of opportunity in the name of equality of results. As Janine Brodie has written, most "key feminist policy demands ... call for more not less government and public spending."[50] Or, to use Abella's formulation, traditional civil liberties require "the state not to interfere with our liberties" while human rights "cannot be realized without the state's intervention." Abella adds that "unlike civil liberties, which re-arranges no social relationships and only protects our political ones, human rights is a direct assault on the status quo. It is inherently about change."[51]

The positive judicial activism required by this "human rights" position — i.e., telling governments what to do, or even doing it for them — is anomalous for libertarians, who think government can infringe constitutional rights only by doing too much, not by failing to act and thus doing too little. For the egalitarian wing of the Court Party, by contrast, a government's failure to act can be just as unconstitutional as its actions, and positive activism thus becomes a logical remedy. A libertarian might well wonder how such an approach to the Charter is possible. How, he might ask, can a document that, on its face, covers only the laws and policies of legislatures and governments apply to the *absence* of law or policy? The answer given by egalitarian theoreticians is that the decision not to impose law or policy is itself a legal or policy decision; i.e., that nonlaw is also law, and thus subject to the Charter.[52]

An example will help to clarify the point. Section 15 of the Charter explicitly prohibits only discrimination by laws. From the libertarian perspective, this means that section 15 does not directly prohibit a private employer from refusing to hire, say, disabled employees. Moreover, although governments are free to address such private discrimination through statutory human rights codes, section 15 imposes no positive obligation to enact such legislation. Someone with this view might well believe that private discrimination against the disabled is wrong, and that legislation to prohibit it would be desirable, but would nevertheless deny that section 15's prohibition of public discrimination requires the state to legislate against private discrimination. If, by contrast, a government's decision not to enact such legislation is understood as legal permission for, even endorsement of, private discrimination, then we have a government policy that would be subject to section 15. As Dale Gibson has put it, "If the term 'law' in section 52(1) of the Charter were interpreted to include [such] permissive aspects of law as well as those which are prohibitory, the Charter would have a very wide range of operation."[53]

A very wide range indeed! Among other things, it would subject all government inaction – all public failures to right private wrongs – to judicial scrutiny under the Charter and would require positive action to remedy any unconstitutional inaction. In our example, it would require any government that had not legislated against private discrimination to do so.

The equality seekers' conflating of state action and inaction involves a rejection of the traditional liberal ordering of state and society. In classical liberal theory the realm of societal freedom precedes the state, which is based on consent. People consent to the establishment of the state, and thus to *some* state-imposed limits on their freedom, in order better to secure a remaining (and significant) realm of freedom. Thus, when classical liberals use the old adage that "whatever the law does not prohibit is permitted," they understand it as protecting an important residue of pre-political freedom, which does not owe its existence to the state.

Modern equality-rights theoreticians understand the same adage very differently. They take it to mean that societal freedom is permitted *by* the law and thus exists *because of* (as opposed to being better secured by) the state.[54] Instead of understanding the state as the creation of a pre-existing society, equality seekers see society as the creation of the state. The societal realm of private freedom is no longer understood as the residue of an original, pre-political freedom, the better protection of which constitutes the very *raison d'être* of the state, but as existing only because, and to the extent that, the state permits it. The state thus becomes responsible for the use and misuse of societal freedom, and can be forced to regulate the latter by courts applying constitutional standards.

The equality-seeking wing of the Court Party has only partially succeeded in persuading the courts to accept its conflation of state and society. The courts have insisted on maintaining the distinction, with the Charter applying only to the state.[55] Since this distinction is undermined by the doctrine that state inaction is essentially the same as state action, the courts have not fully accepted that doctrine. They have not, to be more precise, fully endorsed the view that public failures to redress private wrongs are necessarily subject to Charter scrutiny. The courts have gone part way in this direction, however, holding that *partial* action may be successfully challenged even if complete inaction is permissible. Thus, although a government doesn't have to legislate against private discrimination, if it chooses to do so, the legislation must extend to all the group traits protected against public discrimination by the Charter. Having found that homosexuality was a prohibited ground of discrimination under section 15, for example, the Ontario Court of Appeal, concluded in *Haig and Birch* that the failure of the

Canadian Human Rights Act to include sexual preference as a prohibited ground of discrimination was unconstitutional. In *Vriend* (1998), the Supreme Court came to the same conclusion about the Alberta Human Rights Act.[56]

Logically, of course, finding a partial action to be unconstitutional for not going far enough does not require positive judicial activism if complete inaction is also permissible. Indeed, a perfectly logical response would be to invalidate the entire law, leaving it to the legislature to choose between the two constitutional alternatives: re-enacting the law in a constitutionally comprehensive manner, or enacting no law at all. This is not what equality seekers have in mind, however. Understanding the "staying power of a legal status quo,"[57] such Court Party actors as LEAF argue that the courts should not dismantle desirable remedial legislation, thus establishing ground zero as the legal status quo, a status quo the government might well be tempted to leave in place. Judges "should hesitate," LEAF advised the Supreme Court, "to select a remedy that would leave the disadvantaged dependent on the actions of a majoritarian legislature to restore to them benefits" which have been struck down only because they are "underinclusive."[58] To the contrary, LEAF maintained, judges should not hesitate to read the unconstitutionally missing beneficiaries into the deficient legislation, thus placing the weight of the legal status quo at the interventionist end of the policy continuum. This is the ultimate in positive judicial activism, inasmuch as it allows judges to bypass legislatures altogether and extend policies of state intervention directly, by rewriting legislation themselves.

Here again, the equality seekers' perspective has met with only partial, but nevertheless significant success. The Supreme Court has accepted the legitimacy of reading in, but only when the missing beneficiaries are significantly fewer in number than those already included, thus making it safer to assume that the legislature would rather keep a slightly extended version of the legislation than to abandon it altogether.[59] Homosexuals, it turns out, are a small enough group to qualify for reading into a list of legislative beneficiaries. Thus, in *Haig and Birch*, the Ontario Court of Appeal read sexual preference into the Canadian Human Rights Act, as the Supreme Court later did to the Alberta Human Rights Act in *Vriend*.

The tension between the libertarian and egalitarian wings of the Court Party occasionally results in public and bitter clashes in the courtroom. In such cases as *Keegstra* (hate literature), *Butler* (pornography) and *Seaboyer* (rape shield), LEAF and the CCLA have intervened to take opposing positions. In each instance, LEAF defended the government's policy as necessary to promote the equality of women. The CCLA countered that the censorship of hate literature and pornography unduly infringed freedom of speech and expression, while the rape shield law deprived the accused of procedural fairness. When the Supreme Court struck down the rape shield law in 1991, feminists publicly attacked the CCLA for its role and over 50 CCLA members resigned their memberships.[60]

Libertarians and equality seekers have also clashed about the balance between free speech and anti-discrimination law.[61] For example, Kathleen Mahoney, a prominent feminist lawyer, brought *Alberta Report* before the Alberta Human Rights Commission for publishing a story arguing that the much publicized abuse in Indian residential schools was balanced by the positive experiences many Indians had in these schools. The story suggested that the prospect of federal compensation might fuel exaggerated claims of abuse by Indian leaders. Mahoney charged *Alberta Report* with violating the law's prohibition of publications "likely to expose a person or a class of persons to ... contempt because of" their race. The *Saskatoon Star Phoenix* faced similar charges for publishing an anti-gay advertisement, as did the *Toronto Star* for refusing to publish an ethnic leader's letter to the editor. These challenges to free speech flow from the equality seeking impulse and tend to be opposed by civil libertarians.

Alan Borovoy, longtime Executive Director of the CCLA, became so concerned about the deepening split between libertarians and equality seekers that he wrote a book about it – *The New Anti-Liberals*. Not surprisingly, he defends the libertarian position against what he calls the anti-liberal excesses of the current equality-seeking left. The latter, he claims, has abandoned traditional liberal principles.[62]

The libertarian-egalitarian conflict is not perfectly reflected in the interest group competition between the CCLA and equality seeking groups. The CCLA is decidedly mixed in its commitment to libertarianism. It would hardly agree with the policy positions of the National Citizens' Coalition (NCC), despite the latter's motto: "More freedom through less government." The CCLA has never extended its libertarianism to economic policy. Quite the opposite. The CCLA has early and enduring ties to the labour union movement in Canada and has never challenged the extensive state regime of labour regulation. The NCC, by contrast, frequently challenges labour laws that infringe on individual freedoms of association and speech.[63] The NCC financed Merv Lavigne's Charter challenge against OPSEU. Lavigne, a college teacher in Ontario, objected to portions of his mandatory union dues being used by OPSEU to support left-wing causes that he opposed. (These included the Sandinistas in Nicaragua and the Palestinian

Liberation Organization.) The CCLA intervened to defend the power of unions to contribute money to political causes unrelated to collective bargaining. Lavigne claimed that when combined with compulsory union dues for non-members like himself, this was a violation of his rights to freedom of speech and association.

Social Engineers

A fourth perspective that inclines toward judicial power and thus contributes to the Court Party coalition is captured by the term "social engineer." The social engineers are distinct from the other cohorts of the Court Party in that they are not a physically identifiable group. Nor do they have their own litigation organization; there is no organized group of social engineers' equivalent to the OLMGs, LEAF, or the CCLA. Yet the social engineering perspective informs, to varying degrees, each of these groups, and explains why they favour the empowerment of courts.

Social engineers take the view that the social evils of this world are caused not by human nature but rather by defective social institutions and systems. Cure the institutional ills, they believe, and natural human goodness will prevail. Such a cure, of course, implies comprehensive reconstruction of the defective societal structures; i.e., social engineering. For example, social engineers believe that crime has no natural causes, that it can be explained almost completely by such structural factors as class inequality, and that it can be cured through appropriate structural change.

Underlying the perspective of the social engineers is what Thomas Sowell has called the "unconstrained" vision of human nature and society.[64] This vision is best understood in relation to its opposite, the "constrained" vision, which holds that there are inherent limits or "constraints" on the human capacity to achieve social perfection. Social evil, in the constrained view, has natural causes, which can be checked and ameliorated, but not cured.[65] Human nature, in other words, while not necessarily devoid of admirable social tendencies, has its ineradicably asocial, even antisocial, side. Institutions can channel asocial and antisocial tendencies in more or less productive ways and can affect the relative balance between the good and bad sides of human nature, but no amount of social engineering can eradicate the latter. Improvement is possible; perfection is not.[66]

The constrained vision underlies the traditional liberal separation of state and society. It sees ineradicable human imperfection as the source of both dissatisfaction with the pre-political state of freedom that underlies consent to government and the distrustful insistence on limiting and constraining that government. James Madison most memorably captures this perspective in *Federalist Paper* 51:

> It may be a reflection on human nature that [checks and balances] should be necessary to control the abuses of government. But what is government itself but the greatest of all reflections on human nature? If men were angels, no government would be necessary. If angels were to govern men, neither external nor internal controls on government would be necessary. In framing a government which is to be administered by men over men, the great difficulty lies in this: you must first enable the government to control the governed; and in the next place oblige it to control itself.[67]

According to the unconstrained vision, by contrast, human beings are good by nature but corruptible by society. As Jean Jacques Rousseau, the father of this perspective, put in 1762, "man is born free, and everywhere he is in chains."[68] This view makes it possible to think society could be comprehensively re-engineered to end alienation and conflict and, having restored natural human goodness, make it permanently victorious. For Marx and his followers, to take just one example, the source of man's alienation was class inequality. Abolish private property, they preached, and utopia would follow.

Contemporary (or second wave) feminism has aptly been described as "Marxism without economics," since feminists replace class with gender as the key social construct. Of course, what society constructs can be deconstructed. This is the feminist project: to abolish gender difference by transforming its institutional source – the patriarchal family. Certain streams of the Gay Rights movement have taken this analysis one step further. The problem is not just sexism but heterosexism, and the solution is to dismantle not just the patriarchal family but the heterosexual family as such. As Gregory Hein puts it the "indictment of modern life" brought by such movements "is so scathing" that they "want to transform social attitudes, economic relationships, and political institutions."[69]

The unconstrained vision, which has been and continues to be an influential dynamic in modern politics, can lead to two quite different approaches to democracy: populism and democratic elitism. The populist approach arises when the societal corruption of natural human goodness is understood as affecting only a nefarious elite, in which case the obvious answer is to promote increased democracy. The rule of the "whole uncorrupted portion of the people"[70] can then be seen as an unmitigated good, bringing social and political life to a state of perfection. But, of course, the unconstrained vision does not in principle exclude the systemic corruption of the people as a whole. They too can be deformed by the social system. When this happens, democracy may still be the ultimate end, after the people have been returned to their natural purity, but it cannot be the immediate means. The achievement of true democracy will first require a period of purification through social reconstruction by a vanguard of purifiers. This is the route of major social engineering, and it necessarily involves democratic elitism or "Guardian democracy."[71]

Democratic elitism is the position many proponents of the unconstrained vision are drawn toward today. Wishing to transform the formative system, they cannot entrust power to the people who have been formed by that system and who are likely simply to reproduce it. Thus the vanguard elite must temporarily exercise transformatory power – i.e., it must engage in social engineering – which it can do only through institutions relatively unresponsive to the will of the corrupted many.

This is why Lenin, in his attempt to establish Marxism, had to invent the idea of the Communist Party as the "vanguard of the proletariat" (i.e., the enlightened leaders of the not-yet enlightened masses). For social engineers in Canada's Court Party, the judiciary performs this vanguard role.

Significantly, elements of the social engineering perspective can be found in the thinking of Pierre Elliott Trudeau, the architect of the Charter. Trained as a lawyer and endowed with a Rousseauian view of human nature, Trudeau clearly featured himself as the omnipotent "legislateur" or lawgiver for Canadian society. When he entered federal politics in 1967, he announced a new role for the Department of Justice and its new Minister – himself:

> Justice should be regarded more and more as a department planning for the society of tomorrow, not merely as the government's legal advisor. It should combine the function of drafting new legislation with the disciplines of sociology and economics, so that it can provide a framework for our evolving way of life. Society is throwing up problems all the time – divorce, abortions, family planning, LSD, pollution, etc. – and it's no longer enough to review our statutes every twenty years. If possible, we have to move the framework of our society slightly ahead of the times, so there is no curtailment of intellectual or physical liberty.[72]

Given this ambitious mission, Trudeau's subsequent actions should not surprise us. As Minister of Justice, he introduced reforms that expanded access to legal abortions, decriminalized homosexuality, and made divorce easier. As Prime Minister, his first act was to push through the Official Languages Act (1969) to form a more unified Canada. He pursued his ideal of a more just society through the rejuvenated office of the Secretary of State: the multicultural program (1973-74) and the women's program (1973-74).[73] He also initiated a host of other law-reforming agencies: the Law Reform Commission and the Federal Court (1970); the federal Human Rights Commission (1977), and the Federal Commissioner for Judicial Affairs (1978).[74] For Trudeau the law-giver, the 1982 Charter of Rights was the culmination of a decade and a half of social-transformation.

As the preceding discussion suggests, social engineering is associated more with equality seekers than libertarians. The economic left's attempts to redistribute wealth through social benefit programs (employment insurance, old age security, etc.) and public services (health care, education, etc.) require the construction of the modern welfare state and its legions of bureaucrats. The social left's new but no less ambitious egalitarian projects of moral and social transformation require the institutional engines of democratic elitism, be they vanguard political elites or unaccountable judicial elites. Given the libertarians' scepticism about the benevolence of the "king of the vultures," they are hardly enthusiastic about such state-building projects. This difference explains much of the tension between groups like LEAF and the CCLA, and also the differences between the CCLA and the National Citizens' Coalition.

Postmaterialists

To describe the Court Party as composed of unifiers, civil libertarians, equality seekers, and social engineers is accurate as far as it goes, but it misses the institutional and social nexus that nurtures the coalition. Historians and political analysts have long recognized that inter-institutional struggles reflect competing social forces. As James Mallory puts it, "In a constitutional state with some degree of separation of powers, it may happen that a particular vested interest will capture control of one branch of the government but not another."[75] Often newly emergent government institutions are strongly associated with rising social classes. Thus, the triumph of parliament over the monarchy in the seventeenth century and the eclipse of the House of Lords by the House of Commons in the nineteenth century signaled the rising influence of first the landed aristocracy and then the urban bourgeoisie. Similarly, Canada's nineteenth century struggles for responsible government saw the defeat of executive-ensconced social and economic elites – the Family Compact in Upper Canada; the Chateau Clique in Lower Canada – by democratic and, in the case of Lower Canada, nationalistic partisans of the legislature. The modern Court Party is also rooted in a new class: the so-called postmaterialist or postindustrial knowledge class.

Seymour Martin Lipset has observed that in post-war western democracies, the most dynamic agent of social change has been not Marx's industrial proletariat but a new "oppositionist intelligentsia," drawn from and supported by the well-educated, more affluent strata of society. Inglehart and others explain this change as a consequence of new and growing concerns with noneconomic and social issues – "a clean environment, a better culture, equal status for women and minorities, the quality of education, international relations, greater democratization, and a more permissive morality, particularly as affecting familial and sexual issues."[76]

Lipset and others attribute this political realignment to deeper structural changes in the political economies of most western industrial democracies: historically unprecedented levels of material affluence, education, communication, mobility, and the displacement of the manufacturing and agricultural sectors of the economy by the new service sector. Structural change produces value change. Economic growth, public order, national security, and traditional morality decline in importance. They are replaced by concerns for individual freedom, social equality, and quality of life issues.

These postmaterialist issues have spawned a new kind of interest group. Traditionally, most interest groups have been occupationally based and motivated by the explicit self-interest of their members. Trade unions and manufacturers associations are classic examples. Postmaterialist groups, by contrast, promote "an idea or cause," and thus stand "in contrast to [groups] with an occupational prerequisite."[77] The principal Charter groups – LEAF and the CCLA, for example – fit this postmaterialist mold. Since the 1960s, such postmaterialist groups have been the fastest growing kind of interest group in both Canada and the US.[78] All of the principal postmaterialist groups – feminists, racial minorities, environmentalists, criminal law reformers, anti-nuclear/peace groups – have, to varying degrees, increased their use of litigation as a political tactic.

While postmaterialist interest groups are not occupational groups, they do have a class character. In particular, the new postmaterialist concerns are most prevalent outside the working classes. "The reform elements concerned with postmaterialist or social issues largely derive their strength not from the workers and the less privileged, the social base of the [economic] left in industrial society, but from segments of the well educated and affluent, students, academics, journalists, professionals and civil servants." The latter are all participants in the "knowledge industry" that is a new locus of power in post-industrial democracies. "Just as property was the foundation of elite power in industrial society, so knowledge (based on high levels of education) is the vehicle of power in post-industrial politics of the administrative state."[79]

Of course, it is as difficult today as it has always been for a "knowledge class" to exercise power through majoritarian institutions (consider Plato's philosopher kings). This helps to explain why postmaterialism is attracted to the anti-majoritarian power of the courts. Unlike the progressive reformers of past generations who sought to transfer power from the few rich to the many poor, the postmaterialist left finds itself in the minority and sees the majority as a problem. Inglehart has demonstrated that postmaterialist values are much more prominent among intellectual, bureaucratic, media, and political elites than among the general population. This fact, he argued, created a "tactical dilemma" for "the Left in contemporary society."

> Postmaterialist forces have become powerful at the elite level; they demand major policy shifts in key areas, and they are far too influential among the militants and elites of Left parties to be ignored. But postmaterialists are not equally strong at the mass level – which means that the parties of the Left are in danger of electoral defeat if they swing too far to the Postmaterialist side.

While the postmaterialist left may face a tactical dilemma, it is hardly insuperable. The problem looms large only insofar as the postmaterialist left must compete in the democratic politics of elections and parliaments. To the extent that postmaterialists can move their policy agenda into the courts, the bureaucracy or international organizations such as the United Nations, they can pursue it through the rulings of sympathetic judges and administrators and thus minimize the problem. Inglehart explicitly recognizes that postmaterialists are "better equipped to attain their goals through bureaucratic institutions or the courts than through the electoral process." He points out that, while during the 1960s postmaterialism was symbolized by "the student with a protest placard," it is now symbolized by "the public interest lawyer, or the technocrat with an environmental impact statement."[80]

In Canada, environmental litigation has special significance, because it shows that the attraction of judicial power to postmaterialists exists independently of the Charter. Despite the fact that environmentalists lack any specific constitutional hook (analogous to sections 15 and 28 of the Charter for feminists) and have consequently enjoyed less litigation success, the pace of environmental litigation has increased steadily – from 62 cases in the pre-Charter period to 116 from 1982 to 1995. In just the five-year period between 1990 and 1995, environmentalists initiated 73 actions. This increasing number of cases coincided with the formation of new environmental groups with a strong bent toward litigation – three in the decade preceding the adoption of the Charter in 1982 and another five in the decade following.[81] These groups used an array of legal procedures from writs of mandamus to private prosecutions to advance specific environmental projects. They also lobbied, sometimes successfully, for new legislation that would relax the law of standing, amend the law of public nuisance, fashion new causes of actions, and create mandatory statutory duties – all changes that would facilitate still more use of litigation. In 1986, the Supreme Court opened the door for more environmental litigation by significantly loosening the standing rules governing challenges to administrative actions.[82]

While Mark Silverstein does not employ postmaterialist theory to explain the most recent ascendancy of judicial power in the US, his description of the modern Supreme Court's power base clearly fits the postmaterialist model. "The Warren and Burger Courts," Silverstein writes, "benefited not only the disadvantaged but many affluent, middle and upper-middle class interests.... [E]nvironmentalists, feminists, consumer groups [and] political reformers found in the judiciary an attractive alternative to the other branches in the battle to secure their goals...."[83]

The Elitism of the Court Party

Silverstein says that "[w]hat began as the Warren Court's efforts to empower the underdogs now often serves the interests of the affluent and politically powerful."[84] In other words, the postmaterialist knowledge class is an elite. Furthermore, social engineers engage in democratic elitism. There is, in fact, a symbiotic relationship between these two Court-Party categories: social engineering necessarily involves the transformatory power of a vanguard elite and that elite is drawn from the postmaterialist knowledge class. LEAF provides a characteristic illustration of this Court-Party elitism. Founded by a self-described "elite cadre of professionals," LEAF's initial fundraising efforts targeted "select businesses, well-established law firms, philanthropic institutions [and] upper-class women." With the help of "several large corporations" and Nancy Jackman, the heiress of one of Toronto's wealthiest families, LEAF established an independent endowment fund. In these crucial first years (1985-1988), it also received over a million dollars from Ottawa and the newly elected Liberal government in Ontario.[85]

True, much of the social engineering proposed by Court Party elites is said to serve the interests of disadvantaged Charter-Canadian constituencies, but the rank and file of those constituencies must often undergo "consciousness raising" before they understand their true interests. For the "false consciousness" of the rank and file to be overcome, they must be led by their vanguard, postmaterialist elite. Similarly, the symbolic preoccupations of the unifiers seem most prominent among the same postmaterialist class. The Court Party, in short, is a party of elites. Indeed, it is an important manifestation of what Christopher Lasch calls the "Revolt of the Elites."[86]

The symbiosis of social engineering and the knowledge class, especially with respect to the equality seeking part of the Court Party, should not surprise us. The postmaterialist knowledge class is attracted to the unconstrained vision of the social engineer because that vision places a premium on the concentrated and articulated knowledge of the intellectual. Again, this is best understood against the backdrop of the constrained vision, which emphasizes the dispersed and experiential knowledge of the citizenry at large.

Because the constrained vision views the knowledge of any individual as "grossly inadequate for social decision-making," it conceives of socially relevant knowledge predominantly as "*experience* — transmitted socially in largely inarticulate forms, from prices which indicate costs, scarcities, and preferences, to traditions which evolve from the day-to-day experiences of millions in each generation, winnowing out in Darwinian competition what works from what does not work." Such mechanisms as prices and traditions make a complex society possible by coordinating "knowledge from a tremendous range of contemporaries, as well as from the even wider numbers of those from generations past."[87] The social mechanisms of prices and traditions are much more powerful and effective agents of human progress than articulated intellectual knowledge because they coordinate a much vaster body of social knowledge than any individual or intellectual elite could hope to possess.

For the unconstrained vision, by contrast, experience is "vastly overrated" as compared to "the general power of a cultivated mind," and the "wisdom of the ages" is therefore seen "as largely the illusions of the ignorant." In the words of William Godwin, "The pretense of collective wisdom is the most palpable of all impostures."[88] True wisdom, in this view, is to be found in the articulated rationality, and individual judgment, of intellectual knowledge; i.e., the knowledge of the instructed and cultivated elite. Thus, far from respecting the collective wisdom of the many, as embodied in such mechanisms as prices and traditions, the unconstrained vision emphasizes the role of the intellectual elite in reconstructing the unenlightened many. In other words, it flatters precisely the defining characteristic of the postmaterialist knowledge class.

It is not knowledge *per se* that is being flattered, of course, but knowledge as a prime lever of power. The model of knowledge that has gained prominence among postmaterialists further abets this connection between the knowledge and the power of their class. Postmaterialism is associated with postmodernism, a central tenet of which is that knowledge does not stand apart from power, but in fact *is* power. The reality we purport to understand does not exist independently of that understanding; on the contrary, reality is *constituted* or constructed by our understanding of it. There is no knowledge independent of power; there is only power-knowledge. It is power-knowledge that drives the social construction or social engineering of reality by the knowledge class. The idea that there is no reality independent of human making reflects precisely the perceived lack of limits or constraints that characterizes the unconstrained vision.

The combination of the unconstrained vision and the postmodern model of knowledge is attractive to the knowledge class not only because it flatters its interests, but also because it is consistent with its life experience. Richard Herrnstein and Charles Murray have systematically described and analyzed what others have also observed: the evolution of society's natural cognitive elite from a statistical aggregation into a true class, with its own life experience and distinct interests. They point out that until recently the best and the brightest were distributed throughout society, both geographically and occupationally. Nowadays, by contrast, a variety of sorting mechanisms, particularly the education system, culls them out and concentrates them in high status, knowledge-based occupations and in the communities and networks of what one might call the "internet society," in which they interact mainly with others like themselves.[89] One result, in Christopher Lasch's words, is that "The thinking classes are fatally removed from the physical side of life."

Their only relation to productive labor is that of consumers. They have no experience of making anything substantial or enduring. They live in a world of abstractions and images, a simulated world that consists of computerized models of reality – "hyperreality," as it has been called – as distinguished from the palpable, immediate, physical reality inhabited by ordinary men and women.

This, according to Lasch, helps to explain "their belief in the 'social construction of reality' – the central dogma of postmodernist thought." Belief in this dogma

> reflects the experience of living in an artificial environment from which everything that resists human control (unavoidably, everything familiar and reassuring as well) has been rigorously excluded. Control has become their obsession. In their drive to insulate themselves against risk and contingency – against the unpredictable hazards that afflict human life – the thinking classes have seceded not just from the common world around them but from reality itself.

The knowledge class doesn't believe in a reality that stubbornly escapes human control, in other words, partly because it has seceded from reality. The masses, by contrast, have not seceded from reality because they have not been able to. For the farmer, the assembly worker, the homemaker, and the like, bedrock reality is palpable and inescapable. For Lasch this explains why the political instincts of the masses "are demonstrably more conservative than those of their self-appointed spokesmen and would-be liberators." The conservative instincts Lasch has in mind are largely those of Sowell's constrained vision. In particular, the masses "have a more highly developed sense of limits than their betters. They understand, as their betters do not, that there are inherent limits on human control over the course of social development, over nature and the body, over the tragic elements in human life and history." When Ortega y Gasset wrote *The Revolt of the Masses*, he had in mind a mass man who "looked forward to a future of 'limitless possibilities' and 'complete freedom.'"[90] For Lasch, it is the knowledge elite, not the masses, that now reflect this unconstrained vision of human possibility in western democracies, and it is thus now more appropriate to speak of "The Revolt of the Elites." The Court Party is one manifestation of this revolt of the Elites.

But why is it that these elites present themselves as the self-appointed spokesmen and would-be liberators of disadvantaged groups (in Canada, the Charter groups)? How is it, in other words, that an obviously unequal elite comes to support the cause of equality? For the unconstrained vision, the answer is that the intellectual elite's power of reason – its defining virtue – will lead it to a reasoned support for justice. As Sowell points out, proponents of this vision often assume that intellectual elites are disinterested or "strangers to ambition."[91] This might make sense for some philosophers, under an older view of the disinterested pursuit of knowledge, but it makes little sense within the postmodern perspective of intellectual activity as power-knowledge. In this postmodern view, all knowledge reflects interests, except for an interest in the universal truth, which allegedly doesn't exist, and it thus becomes unclear why anyone's reason would lead him to promote another's interest. We are thus compelled to wonder how the interests of the knowledge classes might be served by projects in the egalitarian transformation of society.[92]

An obvious answer is that such projects serve the power interests of the intellectual elite. Egalitarian social engineering does not give power to the many, whose consciousness needs to be reconstructed, but to the vanguard elite that undertakes the reconstruction. True, the unconstrained vision sees this as *democratic* elitism – i.e., as temporary elitism in the service of more perfect future democracy – but in even the most extreme attempts at societal reconstruction (the Soviet experiment comes to mind), the goal, like a shimmering mirage in the distance, never seems to get any closer, and short of abandoning the reconstructive attempt, the "transitional" period of democratic elitism turns out to be permanent. This is, of course, precisely what the constrained vision would predict: any attempt to achieve the impossible will not end unless those making the attempt recognize and concede its impossibility. A cynic might add that if attempting the impossible enhances one's power, one will be less likely to recognize or concede its impossibility. In this cynical view, the elite's egalitarian rhetoric turns out to be little more than a legitimating cover for its own unending (and unequal) power.[93] The power of the knowledge elite, of course, is best exercised through an institution that emphasizes the articulated rationality of the intellectual. Again, the judiciary is a leading candidate.

The Court Party in Context

The Court Party is interested in the systematic, policy-oriented use of judicial power. It does not, therefore, include such individual litigants as the criminally accused, who raise constitutional issues as part of their defence.

Such individuals certainly try to get the courts to change criminal justice policy, but they do so as a means to their main objective: going free. Policy change may be a byproduct of their courtroom arguments, but such change is not their main concern. Court Party constituencies certainly sponsor or intervene in criminal-justice cases that seem appropriate vehicles for their policy agendas – and it is precisely such cases that tend to end up in the Supreme Court – but ordinary criminal defendants remain responsible for most of the legal rights cases brought under the Charter.

Similarly, corporate litigants cannot be counted as part of today's Court Party. As Hein's review of Supreme Court and Federal Court cases shows, although corporations and Court Party interests generated roughly the same number of legal challenges to cabinet decisions and public policies between 1988 and 1998 – about 100 cases each – there are many more corporations than Court Party associations. Hein finds that one in eight interest groups launched court cases, while only one in 399 corporations did so, showing that corporations have a much lower propensity to litigate than do Court Party interests. In addition, most corporate litigation is directed at other corporations with whom they are competing.[94] When they do challenge government statutes, it is in a defensive, reactive mode. To date, there appear to be no corporate examples of the kind of sustained, systematic Charter litigation undertaken by Court Party interests.

Thus, most Charter litigation is opportunistic in nature; it is undertaken defensively by individuals or corporations out of immediate self-interest. The development of broader policy may be the ultimate outcome of such litigation, but much narrower concerns tend to motivate the individual or corporate parties. For the systematic litigators of the Court Party, by contrast, the bottom-line outcome of the particular case is often secondary to the more general policy reasoning used to justify that outcome.

The comparatively greater attraction litigation holds for Court Party interests should not be exaggerated. Political interests, opportunistic by nature, make use of whatever resources and policy resources they can. Litigation may not figure as prominently in the policy arsenal of corporations, but they certainly make use of it when they can. Similarly, although Court Party interests find litigation more attractive, they do not foolishly ignore other avenues of political influence.[95] Courts have certainly become more important policymaking arenas, but no political interest can afford to ignore the power of cabinets or bureaucracies. Media campaigns and the lobbying of politicians and bureaucrats remain important parts of the overall political strategy of any sensible political interest, and Court Party interests are no exception. The fact remains, however, that Court Party interests are not only more inclined to litigate, but that they generate the main defences of judicial power and devote considerable resources to lobbying the judiciary. It is this comparative attraction to judicial power, not a counterproductive abandonment of other political strategies, that characterizes the Court Party.

If the Court Party doesn't include individuals or corporations that litigate opportunistically rather than systematically, neither does it include all judges. As we have seen, the Supreme Court has accepted many, but definitely not all, Court Party positions. Indeed, the Court Party agenda occasions significant and ongoing disagreement among judges partly because the Court Party is itself divided on certain issues. Explaining why the Court Party is attracted to judicial power and how it has contributed to the growth of that power, as this book tries to do, is one thing. Determining the precise extent to which the Court Party has, to use Mallory's term, "captured" the courts is quite another, and must be reserved to another occasion.

Conclusion

The influence of political institutions reflects the power or weakness of their supporters. The ascendancy of the courts is linked to the ascendancy of the social interests that support the judicialization of politics. In Canada and other postmaterialist western democracies, a new and powerful knowledge class has arisen with an ambitious agenda for social reform.

While the agendas of Court Party interests differ and sometimes even conflict, what unites these groups is a shared commitment to the project of empowering the courts, although not to the exclusion of more traditional political strategies. While many Charter cases are generated by the opportunistic litigation of individuals and corporations, it is the Court Party that has systematically promoted and defended increased judicial power. The Court Party has breathed political life into the Charter, transforming it from a mere parchment barrier into a potent political symbol and resource and making its oracle, the judiciary, a powerful new player in Canadian politics. In theory, the constitution constrains society, but in practice, it is society that shapes – and reshapes – the constitution.[96]

FOUR

THE STATE CONNECTION

What there's money for, you tend to do.

US Civil Rights litigator.[1]

The rapid growth in influence of Canada's Court Party is paradoxical. It has thrived despite good reasons to expect such political interests to fail. In 1965 Mancur Olson published a pathbreaking explanation of why the kinds of postmaterialist interest groups that comprise the Court Party are at a serious organizational disadvantage as compared to traditional, occupation-based interest groups.[2] Postmaterialist groups often pursue relatively "public" goods – for example, clean air or improved gender relations – which by their very nature benefit many people in addition to the group's activists. Under these circumstances, the incentives to become a member of the group are weak. Membership has costs: dues, time, and effort. Since one will get the benefits anyway, why not free ride on the efforts of others? Occupational groups, by contrast, pursue goods that are more private, in the sense that they benefit mainly group members; for example, better wages and working conditions for a union, or a more favourable tax or royalty regime for a producer's association. Here, too, problems of free ridership occur, but they are less acute and easier to manage. Thus, Olson predicted that occupational interest groups would remain more successful than cause-based citizens groups.

Unfortunately for Olson, his thesis appeared to be exploded by events almost as soon as it was published. The 1960s and 1970s saw the rapid growth of precisely the kinds of groups Olson believed would remain rare. Olson was not entirely wrong, however. Indeed, his logic was impeccable. He had simply failed to foresee the extent to which "patrons of political action" would come to the rescue of otherwise weak groups. As Jack Walker and others have pointed out, external aid makes it possible for groups with acute free ridership problems to achieve prominence. Such aid has come from wealthy individuals, private foundations, and the state. In the United States, the first two figure prominently, but in Canada the state is the most significant source. As Leslie A. Pal says of the Canadian context, "The problem of collective action resolves itself into the problem of the state."[3]

The rise of the new so-called "citizens' interest groups," in other words, is not explained by the traditional (or pluralist) view of democracy, which posits the spontaneous generation of interest groups. According to this pluralist view, when a critical threshold of sufficient common interest is reached, a group spontaneously forms and begins to lobby government for policies that protect the group's interests. Dairy farmers come together to lobby for tariff protection against cheaper imports, workers organize to demand maximum hour legislation, students petition for lower tuition fees, and so forth. In these instances, the group always precedes the relevant legislation.

In fact, as Alan Cairns has so vividly explained, the idea of the state as simply responding to an independent societal realm cannot be sustained. The state has become much too thoroughly "embedded" in society, and vice versa. For example,

> It is common, for one state actor to involve segments of society in competition primarily directed against another state actor ... [and] equally common for private socio-economic actors to involve the state to their own advantage relative to other private actors. [4]

In the embedded state, accordingly, interest groups will not necessarily precede their legislation.

Indeed, what is distinctive about recent Canadian (and American) experience is that many "citizens' interest groups" sprang up *after* the passage of legislation establishing public policy in their areas. This trend is attributable in part to the rapid growth of the welfare state since World War II. New redistributive public policy creates incentives for the recipients of these goods to organize. Their interest is obvious: they can lobby to maintain or increase benefit levels. But organizing recipient groups is also in the interest of the state patron or service providers. "Public officials ... [realize] the political value of organized constituents working to promote their programs from outside of government."[5] This reciprocal interest explains the explosion of public interest or cause-based interest groups in recent decades.

In the United States, for example, the elderly organized only after "the great legislative breakthroughs of Social Security, Medicare and the Older Americans Act of 1965." This same pattern held for many of the other US citizens groups formed in the last three decades: the handicapped, mentally ill, children, and other disadvantaged or vulnerable elements of the population. In each instance, these new client-based associations "were more the consequence of legislation than the cause of its passage." Walker describes them as examples of top-down mobilization led by "social services professionals [who acquire] crucial assistance in the early stages from government agencies, private foundations, and elected officials."[6]

Canadian experience has followed a similar pattern. Predictably, the catalyst here was national unity politics and language. After the passage of the Official Languages Act in 1969, the Cabinet authorized the Social Action Branch of the Secretary of State (SOS) to undertake a policy of social animation among francophone communities outside of Quebec. There had been no prior request for such a program from francophone communities, nor had the 1960s Royal Commission on Bilingualism and Biculturalism recommended it. (Indeed, the Commission's report recommended preserving the voluntary private-sector character of such organizations.) The concept of social animation was defined as "a program which ... attempted an in-depth attack on mass apathy and concentrated ... on sensitizing and preparing confirmed or potential leaders."[7]

Ottawa's mobilization of OLMGs illustrates the top-down, state-initiated interest group formation process. While the Official Languages Program funneled new funds to already existing provincial OLMG associations, it also facilitated the creation of several new ones: the Council of Quebec Minorities in 1978 and its successor group, Alliance Quebec, in 1982; the Fédération des francophones hors Quebec (FFHQ) in 1975; and Canadian Parents for French (CPF) in 1977.[8]

The SOS program of social animation for OLMGs became Ottawa's policy template as it set out to facilitate the formation of other groups that purported to represent the various new social movements spawned during the 1960s. In each instance, government passed program legislation (or orders in council) and then charged the SOS to engage in social animation to help organize the client groups that would benefit from these programs. The newly organized clientele groups would then lobby the government to increase the budgets of their bureaucratic patrons.

The rapid growth of multicultural associations occurred only after Prime Minister Trudeau announced multiculturalism as an official government policy in October 1971. Again there was no grass-roots support for the formation of such groups. The programs were based on "elite support from ethnic organizational leaders, politicians and government agencies." The Multicultural Program facilitated the organization of the Council of National Ethnocultural Organizations (CNEO) and later its better known successor, the Canadian Ethnocultural Council (CEC), as well as the National Association of Canadians of Origins in India (NACOI).[9]

In 1967 the Liberal government had responded to the nascent women's movement by creating a Royal Commission on the Status of Women. The Commission's report recommended government funding of women's groups, and Ottawa created the National Action Committee on the Status of Women (NAC) in 1971 to help implement the report's other recommendations.[10] In 1974, the SOS created a new Women's Bureau, which then became a primary funder of Status of Women Councils in every province. The Women's Program subsequently generated the Canadian Advisory Council on the Status of Women (CACSW) in 1973, the National Association of Women and the Law (NAWL) in 1974,[11] the Canadian Congress for Learning Opportunities for Women (CCLO) – which was also supported by the Ontario government – in 1979, and the Canadian Day Care Advocacy Association (CDCAA) in 1983.

Ottawa also encouraged the formation of Native groups during this period. The SOS helped to organize and fund Indian, Métis, and Inuit social and political organizations in the late 1960s, despite opposition from the Department of Indian Affairs. By 1970, taking all funding sources into consideration, Natives were receiving nearly $1 million for organizational activities. The National Indian Brotherhood (NIB) was formed in 1968. By the end of the 1970s, it had become one of largest advocacy groups in Ottawa, with over 50 full-time paid staff. The NIB played a leadership role in challenging the assimilationist thrust of Ottawa's 1969 White Paper on Aboriginal Affairs, with its opposition leading to the creation of the Office of Native Claims in 1974. The NIB acted as a strong advocate for aboriginal concerns during the constitutional negotiations of 1980-81. These efforts culminated in sections 25 and 35 of the Constitution Act, 1982, sections that protected and promoted "existing aboriginal rights." While the NIB was bitterly disappointed that its constitutional lobbying did not achieve more, these sections have subsequently proven to be valuable assets in the hands of sympathetic judges.[12]

In addition to citizenship initiatives coming out of the SOS, the Trudeau government introduced several other important law-reform and law-reforming programs, which had important implications for the adoption and development of the Charter a decade later. While legal aid programs began to appear at the provincial level after 1965, in 1972 Ottawa used its spending power to nationalize the program.[13] In addition to providing "free" legal representation to poorer Canadians, nationalized legal aid created a new constituency of service-providers – lawyers – with a vested interest in promoting the program.

In 1971, Trudeau, "the law-giver," created the Law Reform Commission of Canada (LRC), whose mandate was to make "recommendations for ... the improvement, modernization and reform ... [of] the laws of Canada."[14] The $20 million dollars spent by the LRC over the next two decades helped to create a new generation of criminal law reform specialists. These experts subsequently proved to be a small but influential constituency for the legal rights components of Trudeau's Charter initiative in 1980-81. Two former LRC officers, Antonio Lamer and Gerald La Forest, were subsequently appointed to the Supreme Court. As judges, they used the Charter to implement many of the reforms that they had recommended as commissioners during the 1970s.[15]

The creation of the Canadian Human Rights Commission (CHRC) in 1977 proved to be another federal initiative that subsequently influenced the shaping and development of the Charter. The CHRC culminated two decades of anti-discrimination policy during which all of the provinces had adopted consolidated human rights codes and commissions to administer them.[16] While the CHRC was formed after its provincial counterparts, it quickly became the central node in the new nationwide policy-network of anti-discrimination watchdogs. The CHRC's clientele groups included women, visible-minorities and other "historically disadvantaged groups," so there was considerable overlap with SOS. Like SOS, the CHRC encouraged equality-seeking groups to form organizations that could consult with them and also serve as political allies in the new war on discrimination. During the constitutional struggles of 1980-81, CHRC representatives proved valuable allies to Trudeau. Three different human rights commissions testified in support of the Charter, and especially for a strong version of equality rights, before the Joint Senate-House Committee on the Constitution. Once the Charter was adopted, both federal and provincial commissions played important roles in steering the judicial development of section 15 equality rights away from protecting individuals and toward the group rights approach.[17]

Indeed, all the groups that Ottawa helped to organize during the 1970s lined up to support Trudeau's Charter-project in 1980-81. OLMG groups, multicultural groups, native groups, women's groups, disability groups, and human rights commissions – all came out in force to testify before the Joint Parliamentary Committee on the Constitution in 1980-81. Penny Kome's account of the Charter-making process provides repeated examples of state support for the feminist lobbying effort. Feminist groups spawned by SOS, such as NAWL, CRIAW, and NAC, held meetings so often that there was always an organized feminist presence in Ottawa at critical moments in the patriation process. As Kome put it, "feminist meetings occur so regularly as to be ready for any campaign that might be mobilized.... You could pick almost any month and find a national meeting."[18]

To summarize, the Charter of Rights may be understood as both an effect and a cause of interest group formation. The federal government played the key role of patron for many of the social interests that supported the adoption of the Charter in 1980-81 and that have become active Charter litigators. OLMGs, feminist organizations, multicultural groups, and aboriginal organizations were often as much the result of key public policies as the source of those policies. The laws involved provide the relevant groups with enhanced public status and important legal resources. Even more important, public agencies provided the emerging Court Party with financial and bureaucratic resources. The next chapter focuses on the bureaucratic dimension; the rest of this chapter looks at the major sources of public funding.

Prominent among funding sources are the various programs historically associated with the Department of Secretary of State. During the 1980s, most SOS programs were shifted to the Department of Multiculturalism and Citizenship; presently, they are under the jurisdiction of the Department of Canadian Heritage. For the sake of simplicity, we will refer to them all as SOS programs. The Court Challenges Program, two aboriginal-rights funding programs, and research granting agencies are also important sources of public funding. To round out the story of litigation funding, we also discuss two sources, legal aid and provincial law foundations, that do not as clearly fit the model of state funding for interest groups. Legal aid is certainly a form of state funding, but its recipients are individual criminal defendants who, for reasons set out in the previous chapter, do not fall within our definition of the Court Party. If legal aid benefits Court Party constituencies – civil libertarians, for example – it does so indirectly, by increasing opportunities to intervene in cases. The reverse is true of Law Foundations, which fund interest groups but with funds that are not as obviously public – though they are arguably based on an unacknowledged tax.

Secretary of State Funding

SOS programs have been a longstanding and crucial source of money for groups with official Charter status. From initially modest grants, funding for these groups spiraled upward as Trudeau's obsession with the national unity issue, and thus his need for political allies, grew. Between 1969 and 1973, the SOS budget grew tenfold from $4 million to $40 million as Trudeau launched the bilingual, multicultural, and women's programs.[19]

This was just the beginning. The Official Language Community Grants budget grew sixfold between 1976, the year the separatist PQ was first elected in Quebec, and 1982. At its outset in 1973, the Women's Program had a budget of $223,000. By 1980, its budget had risen to $1.2 million. In the next two years it more than doubled to $3.2 million, and that amount quadrupled again to $12.5 million by 1985. Among the Women's Program's projects in 1992-93 was a $15,000 grant to the Western Judicial Centre to "organize a judges' congress on the role of judges in the 'New Canadian Reality' with specific workshops on issues relating to women." Multiculturalism expenditures kept pace, expanding from $2.5 million in 1976 to $19.6 million by 1987.[20] After the election of the second Mulroney government in 1988, funding for most of these programs was cut back, but none were canceled. For example, the National Association of Women and the Law's annual grant from the Women's Program grew from $64,000 in 1983 to $256,000 by 1987-88. After seven years of cutbacks, NAWL's 1996-97 grant was still $171,000.

The best way to gauge the significance of state funding for Court Party groups, and how they differ from vocation-based groups, is to compare the relative contribution of members and state patrons to the groups' financial coffers. When Walker did this in the US, he discovered that 89 per cent of citizen groups received government or foundation money to launch their organizations, compared to just 34 per cent of the occupation-based groups. Even after initial start up costs, he found that less than a quarter of the citizen groups received more than 70 per cent of their budgets from membership.[21] While private foundations are the main funders in the US, in Canada, governments, chiefly Ottawa, are the primary financial patrons. [22]

Pal's seminal study found that Canadian feminist, multicultural, and official language minority groups typically depend on government grants for 50 to 80 per cent of their budgets. For example, in 1990 Alliance Quebec had an annual budget of $1.7 million, 88 per cent of which came directly from Ottawa. Its counterpart in English-speaking Canada, Fédération des francophones hors Quebec (FFHQ), was dependent on Ottawa for 83 per cent of its budget.[23] Similarly, in its first three years of operation (1985-1988), LEAF received over one million dollars from the Secretary of State and the recently elected Liberal government of Ontario. [24]

In 1988-89, the Canadian Ethnocultural Council – an association whose original purpose was cultural preservation but which has become the leading advocate for employment equity for visible minorities – was dependent on Ottawa for 90 per cent of its annual budget. This actually overstates its independence: that year less that 2 per cent of its revenue came from membership fees and private contributions. The Canadian Day Care Advocacy Association (CDCAA), started in 1982 with a grant from the Women's Program, varied between 84 and 93 per cent dependency on SOS funding.[25]

Pal's findings are replicated in McCartney's 1991 study. McCartney found that federal and provincial funding accounted for three-quarters of the budgets of Native organizations, approximately half for women's groups, and one-third for multicultural and environmental groups. Noting that state funding was the primary source of money for both women's and Native groups, McCartney concluded that, "voluntary organizations in this country are much more likely to receive government moneys that their counterparts in the US."[26]

In theory, there is no necessary connection between SOS-funded interest groups and Charter politics. In practice, however, they are deeply intertwined. When Ian Brodie cross-referenced Charter case interventions with years of SOS funding for the period 1982-93, he found that the top ten interveners, who were collectively responsible for 53 interventions, had all received SOS funding, some of them for many years.[27] The following chart displays his findings.

Intervener	Number of interventions	Years of SOS funding
LEAF	11	8
Alliance Quebec	6	11
Canadian Jewish Congress	6	6
B'Nai Brith	6	2
La société franco-manitobaine	5	11
La fédération des francophones hors Québec	4	11
COPOH	4	11
Canadian Disability Rights Council	3	3
L'Ass'n canadienne-française de l'Alberta	2	11
Canadian Labour Congress	2	3
L'Ass'n francophone des conseils scolaires de l'Ontario	2	1
Roger Bilodeau	2	1

Court Challenges Program

The most important state funder of Court Party litigation, however, is not SOS (or its successors) but the Court Challenges Program.[28] The CCP actually predates the Charter. Created in 1977 in response to the election of the Parti Québécois government, its original mandate was limited to funding language rights litigation by anglophones in Quebec and francophones outside Quebec. It thus provided an additional source of funding for OLMGs who were already receiving core funding from SOS.

Since its inception, the CCP has funded major OLMG Charter challenges to provincial laws in Quebec, Nova Scotia, New Brunswick, Ontario, Manitoba, Saskatchewan and Alberta.[29] In the landmark OLMG education rights case, *Mahé v. Alberta*, the CCP funded the Alberta francophone group that brought the case as well as the intervention of the Association Canadienne-Française de l'Ontario. This funding has contributed to one of the most successful litigation records of any Court Party group. At the appellate level, OLMGs have won all minority-language education rights cases to date. The only language rights losses occurred in two traffic-ticket cases and a claim to be heard by a bilingual judge.[30] A study of 21 appeal court rulings in language rights cases, Charter and non-Charter, revealed a success rate of 81 per cent – more than double the 33 per cent average for Supreme Court Charter decisions.[31]

As noted in chapter 3, the CCP serves the interests of Ottawa as well as OLMGs and other groups that are weak locally but enjoy the support of Ottawa. Especially in the area of provincial language issues, the CCP allows the federal government to achieve indirectly what it could not have achieved directly. Indeed, combining the Charter with CCP and SOS funding was somewhat of a political masterstroke. The financial support ensures that unsympathetic provincial legislation will be challenged, but also provides Ottawa with political cover. Just as the earliest opponents of the Supreme Court had criticized its power of judicial review as disallowance in disguise, the Charter/CCP combination achieves a double indirection, a form of disallowance twice removed from the Cabinet.[32]

No case better illustrates how this works than *Mahé*, the first major OLMG education rights case outside of Quebec.[33] Francophone parents in Edmonton challenged Alberta's provision of French-language education as falling short of the standards required by section 23 of the Charter. Ottawa wanted this claim to succeed. The Court had already used section 23 to strike down the Parti Québécois's restrictions on access to English-language education in Quebec, a decision also favoured by Ottawa, but one that had excited strong criticism among Quebec nationalists. It was thus important to national unity advocates that the Supreme Court balance things out with a similar ruling in support of francophones in English-speaking Canada. Also, a francophone victory in Alberta would, by way of precedent, strengthen the education rights of Anglophones within Quebec, which explains why the Quebec government intervened to defend the Alberta government against the constitutional challenge. Ottawa, in addition to intervening directly in opposition to Alberta and Quebec, used the Court Challenges Program to provide funding to the Quebec Association of Protestant School Boards to intervene on behalf of the French-speaking families in Edmonton. As Ian Brodie has observed, "Here is an example of one arm of the state funding another arm of the state to influence a third, and indirectly, a fourth arm."[34] A unanimous Supreme Court played its role to the letter and ordered Alberta to expand its francophone education programs.

In 1985, after extensive lobbying by feminists and other would-be equality-litigators, the CCP was expanded to include section 15 claims and given a new five-year grant of $5 million. To qualify for funding, a case was supposed to have "substantial importance ... legal merit [and] consequences for a number of people." In other words, the CCP's mandate was to fund cases that could change public policy, not to help unfortunate individuals. Between 1985 and 1992, the CCP funded 178 equality cases.[35]

The CCP, however, did not just fund litigation for existing interest groups. It undertook an active public education campaign (reminiscent of the SOS's social animation of the 1970s) to create new clients for its services. CCP directors "began sponsoring workshops and meetings that created new networks of equality rights groups and, in turn, created new cases."[36] The CCP played a lead role in organizing new interest group litigators such as the Canadian Prisoners' Rights Network (CPRN), the Charter Committee on Poverty Issues, the Working Group on Aboriginal and Treaty Rights, and the Equality Rights Committee of the CEC. In 1989, an internal review of the program remarked that, "To some observers, the kinds of activities carried out might seem more like product promotion than providing public information and education."[37]

The "new" CCP was initially administered by the (publicly funded) Canadian Council on Social Development, whose stated policy was to "emphasize the setting of social justice priorities" in selecting cases to fund. As it turned out, these social justice priorities meant funding only groups that shared the equality seeking perspective of the postmaterialist left. Non-feminist groups such as REAL Women and Kids First saw their applications for litigation funding either ignored or rejected. This was hardly surprising. One of the criteria for selecting members of the Equality Panel was that "each member should be committed to social reform."[38] This was thinly-disguised code for staffing the panel with recognized activists from feminist, gay, disabled, and racial minority groups.

The CCP has been a funding bonanza for LEAF and other equality seek-ing groups on the left. In addition to funding almost every language rights case that has made it to the Supreme Court, the CCP has directly funded the litigants in a number of leading equality rights cases, including *Canadian Council of Churches* (challenging limits on third-party interventions), *Schachter* (authorizing judges to impose affirmative remedies), and *Sauvé* and *Belczowski* (affirming prisoners' voting rights). The CCP has also funded many of the leading homosexual rights cases. These include challenges involving conju-gal visits by homosexual partners for prisoners in a private family visit pro-gram (*Veysey*), family leave for homosexual partners (*Mossop*), and rights of homosexuals in the military (*Haig*).[39]

In some cases, CCP grants appear to have little to do with financial need and much to do with connections and ideology. Toronto feminist lawyer Beth Symes received a CCP grant to challenge the limit on tax-deductible childcare expenses. At the time her case was heard by the Supreme Court, Symes's annual family income was approximately $200,000. She employed a full-time nanny, whose salary far exceeded the allowable limit.[40] Symes, as it turns out, was one of the founders of LEAF and was represented by Mary Eberts, another LEAF founder.

As in the case of OLMG litigation, the CPP funds not only litigants but also interveners in equality-rights cases. It has funded interventions by EGALE (Canada's leading homosexual rights advocacy organization), COPOH, and the Canadian Council for Refugees. The leading recipient of CCP intervener funding is LEAF, whose grants include *Andrews* (the first sec-tion 15 case), *Borowski* (opposing a right-to-life for the unborn), *Taylor* and *Keegstra* (supporting censorship of hate literature), *Seaboyer* (defending the new rape-shield provision), *Schachter* (supporting the power of judges to impose affirmative remedies), and *Canadian Newspapers* (supporting the ban on newspaper publication of the names of victims in rape cases).[41] Janine Brodie, one of Canada's leading feminist scholars, has bluntly referred to the CCP as providing "the financial underpinning for LEAF."[42]

In 1990, when the CCP's mandate ended, it was reviewed by a Parliamen-tary committee. Predictably, all the groups who had been funded by CCP urged its renewal. Other CCP supporters included the Commissioner of Official Languages, the Assembly of First Nations, the Canadian Bar Association, and the Justice Department.[43] Despite the beginning of federal budget cutbacks, the CCP was renewed, and its budget expanded to $12 million over the next five years.

The 1990 renewal legislation further strengthened the *de facto* link between Court Party constituencies and the CCP by moving the CCP's administrative home to the Human Rights Research and Education Centre (also publicly funded) at the University of Ottawa. The Director of the Centre at the time was Professor William Black (on leave from the UBC Faculty of Law), one of Canada's foremost academic proponents of affirmative action and pay equity policies.

Unlike the CCP's OLMG funding, its section 15 mandate prohibited it from funding cases challenging provincial legislation. Despite this restriction, by 1989 CCP was spending more than twice as much on equality cases as language cases. Nor did this restriction stop CCP administrators from funding the intervention costs of LEAF and COPOH in the landmark *Andrews* case, which challenged a British Columbia statute. As noted earlier, the CCP has not been a passive administrator. It has actively facilitated the creation of new equality advocacy groups and then provided them with funding.

While funding Charter litigation is the CCP's primary task, it also serves as an ideological screen for unmeritorious Charter claims. Rejection by the CCP has obvious financial consequences, but the symbolic failure to receive the CCP imprimatur may be equally important. In terms of achieving litigation success, Patrick Monahan has observed, "the credibility and recognition which the Court Challenges Program conferred on funding recipients may well have been as important as the funding itself."[44] Monahan's hunch is corroborated by the facts. The most frequent recipient of CCP funding, LEAF, is also the Charter litigant with the highest success rate before the Supreme Court of Canada.[45]

In its 1992 budget, the Mulroney government unexpectedly canceled the CCP. The official reason was a combination of budget balancing and completed mandate. Cancellation of the CCP was denounced by the Court Party interests, former Supreme Court Justice Bertha Wilson, and the Canadian Bar Association. Critics charged that the action was politically motivated.

In the 1993 election campaign the Liberal Red Book promised to re-instate the CCP. On 24 October 1995, the Liberals made good on this promise, announcing the formation of a new CCP as an independent, limited corporation with an annual federal grant of $2.75 million. This independent corporate status means that Ottawa cannot shut down the CCP in the future. In addition, any money the CPP raises above and beyond its federal grant, such as the $100,000 grant from the BC Law Foundation in 1996, can be used to challenge provincial laws. As a result of intense lobbying by the various equality-advocacy groups, 75 per cent of the new CCP budget is designated for section 15 litigation, and only 25 per cent for OLMG claims.[46] This change reflects the shifting balance of power away from OLMGs to feminists and their equality-seeking allies.

The reorganization of the CCP was guided by the premise that, "The program must belong to those groups that are likely to use it," and its new mandate included the establishment of "partnerships with universities, research centres and various bar associations." This meant that Court Party advocacy groups would have even stronger control of the program than before. Not surprisingly, the first set of directors of the new CCP were all associated with Charter-based interest groups, law schools, or both.[47] The credentials of the seven members of the CCP's first Equality Rights Panel, the committee that screens the applications for funding, read like a who's who of the equality wing of the Court Party. All had either held office or done work for rights-advocacy groups. Five were lawyers, and four had worked for human rights commissions. Two were former members of the Equality Rights Panel, and two were law professors.[48]

By the 1999-2000 budget year, Ottawa had raised the annual CCP grant to $4.4 million and a $5.9 million grant was projected for 2000-2001.[49] In sum, the CCP not only survived the funding cutbacks that characterized federal budgets since 1993, but emerged stronger than ever with a secure funding-source and greater control by Court Party partisans.

Funding for Aboriginal Rights Litigation

Native rights litigation – land claims, treaty claims, Indian Act disputes, C-31 litigation, and hunting and fishing rights – has become a multi-million dollar a year industry in Canada. The surest sign of this is that in the past two decades many major national law firms have added aboriginal rights specialists to their roster in order to get a piece of the action.

There are two readily identifiable sources of federal funding for aboriginal rights litigation. The first is a one-time-only grant of $3 million to pay for legal costs in cases arising out of the implementation of Bill C-31 in 1985. C-31 sought to restore Indian status and band membership to thousands of Indian women and children who had lost their status under a discriminatory section of the Indian Act.

The second is the Test Case Funding Program administered by the Department of Indian Affairs and Northern Development. Established in 1983, the mandate of the TCF Program is "to fund cases in Indian law that result in the setting of precedent(s) with application for a broad number of Indians; and to increase the body of Indian case law."[50] It is administered in a manner similar to the Court Challenges Program. Indian bands or associations apply for grants to bring specific test cases. If the screening committee deems the application worthy, it can grant up to $100,000 per case. However, permission has been granted to exceed this limit in several cases. The *Gitksan* case, for example, was allotted $1.5 million in 1986, $2.1 million in 1987, and another half million dollars in 1988. Similarly the *Meares Island* case was awarded a $674,150 grant . In its first five years, the Program funded 59 cases to a total of $7.5 million dollars.[51]

Academic Research Funding

Less direct but still significant funding is channeled through education and research programs administered by a variety of federal funding programs: the Social Sciences and Humanities Research Council (SSHRC), the Justice Department's Human Rights Fund, and the Canadian Research Institute for the Advancement of Women (CRIAW). In 1990, SSHRC, in conjunction with the Justice Department, launched a new strategic grants program in law and social issues research. Among the thirteen winning grants were four on feminist issues, two on Charter remedies, and one each on aboriginal rights, elder abuse, rights of the mentally-handicapped, and environmental rights. Two of the grants were specifically targeted to create networks that would facilitate the propagation of advocacy research to support feminist and environmental litigation efforts. [52]

After the adoption of the Charter, the federal Justice Department created an internally administered Human Rights Research Fund. In 1984 one of its first grants went to feminist litigator, Mary Eberts, thus assisting her in the founding of LEAF. It also paid for the preparation of briefs by NAC ($40,000), NAWL ($10,000), and other equality seeking groups, for presentation to a parliamentary committee reviewing equality rights. Many of its grants go to Charter experts in the universities. Since most Charter experts are also Charterphiles, to support their research is usually to support the new genre of advocacy scholarship intended to advance the policy agenda of the various Charter groups.[53]

Legal Aid

Provincial legal aid programs are another major source of funding for Charter litigation. Unlike other funding programs, legal aid is not targeted at organized interest groups. Rather, any criminal defendant who meets the financial means test qualifies for legal aid to pay for a lawyer. Since 75 per cent of all Charter cases involve criminal prosecutions, legal aid programs have actually funded more Charter litigation than any other funding source. Predictably, legal aid budgets soared with the advent of the Charter.

Prior to the Charter, the defense of the majority of criminal prosecutions was straightforward and short. Other than plea bargaining (pleading guilty in exchange for a reduced charge), there were usually only two or three possible defenses, all known ahead of time to prosecution, defense, and the judge. This has all changed with the Supreme Court's expansion of the rights of the accused. As one experienced criminal lawyer has observed, "what is on trial is no longer the evidence respecting the guilt of the accused, but the police procedures used to collect the evidence." The result, he continued, is that "the scope of the defense is limited only by the lawyer's own imagination and the client's pocketbook."[54] Until recently, the legal-aid pocketbook was very flush.

The effect of the Charter on legal aid is illustrated by the growth rates in the Legal Aid Plan of Ontario (LAPO). Between 1967, the year it started, and 1982, the year the Charter was adopted, LAPO's cost doubled from $27 million to $56.2 million. Once the Charter was in place, the LAPO budget doubled again in only six years to $113.5 million in 1988 and then doubled again in the next six to over $200 million in 1994![55] These increases cannot be attributed to similar increases in population, crime or economic growth. By 1993, the total bill to Canadian taxpayers for legal aid programs in all jurisdictions was $603 million per year, double the amount only five years earlier.[56]

One of the most dramatic instances of Charter-driven explosion of legal aid costs has been outside the area of criminal law in the field of immigration. In the Ontario legal aid plan for 1994-95, immigration and refugee lawyers received $29.5 million. In 1989, Ontario legal aid issued only 1610 certificates for immigration and refugee cases. The following year, that figure rose to 15,247, a whopping 950 per cent increase in one year. The reason was the new Federal Immigration Act requirement for additional oral hearings, an amendment that was forced on the government by the Supreme Court's ruling in *Singh v. Canada*.[57]

While the lion's share of criminal legal aid goes to garden variety cases, it has also helped to fund many of the landmark legal rights decisions. Taking a criminal case all the way to the Supreme Court of Canada is an expensive proposition, costing a minimum of $100,000, well beyond the means of the average criminal defendant. An experienced criminal lawyer who has argued many cases before the Supreme Court has observed: "[I]t was legal aid, of course. None of those cases could have gotten to the Canadian Supreme Court without it."[58] This is born out by data, which show that legal aid expenditures for appeals to the Supreme Court have more than doubled since the adoption of the Charter. [59]

Partly as a result of the Court's Charter decisions, provincial legal aid programs have experienced a funding crisis in the 1900s. This has not deterred the Supreme Court from continuing to order the expansion of legal aid to new constituencies. In September 1999, the Court ordered a new right to legal aid for poor parents at risk of losing their children to government social service agencies. Feminist and anti-poverty groups applauded this ruling and predicted that it provided a "great precedent" for a future ruling that poor women involved in custody disputes must also be given a government-funded lawyer.[60] The following week, the Court ruled that prison inmates involved in internal disciplinary hearings have a Charter right to free legal counsel.[61]

Provincial Law Foundations

Another increasingly important source of Court Party funding comes from the various provincial law foundations. Created in the early 1970s, these foundations were originally intended to provide funding for legal education, legal aid, law libraries, legal research, and law-reform. The foundations are funded by the interest on lawyers' trust (escrow) accounts held by Canadian banks. Initially modest in size, these accounts can now generate annual interest income in the $13 million (Alberta, 1990) to $23 million (BC, 1990) range. The oldest and most affluent of the provincial Law Foundations is British Columbia's. Founded in 1969, by 1995 it had paid out over $164 million dollars for law-related programs in the province.[62]

Since the lawyers' trust funds consist of their clients' money held temporarily during the course of purchases by corporations and private citizens, skimming off the interest that would otherwise fall to the client amounts to a kind of unofficial tax. The law foundations based on this tax are thus yet another example of citizens subsidizing the Court Party. The general public is unaware of the existence of law foundations, and the grant process is completely independent of government. Save for subsidizing provincial legal aid programs, the law foundations enjoy unfettered discretion in the distribution of grants.

While spiraling legal aid budgets now consume a large percentage of these funds, Court Party interests have successfully captured a healthy share of the balance. The BC Law Foundation has been especially generous to Court Party interests. In 1981, it awarded a $140,500 grant to the BC Public Interest Advocacy Centre to assist the "disadvantaged" and the "underrepresented."[63] The following table shows some of the recipients of BC law foundation grants in 1994:[64]

Law Foundation of British Columbia 1994 Grants [partial listing]

BC Civil Liberties Association	$135,803
LEAF (West Coast Chapter)	$90,240
BC Public Interest Advocacy Centre	$550,000
West Coast Environmental Law Association	$460,000
Comunity Legal Assitance Society	$700,000
BC Coalition of People with Disabilities	$150,678
BC Human Rights Coalition	$109,744
BC Law Reform Coalition	$150,000
Law Clinic and Prison Legal Services (Univ. of Victoria)	$204,676
Native Law Centre (Univ. of Saskatchewan)	$11,000
Total Grants Budget	$5.2 million
Legal Aid	$7.9 million
1994 Total	$13.1 million

Nor is this pattern of funding by the BC foundation likely to change. In 1996, Lynn Smith, arguably the most influential feminist legal advocate in the province, became the new chair of the BC Law Foundation.

It might be thought that British Columbia is an anomaly with respect to Court Party funding. Dominated politically by Vancouver and the lower-mainland, BC politics has always had a more influential postmaterialist element than the other Western provinces. This hunch is disproven by Alberta's experience. The Alberta Law Foundation grants for 1994-95 were equally generous to Court Party affiliates.

Law Foundation of Alberta 1994-95 Grants [partial listing]*

Alberta Civil Liberties Research Centre	$103,940
Calgary Association of Women and the Law	$14,000
Environmental Law Centre	$237,680
Alberta Law Reform Institute (Univ. of Alberta)	$468,847
Centre for Constitutional Studies (Univ. of Alberta)	$149,975
Indigenous Law Program (Univ. of Alberta)	$29,000
Native Law Centre (Univ. of Saskatchewan)	$10,250
Native Counseling Services of Alberta	$160,930
Yellowhead Tribal Comunity Corrections Society	$30,000
Total Grants Budget	$4.4 milion
Legal Aid	$1.3 million
Total	$5.7 million

* Alberta Law Foundation, Twenty-Second Annual Report 1995

In theory, Ontario should be the litmus test for the law foundation-Court Party connection. In fact, it is not. The Ontario Law Foundation's statutory mandate states that a minimum of 75 per cent of its grants must go the Ontario Legal Aid Fund. In 1993, this came to $9.6 million, leaving only $3.6 million for all other grants. Of this, $3.4 million went to Ontario's six law schools ($1.6 million) and the Law Society for Upper Canada ($1.8 million). This left less than $200,000 for grants to individuals and other organizations. Of eighteen grants funded by this $200,000, eight went to familiar Court Party constituencies and/or causes: Aboriginal Legal Services of Toronto, the Canadian Human Rights Foundation, Canadian Journal of Women and the Law, the HIV/AIDS Advocacy Project, the Native Law Centre (University of Saskatchewan), the Advocacy Centre for the Handicapped, and publishing subsidies for two books: "Refugee Determination in Canada" and "Handbook to the Ontario Human Rights Code."[65]

Conclusion

In both Canada and the United States, so-called "citizens groups" have been the fastest growing type of interest group since the 1960s. They have also been the most dependent on non-membership funding. In Canada, the principal patron has been the federal state, and its motives have been transparent. Whether the agenda was national unity in the 1970s or social justice in the 1980s and 1990s, the state patrons and the social interests they fund have a shared agenda. As Pal observes, "By channeling taxpayers' dollars to left-wing organizations, the bureaucracy is merely rewarding its friends and providing support for those who will reciprocate by lobbying for increased programs and budgets."[66]

In Canada, the primary objective of the Trudeau government's policy and spending initiatives was to counter Quebec nationalism by promoting a new sense of Canadian citizenship. But what began as a state attempt to reshape Canadian society ended with a set of newly organized social interests capturing various agencies of the state. As a consequence of their overlapping memberships and shared ideals, these increasingly autonomous social justice bureaucracies soon became advocates for their constituencies. In this sense, much of the institutional infrastructure of the (future) Court Party was already in place prior to the actual adoption of the Charter. While the Charter launched a new era of judicial power and government by lawsuit, it was also the culmination of a decade of state building and social engineering. Thanks to Trudeau's SOS citizenship policies, the minoritarian politics of identity that has thrived under the Charter was already in place by the end of the 1970s.[67]

The aphorism that "Money is the 'mother's milk' of politics" certainly applies to the Court Party. While the absolute dollar value of this state funding may be modest as a percentage of overall government spending, without it, none of the Court Party groups could operate at anywhere near their current levels of influence. In addition to allowing them to pursue extensive litigation, this funding confers the legitimacy that allows these groups to attract favourable media attention as the "official" representatives of whatever social interests they claim to represent. It also provides the permanent office space, paid staff, policy research, and newsletters that are required to be effective. With the assistance of a sympathetic media, state funding has allowed Court Party groups to command a public presence in national and local politics significantly out of proportion to their actual membership.

FIVE

THE JUROCRACY

The problem of collective action resolves itself into the problem of the state.
Leslie A. Pal.[1]

In addition to legislative and financial resources, the Canadian state provides the Court Party with a rapidly expanding rights bureaucracy. This resource is what Les Pal describes as "positional support": "access for some groups and not others to information or to decision-makers or to a formal or quasi-formal role in decision making."[2]

The positional support enjoyed by Court Party interests is illustrated by the revelation in 1997 that EGALE, the homosexual rights lobby and litigation group, was privy to the Justice Department's shortlist of candidates to replace retiring Supreme Court Justice Gerald La Forest. In an internet memo to its supporters, EGALE solicited information about the candidates. The fact that La Forest was leaving the Court was reported as "good news, since [he] has consistently ruled against glb [gay-lesbian-bisexual] equality issues." The memo went on to emphasize how "vitally important" it was for glb communities "that La Forest be replaced by someone more committed to equality issues."[3] EGALE not only had been given the government's shortlist, but clearly expected to exercise some influence on who would be chosen. A quick check with rival conservative groups confirmed that they were not privy to the same shortlist.

Privileged access to the judicial appointment process is only one example of the positional support enjoyed by Court Party interests. The Canadian state now provides a variety of institutional sites in which Court Party interests can be championed. This new rights bureaucracy includes courts themselves, of course, but also administrative tribunals, human rights commissions, legal departments, law reform commissions, law schools, and judicial education programs. Together, these constitute a web of bureaucratic nodes for initiating, funding, legitimating, and implementing the rights claims of Court Party interests.

Courts

Judges occupy the pivotal decision-making position in Charter politics, and it is their greater activism and innovation that has given the Charter the political "bite" that the 1960 Bill of Rights lacked. Partly as a consequence of this growing judicial power, the number of superior court judges in Canada grew from 666 in 1982 to 1011 in 1999, more than a 50 per cent increase. By 1992, the costs of administering the courts in Canada (excluding the $603 million price tag of legal aid) had reached $867 million annually. More significantly, the cost of the judiciary was growing much faster than either the population or the economy. From 1974 to 1994, public expenditures for courts, controlling for inflation, grew at an annual rate of 4.4 per cent, almost three times higher than the 1.5 per cent growth registered by personal income.[4]

Much of this growth has been fuelled by discretionary judicial policy-making. The Court's rewriting of the law of criminal procedure and evidence has increased the complexity and thus the length of many otherwise open-and-shut criminal prosecutions. The Supreme Court's infamous *Askov* ruling on the right to trial within a reasonable time forced Ontario and other provinces to immediately hire dozens of new judges. The *Sparrow* ruling on the non-extinguishment of aboriginal rights and the government's newly discovered fiduciary obligations so increased the incentive to litigate that 500 separate aboriginal cases were before the courts at the end of 1997. In British Columbia for 1997-98, one third of all Appeal Court judges were assigned to aboriginal rights cases.[5]

Judicial costs are going to increase even more in the wake of the Supreme Court's 1997 ruling in the *Provincial Judges Reference*, which gave judges *de facto* control over their own salaries. At issue was the legal authority of several provinces to reduce judicial salaries as part of an across-the-board salary reduction for all provincial employees. Even though they were being treated the same as all other provincial civil servants, provincial judges in Alberta, Manitoba, and PEI claimed that the cutbacks violated the right to judicial independence as guaranteed by the Charter.

The Supreme Court agreed, and ordered each province to create an "independent judicial compensation commission" with the authority to recommend judicial salary increases (or cuts). Any government decision not to follow a commission's recommendations must be justified as "rational ... if necessary, in a court of law."[6]

In a scathing dissent, Justice La Forest denounced Chief Justice Lamer's majority judgment as contrary to "reason and common sense" [and as] "subvert[ing] the democratic foundations of judicial review." The reference to judicial independence in the Charter, he emphasized, appears in a section intended to benefit those accused of crimes, not judges. In the absence of any credible textual basis for the majority's ruling, Justice La Forest characterized it as "tantamount to enacting a new constitutional provision" and ordering the creation of "what in some respects is a virtual fourth branch of government."[7]

Such criticisms notwithstanding, all ten provinces duly enacted new judicial compensation commissions. Even though the decision applies only to provincially-appointed judges, the Chrétien government responded by creating a new and permanent Judicial Compensation and Benefits Commission for federally-appointed judges. Thus, salaries and benefits for all Canadian judges are now set by such commissions, and any government's decision to reject a commission's recommendation is subject to review by other judges.

The consequences have been predictable. By May 1999, provincial judges in three provinces — Alberta, Quebec, and Newfoundland — had already taken their respective governments to court for not accepting the salary recommendations of the newly created commissions.[8] The Alberta case is typical. In 1998, the newly appointed Commission recommended that judicial salaries be increased from $113,964 to $142,000 (24.6 per cent) with an additional 7 per cent boost to $152,000 in 1999. The Klein government rejected this recommendation as too expensive, and offered instead an increase to $125,000 for 1998 with the 1999 increase to be indexed to the average weekly earning figures. The Provincial Judges Association rejected this offer and took it to court. The Alberta Government defended the rationality of its offer by noting that the commission's recommendation would make Alberta provincial judges the highest paid in Canada. By contrast, the government's offer would put Alberta judges in the fifth rank, but in the province with the lowest personal income taxes in Canada. Also, the 31.6 per cent increase was much greater than what the rest of the Alberta public sector had received.

These reasons weren't good enough. In January 1999 Justice Forsyth of the Alberta Court of Queen's Bench ruled that the government's reasons failed the test of "simple rationality." The government appealed, but was rebuffed by the Alberta Court of Appeal. The latter declared that not only did the government's reasons fail the test of rationality, but that they were not even "legitimate."[9] The Quebec provincial judges association also successfully challenged their government's refusal to accept its commission's recommendation of a 20 per cent salary increase.[10] Even before the Supreme

Court's ruling, judges had become the highest paid occupational group in Canada – higher than doctors, dentists or stockbrokers.[11] With judges now sitting in final judgment of other judges' salaries, they can be expected to do even better.

When we think of courts and judicial decision-making, we think mainly of judges. In fact, there is a new set of judicial decision-makers, invisible to the public but increasingly influential. These are the clerks, the scores of recent law school graduates who assist appeal court judges in researching and writing opinions. While all appeal court judges now employ clerks, here we focus on the most influential – those at the Supreme Court of Canada.

In the years following the adoption of the Charter, the number of clerks at the Supreme Court has increased from nine to twenty-seven, that is, from one to three per judge. The clerks play a central role in all major court functions. They recommend which appeals to accept, prepare briefing notes prior to oral argument, and draft portions of the judges' written opinions. In effect, the clerks function as a filter between what comes into the court (factums) and what goes out (written judgments). Lawyers can no longer assume that the judges have actually read their factums, as opposed to selective summaries prepared by the clerks. Lorne Sossin, a former Supreme Court clerk, describes the new clerkocracy as "a research and advisory pool that is analogous in some respects to the Prime Minister's Office (PMO) and the Privy Council Office (PCO)."[12] Sossin's comparison is troubling in light of Donald Savoie's recent book, which argues that the PMO and PCO have effectively eclipsed Cabinet in terms of power.[13] This rapid growth in the number and functions of the clerks has effected a devolution of power from the top (judges) to the middle (clerks) of the bureaucratic pyramid.

While Sossin denies that clerks directly write their judges' decisions, he admits that they have a significant impact on them. As with "any other policy-making institution," he notes, the Court must rely on aides. "Just as the prime minister may have aides to assist him in drafting legislation, clerks play an analogous role. What's more," Sossin adds, clerks "represent the outlook of a new generation." In other words, clerks, whose average age is 27, bring new legal and policy thinking to the Court. The University of Western Ontario's Robert Martin puts it more strongly. "The clerks manage to capture the judges," he argues. "They come along with the latest fancy ideas fresh out of law school. The judges then think, 'I may be old, but I'm still hip,' so they latch on to" those ideas. According to Michael Mandel of Osgoode Law School, one can sometimes detect the influence of new clerks on a judge's opinions. Recalling when a left-leaning student clerked for former Chief Justice Dickson, Mandel discerns a "certain leftist tinge to Dickson's judgments" that year.[14]

Although the substantive work of clerks is enveloped in the "court's shroud of secrecy,"[15] anecdotal evidence illustrates the important impact they have on Supreme Court opinions. For example, Joel Bakan, one of Chief Justice Dickson's clerks in 1985-86, is alleged to have concocted the now famous Section 1 "*Oakes* test." Dickson, it is said, was dissatisfied with the section 1 portion of a draft judgment. He gave the draft to Bakan and asked him to rework the reasonable limitations section. Sensing a long night, Bakan armed himself with a bottle of sherry and set about constructing the now famous three prong balancing test.[16] Thus, what Chief Justice Dickson later described as "the most important section of the Charter,"[17] was given its practical meaning by a 23-year-old clerk.

Another story involved Bakan and Chief Justice Dickson's first administrative assistant, Jim MacPherson. The Chief Justice is supposed to have asked both MacPherson and Bakan to draft opinions for the *Alberta Labour Reference*. At issue was whether the Charter right of freedom of association protected a right to strike for unions. If it did, then Alberta's ban on strikes by essential service public sector unions would be invalid. Bakan, well known for his left-leaning politics – perhaps he is the left-leaning clerk referred to by Mandel – drafted an opinion that took the side of the unions. The more centrist MacPherson wrote a draft upholding the Alberta statute. When a luncheon meeting at Dickson's home failed to resolve this conflict, Dickson pointed to his swimming pool with a smile and announced that they would have to swim a race, and the judgment would go to the winner. Bakan thought this somewhat irregular, but was not prepared to second guess the Chief. What he didn't know, but Dickson did, was that MacPherson had been a competitive university swimmer. Apparently, Dickson was having fun and was not really leaving the outcome to chance. The race proceeded, MacPherson left Bakan in his wake, and Alberta's anti-strike legislation was upheld – the result that Dickson favoured all along.[18]

These anecdotes are consistent with recent American experience. According to Edward Lazarus, a former clerk on the US Supreme Court, "the broadest exercise of what has become politely known as clerk influence occurs ... in the Court's written rulings." "During October Term '88," Lazarus writes, "the vast majority of opinions the Court issued were drafted exclusively by clerks." Only two of the nine American justices allegedly wrote their own first drafts. The others "consigned themselves to a more or less demanding editor's role."[19]

Lazarus's description of "the power of the first draft" applies with equal force to Canada. When they write the first draft, it is the clerks who make the crucial choices with respect to key words, phrases, precedents, structure, and facts. "In the endless ongoing interpretation of Supreme Court opinions," Lazarus aptly notes, "the devil is in these details."[20] In the US, and increasingly in Canada, the details are controlled by the clerks.

The clerks' drafting and filtering functions are coloured by close ties to their law schools. Selected annually from the top graduates of Canadian law schools, they serve as an intellectual conveyor belt from the law schools to the inner sanctum of the Supreme Court. The clerks on the US Supreme Court have been described as a "law school conduit" as they "carry the attitudes of the revisionist academic culture directly to the federal judges.... Professors are likely to have been clerks to federal judges, and they send their best students to clerkships."[21]

This pattern has replicated itself in Canada.[22] For example, Katherine Swinton and Kent Roach clerked for Justices Brian Dickson and Bertha Wilson, respectively, and both became professors at the University of Toronto, the law school that sends more clerks to the Supreme Court than any other. Swinton is now a judge in Ontario, while Roach became Dean of Law at the University of Saskatchewan. Professor Wayne MacKay, now at Dalhousie University, clerked for former Chief Justice Bora Laskin, as did Joseph Magnet, now a law professor at the University of Ottawa, and Allan Young, who now teaches at Osgoode Hall Law School. Joel "Oakes" Bakan clerked for Chief Justice Dickson before becoming a professor at the University of British Columbia. Jamie Cameron, another Dickson clerk, teaches at Osgoode. The "swimming clerk," Jim MacPherson, went on to become Dean of Osgoode Hall Law School. Today he is a judge on the Supreme Court of Ontario. With the most recent appointment to the Supreme Court, the circle was completed. Louise Arbour clerked for Justice Pigeon in 1971-72, worked briefly for the Law Reform Commission of Canada (and her former law school professor, Antonio Lamer), taught at Osgoode Hall for thirteen years, served as a Director for the Canadian Civil Liberties Association, and was then appointed to the Supreme Court of Canada (where she again rejoined Antonio Lamer). Like many other Canadian elites, the judicial elite is small and cozy.

While the law school connection does not necessarily mean sympathy for the Court Party, Sossin reports that, "the clerks, by and large, shared the optimism espoused by progressive voices who have advocated more innovation under the Charter to redress social wrongs." This orientation was especially true among what what Sossin calls "programmatic clerks." More than others, programmatic clerks are result oriented, arguing for either judicial activism or judicial self-restraint, whichever is most likely to help disadvantaged groups. Sossin stresses that "this applies especially to Charter cases."

> Rather than 'striving for neutrality' in their analysis of a case, these clerks are much more likely to strive for what they consider just. What programmatic clerks have in common is a belief that the Charter can accomplish policy ends....[23]

Again, if American practice is any guide, the advent in Canada of programmatic clerks is not surprising. Lazarus has described the US clerks' power as "very significant" and detailed the "very conscious and abusive manner in which clerks exercise that power for partisan ends."[24]

Sometimes the clerks' support for Court Party interests goes beyond advocacy. In December 1988, LEAF's co-founder and leading litigator, Mary Eberts, gave a series of lectures at law schools around the country. Eberts was received as a sort of conquering hero in the heady aftermath of the feminists' triumph in the *Morgentaler* abortion case. Emboldened by the celebratory mood that surrounded her lectures, Eberts recounted how LEAF had been able to seek intelligence from contacts inside the Supreme Court when it refused to dismiss as moot the pending appeal of pro-life crusader Joe Borowski.[25] Since private contact with a judge on such a matter would have been a gross breach of judicial independence, LEAF's insider contacts could only have been with sympathetic clerks, some of whom Eberts would have known earlier as students at the University of Toronto.

Sossin's explanation for the clerks' partisan advocacy is straightforward and plausible. Unlike the judges for whom they work, the clerks have "studied the Charter in high school, university, and law school." This "formative period of their legal education has been one in which the rights of women, linguistic and ethnic minorities, refugees, prisoners and other groups are perceived to have been enhanced as a direct result of Supreme Court action. With some exceptions, clerks tended to applaud these developments and sought to extend them further."[26] In sum, the influence of clerks has been an important factor in the Court Party's success before the Supreme Court. As in all dealings with government bureaucracies, having supporters on the inside is the ultimate form of positional support.

Administrative Tribunals

While the nine judges of the Supreme Court of Canada are the final and authoritative judicial interpreters of the Charter, the same power of judicial review is exercised by Canada's 2100 other judges. Although this is similar to the US practice, it stands in sharp contrast to the European approach. The Europeans believe that the power of a judge to overrule elected legislatures is so anti-democratic that they restrict it to a single specialized constitutional court.

In France, only the Constitutional Council has such authority, and only politicians can trigger review by the Council. In Germany, any citizen or interest group can initiate a constitutional challenge, but all such issues must be expedited to the Federal Constitutional Court for resolution. The United Kingdom, one of the last democracies without a written constitution, did not even recognize the power of judicial review until 1998, when it granted its judges the power to enforce the European Convention of Human Rights. Even under this arrangement, however, British judges are not given the power to declare a conflicting statute invalid. The most they can do is issue a declaration of incompatibility, which is intended to elicit the government's attention to the problem.[27]

Under the Charter, the Supreme Court is pushing Canada in the opposite direction, beyond what is allowed even in the US. In its 1991 *Cuddy Chicks* judgment, the Court ruled that certain kinds of administrative tribunals may join judges in enforcing the Charter. Examples abound. The earliest rulings that section 15 should be interpreted to include sexual orientation came from human rights tribunals and administrative adjudicators. In 1991 an adjudicator in the Immigration department ruled that the delays in the refugee determination process were so long as to violate the claimant's Charter right to be heard within a reasonable time. Lawyers for church and immigration groups had been urging such a ruling since the *Askov* decision was handed down in the criminal law field. Ironically, the principal cause of the delays in the refugee determination process was an earlier Charter ruling that all refugee claimants are entitled to a full, oral hearing before the decision-making board.[28] In effect, the backlogs caused by the remedy to one Charter violation created another violation.

The extension of the power of judicial review to administrative tribunals is wrong in theory and in practice. It inverts the normal hierarchy between Parliament and the executive bureaucracy. In theory, Parliament makes the laws and the bureaucracy administers them. As a result of the Supreme

Court's ruling, administrative agencies now sit in judgment of the legislatures that created them. As a practical matter, this radical decentralization of the power of Charter enforcement creates an almost infinite number of veto points in the regulatory process from which aggrieved interests (and their bureaucratic sympathizers) can frustrate government policy.

These criticisms have prompted the Court to rethink the issue. In its 1996 *Cooper* ruling, the Court tried to reduce the scope of the *Cuddy Chicks* precedent. Four judges attempted to restrict the scope of *Cuddy Chicks* without, however, overruling it. In a concurring opinion, Chief Justice Lamer went further. Citing his concerns for the constitutional principles of democracy and separation of powers, Lamer declared that *Cuddy Chicks*, a judgment he had signed, was "deeply flawed" and "profoundly illogical," and should be overruled. The problem, according to Lamer, was that the Court's decision in *Cuddy Chicks*,

> instead of putting the intent of the legislature into effect ... enables tribunals to challenge the decisions of the democratically elected legislature.... Instead of being subject to the laws of the legislature, the executive can defeat the laws of the legislature.[29]

Lamer's change of mind fell on deaf ears. Not only was *Cuddy Chicks* upheld by the four-judge majority, but in a dissenting opinion, the two other justices on the *Cooper* panel, McLachlin and l'Heureux-Dube, opposed any reduction in the power of administrative tribunals.

Among administrative tribunals, Human Rights Commissions have become an especially important institutional site for rights advocacy. The commissions are staffed preponderantly by human rights enthusiasts drawn from the same circles as the major section 15 equality seekers.[30] A representative of the Ontario Human Rights Commission has spoken approvingly of the "cross fertilization between human rights decisions and Charter jurisprudence" and declared that "we [the Commission] are part of an extended family of equity forums."[31]

HRC activists were an important part of Trudeau's Charter-coalition during 1980-81. Since 1982, they have been particularly influential in shaping the activist judicial interpretation of section 15. The concepts of systemic discrimination and preferential treatment for historically disadvantaged groups that the Supreme Court embraced in its 1989 *Andrews* decision both have their origin in jurisprudence under human rights legislation. As one enthusiast observed approvingly, "It is ironic ... that the Supreme Court has been a leader in the last few years in articulating progressive equity concepts. Such was once the preserve of human rights commissions and adjudicators. Certainly with the *Andrews* decision, the Supreme Court has made a significant contribution."[32]

In one instance, the cross fertilization between courts and HRCs verged on incestuous. The Ontario HRC took the lead in an early gay rights challenge to a government benefit program that restricted dependent coverage to spouses of the opposite sex. The HRC supported the claim that this restriction constituted unlawful discrimination under section 15 of the Charter. The complainant was a lawyer in the office of the Ontario Attorney-General, and, despite the fact that there were not yet any appeal court rulings on this issue, lawyers representing the same Attorney-General conceded that sexual orientation is protected by section 15 under the analogous ground rule. The only defence was that the restriction should be allowed as a reasonable limitation per section 1 of the Charter. Predictably, the three-person board of inquiry, which was hand picked by the Ontario HRC, rejected this defence.[33]

In a similar vein, the federal HRC intervened in the 1995 Alberta Court of Appeal's hearing of *Vriend*, another homosexual rights case. Government lawyers for the federal HRC argued that the failure of the Alberta HRA to include sexual orientation among its prohibited grounds of discrimination violated section 15 of the Charter and could not be saved by section 1. This occurred in 1995, one year before the Chrétien government amended the federal HRA to include sexual orientation. In other words, the cross fertilization between courts and HRCs cuts both ways. Just as judges have used HRC rulings to expand their monitoring of government policies under the Charter, so HRCs have used the Charter to expand the scope of their own superintendence of private sector discrimination.

The cross-fertilization of equity concepts and their extension into the private sphere illustrates the willingness of Court Party equality seekers to sacrifice liberty in the name of equality. As we observed in chapter 3, the traditional purpose of constitutional bills of rights is to protect individual liberty by restricting what the state can do and how. The explicit purpose of the HRAs is not to protect society from the state but to reform society through the state.[34] That is, the Charter controls state actions, while an HRA regulates private actions. Interpreting the Charter to require the expansion of HRAs, as the Federal HRC urged in *Vriend*, makes the Charter a state expanding rather than a state limiting document.

Government Legal Departments

Next to judges themselves, the most influential government players in Charter litigation are the crown counsels charged with defending the laws of their governments against Charter challenges. Many Canadians will be surprised to learn that sometimes these crown counsels, rather than defending their (elected) government's policies, actually join in the attack.

Historically a crown counsel is expected to defend government policy from constitutional attack. This was true under the law of federalism prior to 1982, and there was no reason for it to change with the advent of the Charter. In fact, this is still what most government lawyers do most of the time. However, the exceptions are important. There has been considerable grumbling among tradition-minded federal crown counsels, especially those based outside of Ottawa, that the defense of federal statutes against Charter challenges has been intentionally weak. These charges include conceding Charter violations too readily, providing weak (or even no) evidence to support a section 1 defense, and not appealing a loss. We have personally heard off-the-record crown-counsel complaints with respect to gay rights cases, prisoners' voting rights cases, and feminist cases.

Clearly on the record are instances in which an attorney-general has refused to defend a government policy. Ottawa has virtually invited the courts to rule in favour of gay rights claims against federal laws. In the first gay rights challenge to a federal law, lawyers for the Justice Department conceded the most important issue: whether the equality provisions of section 15 of the Charter extend to sexual orientation.[35] Gay rights activists "anticipated this initial obstacle would be difficult to surmount," and rightly so. Sexual orientation is not listed as one of the prohibited grounds of discrimination; attempts to add it to the Charter in 1981 had been soundly defeated.[36] However, government lawyers did not even mention this legislative history. Indeed, Justice had for some time been circulating studies predicting that the courts would read sexual orientation into 15 of the Charter, and its lawyers now set out to turn this into a self-fulfilling prophecy. Ignoring legislative history, they conceded that the judges should add sexual orientation to section 15. In a gesture to their traditional role of defending government legislation, they then asked the court to uphold the statute as a reasonable limitation on the new right. Not surprisingly, the judges accepted the first argument and rejected the second. Justice Minister Kim Campbell chose not to appeal her "loss" to the Supreme Court,[37] thereby using the courts to add sexual orientation to the Canadian Human Rights

Act at a time when her party caucus strongly opposed such an amendment.[38]

In 1998 a new Liberal Justice Minister, Anne McLellan, used the same trick of not appealing an Ontario Court of Appeal's pro-gay rights ruling against the federal Income Tax Act (ITA). In this case, Rosenberg, a lesbian, and her union, CUPE, successfully challenged the ITA's definition of spouse as "a person of the opposite sex."[39] There was reason to expect that, had the government chosen to appeal the case, it would have won. Only three years earlier the Supreme Court had ruled in *Egan* that the traditional heterosexual definition of spouse was constitutionally permissible. More significantly, until this case the government had never lost a Charter appeal involving a discrimination claim against the ITA. McLellan's failure to appeal *Rosenberg* to the Supreme Court broke this trend and signalled her government's willingness to let the courts legislate on gay rights. Even when the Official Opposition Reform Party forced a vote on whether to appeal the *Rosenberg* decision, McLellan and the Liberals stood their ground.[40]

Rosenberg is an excellent example of government/Court Party collaboration in other respects. The Ontario Court of Appeal decision was authored by Justice Rosalie Abella, a well-known feminist activist and equality advocate prior to – and clearly even after – her appointment to the bench. Rosenberg was joined in her Charter challenge by her union, CUPE, which, like many other public sector unions, has strongly supported the gay rights movement. Finally there were thirteen "equality seeking" groups – all funded in part by the federal government – that intervened in support.[41] With a line-up like this – Abella, Crown attorneys, CUPE, and a swarm of state-funded equality seeking interest groups – it is hardly a mystery why Rosenberg won and why McLellan refused to appeal the government's "loss."

At the provincial level, Ontario has the most public record of crown lawyers cooperating with Court Party groups by refusing to defend public policy. In 1983, Ontario's Conservative Attorney-General, Roy McMurtry (now the Chief Justice of the Ontario Court of Appeal), defused opposition to the extension of francophone education services by referring the existing, unamended policy to the courts. When the courts declared this policy unconstitutional, McMurtry did not appeal. Instead, he used the ruling to justify his desired amendment of the act. In the 1985 case of *Justine Blainey v. the Ontario Hockey Association*, Liberal Attorney-General Ian Scott refused to defend Ontario's policy of permitting single-sex hockey leagues, despite the defense of this tradition by the official spokesmen for both the male *and female* leagues. The policy was declared unconstitutional. Scott went on to write an article defending an attorney-general's discretion not to defend a government policy.[42]

Scott's actions pale in comparison to his NDP successor, Marion Boyd. In 1994, Boyd introduced a bill extending various rights and benefits to homosexuals. After much debate, it was rejected in a free vote by the Ontario legislature. Not to be deterred, Boyd then told her crown counsel to try to win in the courts what she failed to win in the legislature. In a 1995 case challenging the Ontario Child and Family Services Act's prohibition of homosexual adoption, Boyd instructed government lawyers to argue the law was unconstitutional. Not surprisingly, the judge agreed, and allowed four lesbian couples to proceed with their adoptions.[43]

In a separate gay rights case challenging the Ontario Family Law Act's (FLA) definition of spouse as a member of the opposite sex, Boyd instructed crown counsel to intervene and to argue that the act violated the equality rights section of the Charter. When the Tories defeated the NDP later in 1994, the new Harris government submitted a revised factum defending the existing FLA.[44] This did not deter Judge Gloria Epstein from ruling that the FLA discriminated illegally against homosexual couples. Judge Epstein's respect for democracy was illustrated in her dismissal of the results of the 1994 free vote as being "strongly affected by perceived gains and losses in the then pending election."[45] Evidently Judge Epstein does not share the view of most Canadians that it is generally a healthy sign of democracy when elected representatives pay attention to voters' views.

While most Attorneys-General are reluctant to be this blatant, it is not uncommon for Ontario and New Brunswick to intervene in language rights litigation involving other provinces to support OLMG Charter claims.[46] In so doing, these provinces know full well that the decision that they are encouraging the courts to impose in another jurisdiction will force a similar policy in their own. The political advantage of this technique is that public criticism of the policy can be deflected to the courts.

Government legal departments function as an institutional site for rights advocacy in a second, less visible, but equally influential way: through the Charter-screening (or risk management) process. This new process occurs at the pre-legislative, policy development stage, when governments consult with their justice department lawyers to identify potential constitutional problems in new policy initiatives. This practice pre-dates the Charter but has expanded exponentially as a consequence of the courts' activism under the Charter.

Charter-screening occurs informally in all governments, and has been institutionalized in Ottawa and Ontario. In 1986, Ontario's Liberal government instituted a new policy requiring all policy submissions to Cabinet to first be reviewed for Charter concerns. To meet this demand, Attorney-General Ian Scott created a new division of Constitutional Law and Policy with its own assistant-deputy minister. This new division was designated as a "clearing house" for all Charter concerns, and consultation procedures were put in place to insure its involvement at the "earliest possible stages" of the policy development process. The Federal Justice Department has similarly created a new Human Rights Section that is responsible for "research, policy work, advisory services and litigation support in matters relating to the Charter and other human rights instruments."[47] By 1992, the Human Rights Section had grown to 22 full-time lawyers.

While in theory the advice provided by such Charter-screening units is objective and legal, it provides an opportunity for legal advisers to shade their advice in a manner that advances certain interests and harms others. As Patrick Monahan points out, the indeterminacy of Charter law means that "it will be very difficult for government lawyers to avoid colouring their legal analysis with their views of the substantive merits of the legislation."[48]

Monahan's interviews led him to conclude that in-house government Charter-experts did not exercise a "Charter veto" over policy development.[49] This view was contradicted by one Ontario crown lawyer who said the Charter's "biggest impact" has been not in the courts but at the pre-cabinet stage, adding: "I can't tell you how many legislative proposals I've turned back."[50] While the degree of influence may be open to debate, there is no disputing that the Charter-screening process has created a new site for Court Party rights-claiming.

In the context of this new Charter-screening process, government lawyers sympathetic to the policy objectives of Court Party interests, can — and often do — use their advisory role to influence the substance of government policy. In interviews federal lawyers stressed that they tried to "live up to the spirit, and not just the letter, of the Charter" by providing "large and liberal" — as opposed to "narrow and technical" — interpretations of Charter rights.[51] In Charter-speak, these phrases have become code-words for policy results desired by the Court Party. Large and liberal interpretations are to be applied to the claims of feminists, OLMGs, homosexuals, criminal defendents (except in rape cases), and aboriginals and other visible (non-European) minorities. Narrow and technical interpretations are reserved for Charter claims advanced by those outside this charmed circle of "disadvantaged groups."

A recent example of the ideological bias of the Justice Department's "Charter screening" process may be found in the shaping of Bill C-3, "The DNA Identification Act." The Liberal government introduced Bill C-3 in 1998 to authorize the creation of a national DNA databank that would aid police investigation of crimes, by authorizing them to compare DNA samples found at a crime scene with samples previously collected from those already convicted and in prison. Police, other law-enforcement groups, and the opposition Reform Party wanted the latter category expanded to include pre-conviction samples from persons charged with a criminal offense. This change would have followed long-standing police practice with respect to fingerprinting, which is also done upon charge. Supporters of this amendment testified that it would have significantly enhanced the utility of the DNA database with respect to repeat sex offenders and serial killers such as Clifford Olson.[52]

On the advice of the Justice Department, the Liberals rejected this amendment. According to Justice Department lawyers, the Supreme Court would invalidate the pre-conviction taking of DNA. They pointed to the 1997 *Stillman* precedent, in which the Court threw out DNA evidence collected by the police as a violation of the accused's Charter right against self-incrimination.[53] Proponents of the amendment pointed out that *Stillman* was hardly conclusive, since the Court had emphasized the absence of any "valid statutory authority" for the police taking of DNA evidence from the accused. Bill C-3 would supply this condition, proponents argued, and thus the *Stillman* precedent could be distinguished. As a last resort, they challenged the Liberal government to refer the issue to the Supreme Court for an expedited answer. The government refused. In sum, the Justice Department used its "Charter screening" role to significantly reduce the scope and thus effectiveness of the new DNA database.

Brodie has marshalled five examples of how policy networks connect Court Party groups with crown attorneys in the Federal Justice Department.[54] These include the Department's 1986 report on equality rights, which endorsed the feminist concept of systemic discrimination; the elimination of discrimination based on sexual orientation; and the establishment of affirmative action and pay equity programs.[55] Federal Justice used its internal Human Rights Fund to pay for the preparation of briefs by NAC ($40,000), NAWL ($10,000) and other equality seeking groups, for presentation to a parliamentary committee reviewing equality rights. Its Human Rights Section authored a paper on systemic discrimination that claims that courts are authorized under section 15 of the Charter to order governments to implement affirmative action programs. In 1991 the Department organized a national symposium on women and the law and invited the leading feminist scholars and organizations. Finally, in the aftermath of the Supreme Court's *Seaboyer* decision, Justice Minister Campbell met with feminist groups to discuss a revised law but refused to meet with REAL Women, an anti-feminist women's group.[56] All of these incidents illustrate Pal's concept of "positional resources."

Similar positional resources have been supplied by the Ontario attorney-general's office. Ontario was the first to set up a provincial counterpart to the CCP to fund equality challenges to provincial statues. In addition, Ontario has frequently intervened to support OLMG and feminist Charter attacks on the statutes of other provinces. Unlike other provinces, Ontario's intervener factums in Charter cases until recently tended to urge interpretive choices that expand the scope of judicial review – and thus judicial power – under the Charter.[57]

Indeed, a recent study found that Ontario's interventions have been a crucial factor in LEAF's high success rate before the Supreme Court of Canada. When LEAF's position is seconded by Ontario's, LEAF almost always wins.[58] Ontario's intervener record is a predictable consequence of the centralized Charter-coordinating process instituted by its former Attorney-General Ian Scott. Scott's concentration of responsibilities for Charter litigation, planning, and policy-development all in one new division maximized the Ontario attorney-general's policy influence. Brodie concludes that, "Scott was essentially trying to carve out a veto within the Ontario public policy process. His reforms ... gave him and his staff the maximum influence in the wider policy process."[59] Although Scott intensified it, however, the pattern of Ontario support for broad interpretation of Charter rights both pre-dates and survives him. In fact, the pattern persisted over three different party governments – the Davis Tories, the Peterson Liberals, and the Rae NDP. It appears to have ended with the election of the Harris Conservatives in 1995.[60]

In sum legal departments' historical monopoly on legal advice to governments, combined with the new opportunities for constitutional challenges under the Charter, has dramatically expanded government lawyers' advisory role in the policy process.[61] As a senior Justice official observed, "the Charter has involved the Department of Justice in the policy development process of its client departments to an extent that would previously have been considered unnecessary and inappropriate."[62] Indeed, most analysts conclude that the Charter – or more accurately, the Court's activist interpretation of the Charter – has turned the Federal Justice Department and its Ontario counterpart into central agencies like the Privy Council Office or Treasury Board.[63] Brodie, who agrees that legal departments have become much more influential, has modified this claim. He points out that the defining purpose of the other central agencies is to enhance cabinet's control of the bureaucracy and policy development. In contrast, legal departments sometimes use their relative autonomy and expertise to frustrate cabinet policy directives, generally at the urging (and to the benefit) of Court Party interests.

Law Reform Commission of Canada

The Law Reform Commission (LRC) is another federal bureaucracy that has become an influential player in Charter politics. Created by the Trudeau government in 1971, the LRC undertook a comprehensive study of Canada's criminal law and law of evidence. Its studies usually included theoretical analysis followed by empirical studies. Most of this research was conducted by law professors and criminologists.

By the end of the 1970s, the LRC was issuing numerous recommendations for reform, most of which were designed to expand the rights of the accused by placing new restrictions on police and prosecutors' discretion. Many copied the criminal law reforms ordered by the Warren Court in the US during the 1960s, such as the Miranda warning (the right to remain silent) and the exclusion of illegally obtained but reliable evidence. While these reforms were popular with the academic experts who proposed them, they had little public support. They were especially opposed by provincial law enforcement agencies as being too inefficient, too costly, or both. As one former LRC commissioner put it, provincial officials viewed the LRC's proposed reforms as "an expensive pain in the ass."[64] While criminal law is a federal jurisdiction, provinces enforce it and their consent is thus often considered a prerequisite for major reforms. As a result, the LRC's reform proposals were never adopted by parliament.

However, the Supreme Court subsequently enacted what parliament failed to legislate. The single most active field of judge-led policy reform under the Charter has been criminal law. As noted in chapter 1, those accused of crimes in Canada now enjoy procedural protections not found in the US.[65] A 1996 study found that most of the Supreme Court's reforms in this area closely follow the earlier recommendations of the LRC.[66] By 1992, LRC reports had been cited as authorities in 225 reported Charter decisions,

48 of them by the Supreme Court.[67] Using its power of interpreting the Charter, the Court implemented LRC recommendations on such policy issues as unauthorized search and seizures, electronic and video surveillance, custodial interrogations, reviewability and disclosure of information on police wire-tap affadavits, pre-trial disclosure of Crown evidence, court delay, exclusion of illegally obtained evidence, *mens rea* and "constructive murder," and the intoxication and insanity defenses.[68]

Most of the key Charter rulings were written by Chief Justice Lamer, a former chairman of the LRC (1971-78), and Justice La Forest, a former commissioner (1974-79). Indeed, both Lamer and La Forest continued to consult with the LRC after their appointment to the Supreme Court. The 1996 study found that La Forest and Lamer had authored more search and seizure, right to counsel, and exclusion of evidence judgments than any other judges.[69] La Forest's discovery of a section 8 privacy component in *Dyment* (1988) laid the basis for his subsequent ruling that prior judicial authorization is required for all forms of surveillance. Lamer clearly led the court in his opinions on right to counsel, trial within a reasonable time, exclusion of evidence, and most of the *mens rea* cases.[70] To support these rulings, both judges referred frequently to LRC studies that were done during their tenure at the Commission.[71]

While the evidence is circumstantial, it suggests that Justices Lamer and La Forest used their new influence under the Charter to implement the reforms they had recommended while on the LRC but that were never accepted by parliament. By the end of the 1980s, professor Dale Gibson, a Charter expert/advocate and former consultant to the LRC, sought to legitimate this trend by recommending that the LRC develop reform "proposals designed to be implemented by the courts rather than by the legislatures." Legislators, Gibson claimed, "lack the time or interest to deal with them properly."[72] This reasoning conveniently omits a third possible reason: legislators' (and voters') opposition to reforms that increase the difficulty and costs of prosecuting criminals.

Ironically, Gibson's recommendation would take Canada back to the era of judge-made criminal law, the target of the nineteenth-century Benthamite reformers, who, under the banners of democracy and accountability, gave Canada one of the commonwealth's first criminal codes. Gibson's recommendation is a discouraging but accurate barometer of plummeting support for parliamentary democracy and responsible government among intellectuals.

Most Charter commentators argue that the Court's legal rights reforms are different from its other Charter-based reforms in that they are not the product of interest group test cases and strategic litigation. This is true but not conclusive. Other aspects of the Court's reform of Canadian criminal law under the Charter fit comfortably within the Court Party paradigm. Without public funding in the form of hundreds of millions of dollars of legal aid most of these cases would never have made it to the Supreme Court.

More telling is the close connection between the Court's criminal law reforms and the LRC. The LRC was a quintessential postmaterialist policy elite, and its reformist agenda, rejected in the legislative arena, was effectively enacted by the Court, indeed, by two of the LRC's own former officers.

National Judicial Institute and Western Judicial Education Centre

Two of the least visible but most influential institutional nodes on the Court Party network are the judicial education programs run by the National Judicial Institute (NJI) in Ottawa and the Western Judicial Education Centre (WJEC) in Vancouver. The NJI was established in 1988 by the Canadian Judicial Council, which funds it with an annual grant of approximately $500,000.[73] Its administrative office is at the University of Ottawa, which also housed the Court Challenges Program from 1990 to 1992. The NJI's mandate is to provide continuing education courses for federally appointed superior court judges. The WJEC was founded in 1983 by the Canadian Association of Provincial Court Judges to provide similar continuing education courses to provincially appointed judges.

While these programs began primarily as vehicles for continuing professional development, they have become indoctrination centres for Court Party orthodoxy. Since 1992, both programs have included gender sensitivity seminars as regular components of their judicial education efforts.[74] In 1991, then Justice Minister Kim Campbell hinted that "newly appointed judges will likely get 'mandatory' training to sensitize them to gender-related issues in their courts."[75] Thus far the idea of mandatory participation has been resisted, but indirect pressure is high. Both programs report 80 per cent participation rates.[76]

These developments have not occurred by accident. Both programs were designed in the years following the adoption of the Charter and were targeted by Court Party activists as a key element in their influencing the influencers campaign. The Advisory Council of the Status of Women's (CACSW) 1984 report calling for the creation of LEAF also stressed "participation in judges' training sessions" as an important "means of disseminating and legitimating such [feminist] theories of equality."[77]

LEAF's influencing the influencers strategy clearly worked with the WJEC. Three of Canada's leading feminist law professors – Lynne Smith, Kathleen Mahoney, and Sheilah Martin – were involved with the WJEC from the start. All three are active in both LEAF and NAWL and gave the WJEC's gender program a strong feminist orientation. In 1992, the SOS Women's Program gave WJEC a $15,000 grant "to organize a judge's congress on the role of judges in the 'New Canadian Reality' with specific workshops on issues relating to women." In 1993 WJEC sponsored such a conference, attended by 300 judges and devoted to issues of "aboriginal justice, gender equality, and racial, ethnic and cultural equity."[78] One participant reported that, "the message to the judges [at this conference] was: 'The system is failing us, so please fix it.'"[79] That same year the Canadian Bar Association reported that "[WJEC's] gender equity program has been called 'the best' by top consultants in the field and judicial educators have come from as far away as England to study its program on racial, ethnic, and cultural equity." This success was attributed to the Centre's ability to attract "leading experts to assist in developing the gender equity program."[80] These "leading experts," of course, were Professors Smith, Mahoney, and Martin.

The NJI has also been a target of the feminist lobby. During the formative period of the NJI, the CACSW lobbied its interim chairman, then Chief Justice Brian Dickson, "to convey the Council's concern on how the new equality rights would be interpreted by the judiciary."[81] The CJI's curriculum still includes technical courses such as computer literacy, court administration, and case flow management, as well as refresher courses in rapidly changing areas of law such as the Charter. However, the NJI has increasingly gone into the business of offering social awareness courses on such topics as "gender bias, cross cultural, and native perspectives."[82]

The institute's program on gender equality "consists of a 30-minute video, printed materials and an afternoon panel discussion." (The video is also widely used in bar admission programs.[83]) Both the video and printed materials exclusively present the feminist version of section 15, plus issues such as domestic violence, custody and support, sexual assault, and systemic discrimination. This heavy feminist bias is hardly surprising. Most of the supporting materials are taken from *Equality and Judicial Neutrality*, a book edited by law professors Sheilah Martin and Kathleen Mahoney. It consists of papers presented at a 1986 feminist conference on the same topic.[84]

The contributors read like a who's who of Canadian legal feminists. In addition to the editors, they include Barbara Knoppers, a well-known feminist from Montreal, and Freda Steel, a LEAF board member in Manitoba.

The two lead articles on section 15 of the Charter are by Sheilagh Day and Gwen Brodsky. Brodsky is a former LEAF litigation director and also chaired the Gay/Lesbian Section of the Canadian Bar Association. Day, a past president of LEAF, co-chaired the lesbian caucus at the United Nation's 1995 Women's Conference in Beijing, and is the new chairperson of the CCP's Equality Panel.

The unbalanced character of judicial education seminars and the heavy involvement of LEAF activists have raised concerns about judicial independence. In December, 1991, the Alberta Provincial Judges' Association passed a resolution protesting judicial education programs that provide "unilateral views on socio-political sensitization issues."[85] This charge was carried forward by REAL Women, a conservative, non-feminist women's group. REAL strenuously objects to the fact that LEAF activists have been given special audiences with judges at the same time that LEAF frequently appears as a litigant before the same judges on the same issues.[86]

The original director of the NJI, David Marshall (now a superior court judge), has expressed related concerns. Inadequate government funding for judicial education, Marshall contends, has made the CJI and WJEC dependent on "funded interest groups" who use their superior resources to place their agendas into the judicial education programs. "The fact that program content is often selected by the interest group with sufficient clout to encourage government sponsorship is entirely inimical to judicial independence," he wrote in 1995.[87] The Women's Program's 1992 grant to the WJEC is a good example of how feminists have bought their way into Canada's judicial education programs.

This privileged access to Canada's judges, the ultimate Charter decision-makers, represents the fulfilment of NACSW's 1984 strategy of influencing the influencers. It represents a resource that is denied to all other social interests. While some senior judges have protested against what they perceive as an erosion of judicial independence, the seminars send a subtle but powerful message to new and younger judges: if you aspire to further judicial appointments, then get on side – the Court Party side.

Sometimes the message is not so subtle. Consider Kathleen Mahoney's remarks in May 1999, in the wake of the Canadian Judicial Council's reprimand to Alberta Court of Appeal Judge John McClung. In February 1999, McClung had written a letter to a national newspaper protesting a Supreme Court opinion by Justice l'Heureux-Dubé that not only overruled McClung's judgment in the case but accused him of gender bias. Formal complaints were filed with the Canadian Judicial Council against McClung by a number of feminist groups. Anti-feminist women's groups filed counter claims against L'Heureux-Dubé. The Judicial Council dismissed the charges against l'Heureux-Dubé almost immediately. As for McClung, after lengthy private hearings, the Council issued a formal reprimand but did not recommend removal from office.[88]

Mahoney concurred with the Judicial Council's decision, but made it clear what she thought the Council was saying: "There is no great purpose in firing Justice McClung at this stage in his career, but the educative value of this decision is critically important. It sends a very, very important message ... that we do live in an equalitarian society and we must respect the equality rights of women, of girls, of gays, and lesbians." Just in case anyone did not get the message, Mahoney spelled it out: "the federal government should not appoint or promote judges unless they have taken gender sensitivity courses to root our anti-female bias in the courts."[89]

Conclusion

The Court Party enjoys significant positional support at both levels of government. It has allies in the federal and provincial legal departments, federal and provincial human rights commissions, federal and provincial law reform commissions, the judicial education programs at CJI and WJEC, and the courts themselves. These alliances transcend and thus dissolve the traditional distinction between state and society and render inaccurate the libertarian view of the Charter as protecting individuals against the overbearing state. The common assumption that the Charter creates an adversarial relationship between courts and legislature is too simplistic. As often as it "checks" the federal government, the Supreme Court acts as its agent in support of issues and clientele groups that Ottawa supports. The issue is not whether courts use the Charter to help minorities, but *which minorities*.

The Court Party, in other words, is not only heavily funded by the state; it is to a considerable extent part of the state through a set of alliances or policy networks that connect its interests and the various rights bureaucracies. Indeed, as the next chapter shows, their personnel are often interchangeable.

SIX

POWER KNOWLEDGE:
THE SUPREME COURT AS THE
VANGUARD OF THE INTELLIGENTSIA

There was, throughout his entire judicial career, a very special relationship between Chief Justice Dickson and the Canadian academic community. . . . [H]e devoured much of the literature produced by the Canadian legal academic community and drew upon it as he decided cases and wrote judgments. . . .[T]he Chief Justice's . . . law clerks . . . were under instructions to watch the law reviews and bring good articles to his attention.

James C. MacPherson,
Executive Legal Officer, Supreme Court of Canada, 1985-87.[1]

In the 1960s, the heyday of the Warren Court, there was a popular joke in American universities about where to locate sovereignty in the US. The American people seized sovereignty from King George III in 1776 and transferred it to the Constitution in 1787. But since the Constitution has come to mean only what the judges say it means, and since the judges say only what they read in the *Harvard Law Review*, sovereignty in the US now rests with the faculty at the Harvard Law School. As recently as 1994, Mary Ann Glendon (of Harvard Law School) confirmed the underlying truth of this joke. Writing about the "powerful synergy [that] links the appellate judiciary and the legal academy," Glendon maintained that just as "[m]any professors strive mightily to influence the course of judicial opinions, [so] many judges reach out in their opinions to 'constituents' in the professoriate."[2]

Like so many other things in recent years, this American anecdote now applies equally to Canada. Peter Russell has noted that "a phalanx of academics" played a key role in mobilizing support for the Charter during 1980-81.[3] In 1992, on the tenth anniversary of the Charter, the late Walter Tarnopolsky – then a judge, formerly a law professor – was asked to explain the success of the Charter. One of the reasons he gave was "the support of the academic community for an 'effective' Charter."[4] Marc Gold, formerly of Osgoode Hall Law School, has observed that sometimes it "appears as if the court is writing for the academy."[5] According to University of Victoria law professor Hamar Foster, the Court's Charter activism in the field of criminal law is the consequence of "three decades of academic support for American-style rights review."[6] This view is not just the conceit of legal academics. It has been endorsed by Supreme Court Justice l'Heureux-Dubé, who told a law school audience that important "judicial decisions [are] buttressed by professors and their writings."[7]

While the conjunction of power and knowledge in legal academics may surprise most Canadians, it is not a phenomenon limited to Canada and the US. In his study of the rise of judicial power in France and Germany, Stone observes that "[constitutional] discourse ... is dominated by law professors who, by training and inclination, have sought not only to influence jurisprudential development in explicit partnership with the judges but also to bolster the legitimacy of the court and of judicial review."[8]

The role of legal academics in promoting the Charter, and thus judicial power, represents the confluence of several factors: the collective self-interest of lawyers, the recent independence of Canadian law schools from the legal profession, and the new postmodern orthodoxy that has captured the universities, and especially the law faculties, in the past decade.

The support of legal academics for the Charter is part of a modern trend of the transfer of political influence to professional experts. Keren has observed that all professionals "derive their status from their possession of esoteric and easily monopolized skills and their political engagement may be seen as a means to increase the scope of issue areas in which those skills can be demonstrated.... The more social matters are discussed in professional terms, the more symbolic assets are translated into economic and political gains."[9] In the context of the Canadian Charter (and rights instruments in other Western democracies), lawyers have a vested interest in redefining policy issues as rights issues, since the latter call into play their expertise and marginalize the non-expert opinions of most legislators and voters. This incentive becomes even greater when the normal impulse toward self-aggrandizement is linked with an ideological agenda, as it clearly is with Court Party lawyers and professors.

The role of legal academics in promoting the Charter also reflects the new independence of Canadian law schools from the legal profession. Until the 1960s, legal education in Canada followed a traditional apprenticeship training model, an approach that reflected and reinforced the relatively conservative interests of the legal profession. In 1951, Bora Laskin – then a professor, later to become the Chief Justice of Canada – attributed the historical conservatism of the Supreme Court in part to "the late development of university law schools."[10] The more recent political activism of law professors came with the growth of law schools that were economically and ideologically independent of the more conservative profession.

The development of law schools may have been late, but it has been vigorous. The number of law schools in Canada has doubled since 1945 from ten to twenty with five founded since 1967. There has been a corresponding increase in the number of law professors: 660 by 1987, an increase of 75 percent since 1971. This rapid growth produced a relatively young faculty: the median age of Canadian law professors in 1982, the year the Charter was adopted, was only 38.[11] Thus, a significant cohort received their undergraduate and/or graduate education during the formative period of the 1960s and 1970s.

Accompanying the quantitative growth in law schools is a qualitative change in legal education: the displacement of the old vocational training approach by an emphasis on theoretical and constitutional issues. The social movements that were born in the 1960s were soon carried into the law school curriculum by the new cohort of young professors hired during the rapid post-war expansion. They introduced new courses that embraced a human rights curriculum: feminism, aboriginal rights, gay rights, prisoners rights, critical legal studies, and environmental law. In addition, as Stagers and Arthurs found, during the 1970s significant numbers of law professors worked for law reform commissions, human rights commissions, and public interest groups,[12] the training grounds for the Court Party activists of the 1980s. Just as "Lawyers from the corporate sector helped translate the philosophy of laissez-faire [economics] into legal terms and constitutional doctrines"[13] in the late nineteenth and early twentieth centuries, so law professors and public interest lawyers are doing the same for the philosophy of the Court Party today.

The new autonomy of Canadian legal education coincided with the triumph of postmodernism among university-based intellectuals. Postmodernism rejects the possibility of scientific or objective knowledge, claiming that all knowledge is self-interested and reflects (and supports) unequal power relationships based on class, gender, race, and so forth. It portrays the political, legal, and cultural traditions of western civilization as the corrupt legacies of "dead, white, heterosexual, male" privilege. For example, deductive logic and concepts of evidence are often dismissed as phallocentric modes of reasoning. Postmodernism provides the intellectual grounding for many of the new postmaterialist social movements: feminism, multiculturalism, gay and lesbian rights, and the more radical forms of environmentalism.

Convinced of their own unique virtue and the corruption of all who disagree or question, postmodernists fuel the new reign of political correctness that has stifled intellectual freedom at Canadian universities over the past decade. Ontario's zero tolerance policy for universities and the much publicized incidents at the University of Victoria, UBC, and Simon Fraser are just the tip of the iceberg. Robert Martin, a professor of law at Western Ontario, has described in detail the intellectual corruption that has infested legal and social science research on Charter-related issues. Traditional standards of scholarship, Martin writes, "are being abandoned, replaced by nothing more than a determination to propagate orthodoxy."[14] John Fekete has filled two chapters with short accounts of "professors on trial" for "lookism" and "thought crime" at various Canadian universities.[15] As Fekete has observed, "The university, with its 'anti-' codes and its new and expanding policies of positive obligation, is coming to resemble a creed state…. Creed states impose state creeds; they profess and practice zero tolerance of other creeds."[16] These developments explain the title of CCLA Executive Director Alan Borovoy's recent book, The New Anti-Liberals, and why he devotes two chapters to universities and academics.[17] Similar concerns are what led Peter Russell to observe in 1992 on the tenth anniversary of the Charter that "in thirty-five years of university teaching, I have never sensed as much pressure to conform to certain political positions as I do at the present time, particularly when objection is made to the expression of ideas that are offensive to certain groups."[18] (He added, correctly, that, "professors of political science cannot really function if they are not permitted to be offensive.")

Postmodernism in the form of the "Critical Legal Studies" (CLS) movement has been particularly influential in the law schools. The postmodernist contention that all knowledge is constructed found a receptive audience among lawyers trained in the adversarial method of argument. Constructing one-sided and self-serving accounts of conflicts is what common-law lawyers are trained to do. Under the CLS banner minority, multicultural, native, feminist, and gay-rights advocates have deconstructed such traditional legal norms as judicial independence, judicial impartiality, and the rule of law as nothing but disguises for class privilege, racism, sexism, and heterosexism. By the 1980s, the "Crits," as they are known, had become the dominant faction at the most prestigious American law schools. CLS was carried back to Canadian law schools by the increasing number of law graduates choosing to do their LL.M.'s at Harvard and Yale rather than Cambridge or Oxford. If, as Charles Sellers maintains, "lawyers were the shock troops of capitalism" in the nineteenth century,[19] "crit" lawyers form the shock troops of today's Court Party.

It thus comes as no surprise that those outside the academy often find shocking the virulence of CLS attacks on traditional legal norms. (Those inside have become numbed by overexposure.) In the US, the most radical expressions of CLS concern race relations. The prestigious *Yale Law Journal* recently published an article by Paul Butler, a black law professor, who defended the right of black jurors to ignore evidence and to acquit black defendants in non-violent cases as a way of protesting racism in the criminal justice system.[20] Patricia Williams, a black law professor at Columbia University, has defended a young black woman who made up a story about being raped by a gang of white men. This lie was justified, Professor Williams argues, because "her condition was clearly the expression of some crime against her, some tremendous violence, some great violation that challenges comprehension." The lie was justifiable, the Columbia University professor continued, because it "has every black woman's worst fears and experiences wrapped into it."[21] In Canada, the postmodern angst has focused more on gender and sexual orientation than race. Recently, however, the Canadian Bar Association released a report alleging wide-spread racism throughout the legal system. A subsequent inquiry revealed that the CBA's finding was based not on reliable data, but on the committee's embrace of "critical race theory."[22]

In short, higher education, especially postmodernist legal education in the law schools, is very much in tune with the Court Party. The contribution of universities to the Court Party goes well beyond harbouring intellectual sympathizers, however. Universities supply three tangible and crucial ingredients to the Court Party effort: administrative support, rights-experts, and advocacy scholarship.

Administrative Support

University law faculties host a wide variety of Court Party organizations and projects. While these relationships are promoted as enhancing the profile of the host institution, they are yet another way of covertly funneling taxpayers' dollars to Court Party interests. Furnished office space; telephone, fax and computer services; secretarial support; access to libraries and student research assistants – these are all resources for which other interest groups have to pay. Equally important, a university affiliation lends credibility to a rights-advocacy organization, legitimizing it in the eyes of the media and helping it to attract grants from government funding agencies and private foundations.

The Human Rights Research Centre at the University of Ottawa has served as an important research resource and Court Party networking centre since Walter Tarnopolsky founded it in 1980. In 1987 it became the first home of the Canadian Judicial Institute (CJI) and in 1990 was made the host institution of the Court Challenges Program. The then Director of the Centre, Professor Bill Black, was the former director of the CCP.

The universities' embrace of professional feminism is particularly evident in the law schools' close relationship with the National Association of Women and the Law (NAWL). Ten law schools in six different provinces host NAWL by providing office space and other support services.[23] NAWL is much more than just a women's professional organization. In 1984, it launched the *Canadian Journal of Women and the Law* to promote feminist scholarship. NAWL lists among its other accomplishments successfully lobbying for "gender sensitivity training" for sitting judges, supporting the re-instatement of the Court Challenges Program, and routinely lobbying for the appointment of pro-feminist judges.[24]

The distinction between education and political action is dissolved completely in the Charter litigation projects within some law schools. The law school at Queen's University runs a prisoners rights project. The Faculty of law at the University of Toronto has a similar rights litigation project.

Rights Experts

The role of law schools in promoting judicial activism was predicted even before the Charter was legally proclaimed. Writing in 1982 about the probable impact of the new Charter, Peter Russell observed, "A generation of Canadian lawyers has been exposed to the influence of professors who have contrasted unfavourably the Supreme Court of Canada's restrained treatment of the Canadian Bill of Rights with the much more activist approach of the US Supreme Court, particularly during the era of the Warren Court."[25]

These words proved prophetic. Today, universities recruit, shape, and pay the salaries of the *engagé* intellectuals whose ideas drive the Charter movement. Law schools now produce a steady stream of rights experts to staff the interest groups, bureaucracies, and courts that pursue the politics of rights. In the new constitutional politics of gender, race, ethnicity, and language, each of the official constitutional groups draws extensively on academic sympathizers for legal and political support. Of special significance are the scores of committed law professors who serve on the boards and litigation committees of Charter-oriented interest groups. The research interests and legal expertise of these professors usually dovetail with the cases on which they work. Their research supports their politics, and their politics feeds their research.

This mutual penetration of politics, education, and government is reflected in the career paths of most Court Party activists. These typically include multiple (and often simultaneous) appointments to universities, administrative positions within the rights bureaucracy, and executive positions within the new rights-advocacy groups.

No career path better illustrates the symbiotic relationship between universities and the Court Party than that of the late Walter Tarnopolsky. Tarnopolsky began his career as a law professor in the 1960s. One of his early books established him as the leading critic of the Supreme Court's self-restrained interpretation of the 1960 Canadian Bill of Rights. This led him to become President of the Canadian Civil Liberties Association (1977-81), in which role he influenced the framing of the Charter through his testimony before the Parliamentary Committee on the Constitution. Once the Charter was adopted, he was part of a roving team of rights experts, sponsored by the state-funded Canadian Institute for the Administration of Justice, that toured the country during the first half of 1982 promoting an activist approach to the Charter to judges and lawyers. During this same period Tarnopolsky also served as a Commissioner of the Canadian Human Rights Commission (1978-83), wrote what was then the definitive book on Canadian human rights legislation,[26] and founded and became the first Director of the Canadian Human Rights Centre at the University of Ottawa (1980). (The Centre became an important clearing house for Court Party litigation in the decisive first decade of the Charter.) Once the Charter was safely in place, Trudeau rewarded Tarnopolsky with an appointment to the Supreme Court of Ontario in 1983.

A similar interplay between university employment and interest-group activism is evident in the careers of many other Court Party stalwarts, including Mary Eberts, Dale Gibson, Bill Black, and Lynn Smith, all influential equality seekers. Eberts, after post-graduate work at Harvard, became a full-time professor of law at the University of Toronto in the mid-1970s and has taught there part-time ever since. From 1979 to 1983, she was vice-president of the CCLA and in 1984 helped to found LEAF. Gibson, formerly a Manitoba Human Rights Commissioner and a member of the Canadian Judicial Council's Charter Education team, was a long-time law professor at the University of Manitoba and is currently Belzberg Professor of Constitutional Law at the University of Alberta. Black, a professor at the UBC law school, has served as director of both the Court Challenges Program and the Canadian Human Rights Centre at the University of Ottawa. Also at the UBC Law School, and until recently its Dean, Lynn Smith has chaired the BC Law Foundation, headed its Policy and Planning Committee, and served as a member and consultant to the Western Judicial Education Centre. In 1998 she was appointed as a judge by the Chrétien government. All four of these activist scholars have contributed extensively and influentially to the advocacy scholarship on equality rights under the Charter. In addition, Eberts, who has been lead counsel on numerous feminist test cases, has frequently been touted as a possible Supreme Court appointee.

Rosalie Abella, currently a judge with the Ontario Court of Appeal, is another prominent equality seeker who is often rumoured to be bound for the Supreme Court. Abella headed the Royal Commission on Equality in Employment (1983-84), which produced the controversial Abella Report recommending the government adoption of mandatory employment equity programs. From 1989-92, she chaired the Ontario Law Reform Commission. Although she has never been a full-time university professor, her university connections are long-standing. From 1976-84, she co-chaired the University of Toronto's Academic Discipline Tribunal. She was visiting professor at the McGill Law school from 1988-92 and senior fellow at Toronto's Massey College from 1989-92. In addition, universities have awarded her 15 honorary doctorates in seven years! Another example is Mary Ellen Turpel, a law professor/aboriginal rights activist who was appointed a provincial court judge in Saskatchewan in 1998. A year and a half later, *Time* magazine named Turpel as a future leader in its section on "politicians and activists … people who are trying to move the country."[27] One could easily multiply such examples of the university connection in the career of Court Party leaders.

University-based rights experts serve the Court Party in a particularly useful way when they are called upon by the media as "authorized knowers" who can explain the meaning or significance of a judicial decision.[28] An authorized knower is a specialist in the subject of the story. When the media want to report on Charter decisions, they tend to suffer the same disabilities as the rest of us: length of judgments, lack of time, and highly technical language. The media try to short-circuit these difficulties through interviews with Charter experts who are expected to cut through the legalese and give the public a concise, plain-language version of the judges' decision. However, the experts are typically themselves partisans on the issue at stake, and tend to provide interpretations that favour their political views. The public is thus twice removed from the actual Charter: the judges interpret the Charter, and then the media-designated authorized knowers (i.e., law professors) interpret the judges. The professors enjoy as much discretion as the judges, and, like the judges, they typically use it to advance Court Party interests.

The television reporting of the *Morgentaler* decision provided a clear example. All three main networks relied heavily on interviews with women lawyers and law professors, almost all of whom were active feminists. Consciously or not, there was a decided tendency to overstate the scope of the Court's decision: quoting the more radical opinion of Madame Justice Wilson at length; minimizing the narrow, procedural basis of the other two majority opinions; and ignoring the two dissenting judges altogether. Some experts also extended the meaning of *Morgentaler* to include public funding of abortions, an issue that was neither addressed nor answered by the Supreme Court's decision.[29]

Advocacy Scholarship

The expertise brought to the media by rights experts is, of course, based on their scholarship, which does much more than establish their credentials. In important ways, it directly influences and shapes judicial opinions. In effect, the judgments that authorized knowers explain to the media have often been profoundly influenced by their own prior writings. While the simple view is that interpreting the Charter is the responsibility of the judges, the interpretive community is in fact much broader and clearly includes legal academics. Imagine three concentric circles. Judges occupy the centre but draw from the outer two rings. Counsel for parties and interveners constitute the second ring. Their written factums provide judges with competing interpretations of key Charter sections. Judges often rely heavily on these written factums. The third ring consists of the scholarly commentary published in the law reviews and books. Both judges and counsel look to this commentary for guidance. The clerks who work for the Supreme Court – all recent law school graduates – also bring current legal scholarship to the attention of the judges.[30]

Scholarly commentary did not always enjoy its current prominence in the development of law. Four decades ago, the Supreme Court had an unwritten presumption against using contemporary academic sources. At the end of the 1960s the Supreme Court Reports contained "barely a dozen references a year to academic texts, and virtually none to legal journals." In the 1990s, by contrast, the Supreme Court cites hundreds of books and articles a year, most written by living authors. Although most references are to Canadian authors, US writers now account for about one half as many citations as Canadians. This new judicial reliance on contemporary legal scholarship is most prominent in three categories of cases: Charter, family law, and tort.[31]

Legal commentary has taken on added significance in the case of the Charter. In 1982 the Charter was new. Law professors sympathetic to the

Court Party coalition promoted it as a break with past Canadian jurisprudence – a sort of legal *tabula rasa*. On this understanding there were few past
precedents that were unambiguously applicable to Charter interpretation.
As the deputy minister of justice told a conference in 1991, "Imagine the difficulty of advising the government what the Charter means when there have
been no decisions."[32] This left a legal vacuum that was quickly filled by the
avalanche of new, reformist Charter scholarship.

Under these circumstances, Martin Shapiro's observation about American legal scholarship is even truer in the Canadian context: "[T]he study of
law and courts [is] part of the process of making the [law]; that is, [part of]
the public discourse that continuously constitutes and reconstitutes constitutional and other law."[33] Legal scholars follow and comment on what the
courts are saying, and the judges take note of what the law professors write.
Even under normal circumstances, which the first decade of the Charter
was not, legal academics are important partners in the development of the
law.

The burst of advocacy scholarship that followed the adoption of the
Charter was a calculated component of Court Party strategy to maximize
the political utility of Charter litigation. The 1984 report that led to the
creation of LEAF declared that "a critical component of this [systematic liti-
gation] strategy [is] to build a theory of equality which is accepted by academics, lawyers and the judiciary. Legal writing in respected law journals,
presentations of papers at legal seminars, and participation in judges' training sessions are all means of disseminating and legitimating such theories of
equality."[34] Marilou McPhedran, a LEAF founder, even lobbied Peter Hogg,
author of Canada's most influential constitutional law commentary, to try
to persuade him to adopt the "correct" interpretation of section 28 of the
Charter. McPhredran later recounted that even after three hours, Professor
Hogg "still got it wrong" (i.e., he disagreed with the feminist position).[35]

Once LEAF was established, it adopted a self-styled campaign of influencing the influencers that included fostering supportive legal scholarship.
LEAF organizers clearly considered this to be much more than an academic
exercise. "The shaping of the Charter will be an intensely political process,"
Sheila McIntyre explained to fellow feminists, [one that is] "far more respon-
sive to public pressure than [to] constitutional law."[36]

To implement this strategy, the ubiquitous Mary Eberts hastily organized
a conference on equality rights, invited academic advocates of all the section
15 constituencies, and published the papers as a book. The book does not
include a single article that challenges the concepts of systemic discrimination or unequal impact, concepts that vastly increase the scope of section 15

and thus its utility to equality-seeking interest groups. One reviewer summed up the book as "legal scholarship in the service of a social movement."[37] That same year, NAWL launched the *Canadian Journal of Women and the Law*.

The influencing the influencers strategy was not limited to organized feminists, but is also reflected in the growth of new law journals and reporters that cater to a variety of Court Party concerns and clientele groups. Of the 136 law-related Canadian journals and reporters, 48 – or 35 per cent – have been started since 1980. Twenty-one of these 48 are postmaterialist in content, and 14 of these 21 are Charter or rights-related.[38] Since most of the explicitly rights-oriented journals are founded and funded by Court Party activists, they actively recruit, publish, and thereby legitimate advocacy scholarship that advances their political agenda.

Fifteen of the 21 postmaterialist journals are published in Ontario, the political heartland of the Court Party, and only six are subscriber supported. The other 15 are all state-funded, directly or indirectly. Five are university-based and/or funded by annual grants from provincial law foundations. In terms of multiplicity of state-funding sources, it is difficult to match the *Canadian Journal of Women and the Law*. Since it was founded in 1985, *CJWL* lists the following funding sources:

Federal:	Justice Department's Human Rights Law Fund; SOS-Women's Program; SOS-Multiculturalism and Citizenship; SOS-Promotion of Official Languages; SSHRC.
Ontario:	Anti-Racism Secretariat; Women's Directorate.
Law Foundations:	Ontario, Nova Scotia, PEI, Newfoundland, New Brunswick, Manitoba, Saskatchewan, and British Columbia
University Law Faculties:	Windsor, Queen's, Laval, and Ottawa.
Other:	National Association of Women and the Law Trust Fund.

The "extensive intermingling of the academic and political spheres," Alan Cairns has observed, has produced a Charter "scholarship" that is increasingly "purpose driven and laced with advocacy." Cairns has called attention to the parallel trend of "insiderism" – the belief that only a member of an ethnic, linguistic or gender group can speak with any authority about its constitutional interests.[39] For example, in 1991 a conference was held at the law school at the University of Alberta entitled "Conversations

Among Friends: Women and Constitutional Reform." The program listed 19 panelists, all women, half of them lawyers.[40]

The growth of advocacy research in the field of legal scholarship is a predictable consequence of the Charter's empowerment of judges. One of the iron rules of politics is that "where power rests, there influence will be brought to bear."[41] Patrick Monahan has correctly identified the incentives that encourage advocacy scholarship: "Because of the political potency of Charter arguments, there is a tremendous incentive to try to shape perceptions of the Charter's meaning so as to advance one's political goals."[42]

American political scientist Martin Shapiro has more bluntly described constitutional scholarship in his own country as a form of "lobbying the courts." "The distinction between scholarship and advocacy," Shapiro writes,

> has always been uncertain or nonexistent in most of the legal scholarship produced in law schools. Much of that scholarship consists of doctrinal analysis that purports to yield the correct or a good, better or best statement of the law. *The central strategy is a massive and deliberate confusion of is and ought.* The previous cases are examined to show that, properly interpreted, the body of existing law really adds up to the law as the author thinks it ought to be. In short, most such writing consists of expanded and embroidered legal briefs. The key question in understanding such work is, "Who's the client?"[43]

In Charter commentary, the client is invariably one of the Court Party constituencies. Treatment of Charter issues tends to be one-sided. Counterarguments and contrary precedents are portrayed negatively or ignored altogether. At a time when the debate over judicial activism defines the core of the conservative/liberal conflict over appointments to the American Supreme Court, it is all but impossible to find a Canadian law review article that argues for judicial self-restraint or narrow interpretation of Charter provisions.[44]

In a systematic study of Charter scholarship Troy Riddell examined legal commentary on the section 1 reasonable limitations clause.[45] Former Chief Justice Brian Dickson aptly described section 1 as "the most important section of the Charter,"[46] since its interpretation usually makes or breaks a Charter claim. Predictably, Court Party interests have invested heavily in efforts to shape the scope of section 1, first at the framing stage, then in litigation.[47] A narrow interpretation of what constitutes a reasonable limitation of a right invites strict judicial scrutiny of legislative policy decisions, enhancing the odds of winning a Charter claim. Conversely, a broad interpretation invites judicial deference, minimizing judicial intervention in the policy process, and reducing the potential for successful interest group litigation.

In his study of 20 pieces of English-language legal scholarship dealing with section 1, Riddell found that they overwhelmingly endorsed interpretive choices that would make it easier for rights claimants to win their cases. Nine of 13 commentators who addressed the issue argued that, given the prospect of justifying reasonable limits on rights under section 1, the rights themselves should be given the broadest possible interpretation, an approach that makes earlier Bill of Rights precedents less relevant. This approach also makes it very easy to claim a rights violation and thus trigger the necessity of a section 1, reasonable limits defence. Having endorsed such easy rights claiming, 18 of 19 (95 per cent) of the commentators who addressed the burden of proving the reasonable limits defense recommended placing that burden on the government. Eighty-one per cent (13/16), moreover, insisted that the test of adequate proof must be stricter than the lenient "valid federal objective" test employed under the Bill of Rights.[48] By favouring interpretive choices that maximized the scope of judicial scrutiny of public policy, these commentators encouraged the kind of judicial activism that Court Party interest groups would need to succeed in their Charter test cases. In its 1987 landmark section 1 ruling of *R. v. Oakes*,[49] the Supreme Court – with a big assist from clerk Joel Bakan – adopted all of these recommendations.

The same pattern exists in the scholarship on the issue of intervener participation in hearings before the Supreme Court. This is a strategic issue for Court Party interest groups, because it represents the most direct channel of communication they have with the Supreme Court. As we noted in chapter 2, the Court had historically been stingy about intervener access, since it contradicted its traditional adjudicative role. Academic commentary, however, unanimously urged the Court to adopt an open door approach to intervention, and after some initial hesitation, the Supreme Court followed this advice.[50]

Advocacy literature has played a similarly important role in gay rights litigation. Gay advocates (and postmodernists generally) view law as an important formative and pedagogical force. Just as the traditional family has been constructed by the law, so changing the law can deconstruct it. Jodi Freeman, an activist who helped develop EGALE's CCP-funded factum in the ground-breaking gay rights case, *Mossup*, has written that, "rights litigation can be a useful tool in the pursuit of social change, as part of a broader strategy."[51] Didi Herman, Canada's most published gay rights lawyer/professor, has stated it more strongly: "law reform is part of an ideological battle, and fighting over the meanings of marriage and family constitutes resistance to heterosexual hegemony."[52]

To use the Charter as part of such an ideological battle, gay and lesbian activists had first to overcome the intentional omission of sexual orientation from the list of prohibited grounds of discrimination in section 15 of the Charter. They thus began publishing articles advocating that it be added by way of judicial interpretation. According to Didi Herman, this publishing strategy aimed to supply "the appropriate argument for lesbian and gay litigants to make."[53] Greener's 1997 study of 22 law review articles discussing the definition of the family (all published since 1982) found a pattern similar to the law journal scholarship on section 1 and intervention. While the broader literature revealed a lively debate about the merits of the family, including defences of the traditional family, the law journal articles were "uniformly critical of 'familial ideology' ... [especially] the 'traditional family,'" which was portrayed as "the ideological centrepiece of heterosexual supremacy."[54]

The only serious disagreement in this literature was whether to seek a partial deconstruction of the heterosexual definition of family so as to allow homosexual marriage, or to pursue "a more radical deconstruction that aims to abolish any meaningful distinction between family and non-family."[55] According to Jody Freeman, "recognizing marriage between gay men or lesbians would revolutionize its meaning."[56] The Supreme Court has not responded to the most radical strain in this literature, but it has read "sexual orientation" into section 15 of the Charter and has begun redefining family so as to include homosexual relationships.[57]

In addition to the law journals, there is a second type of advocacy scholarship that has played an influential role in Court Party litigation: social science studies that present one-sided and partisan views of social policy issues. Because of the heavy reliance the Court has placed on the section 1 reasonable limitations clause in resolving Charter claims, judges must frequently review extrinsic evidence (or social facts) in order to determine if the challenged law has a "compelling public purpose" or uses the "least intrusive means" to achieve that purpose – two components of the Oakes test.

This new reliance on social facts to resolve Charter cases introduces a myriad of problems. The adversarial process was not designed to elicit or test the reliability of social facts, since there is no guarantee that the relevant social facts will be brought before the court. Even when they are, there is a question of whether judges will understand them, especially when they are presented in statistical form – a field of knowledge in which judges have little to no training. In the *Askov* case, dealing with the right to trial within a reasonable time, the Court's failure "both to test facts and to find facts" resulted in the dismissal of over 40,000 pending criminal prosecutions, many of them for violent indictable offenses, and a subsequent about face by the Court in the face of angry public opinion.[58] The *Askov* fiasco highlights the problems judges face in determining the validity and reliability of the evidence put before them.

These problems are not academic. Both sides have a vested interest in presenting self-serving accounts of the policy problem before the court. There are many social scientists willing to work as expert witnesses who, for a price or out of ideological conviction, will present skewed or misleading evidence to the court. The hired-gun syndrome was a problem prior to the Charter, but the recent trend toward self-proclaimed advocacy research in policy studies has exacerbated it. Anyone who has participated in Charter litigation knows this syndrome only too well. For present purposes, a single example will have to suffice.

In a 1996 address on the topic, "Does the Charter make a difference?," Mary Eberts dismissed the "male strategy of neutrality" in favour of the "advocacy research" practiced by feminists.[59] She boasted of the influence of feminist advocacy research on several Supreme Court decisions. She could have pointed to several cases. In *Norberg*, LEAF introduced studies about unequal bargaining power to undermine the defense of consent in sexual assault cases. In *Moge*, a spousal support case, LEAF introduced studies about the "feminization of poverty." But Eberts chose to focus on Justice Wilson's heavy reliance in the *Lavallée* case on the work of social scientist Lenore Walker.[60]

Having fatally shot her husband in the back of the head as he left the room, Angelique Lynn Lavallée claimed self-defence. Since the rule of self-defense is, for obvious reasons, strictly limited by the requirement that grievous bodily harm to the accused be imminent and that there be no alternative to the use of deadly force, it would not normally have been available to Lavallée. True, her husband had threatened to kill her during the argument that preceded the shooting; nevertheless, he was leaving the room when Lavallée pulled the trigger, and thus did not appear to pose an imminent threat, especially since she could presumably have left.

Lavallée's lawyer countered these damaging facts with a theory known as the "battered-wife syndrome" (BWS). BWS holds that abused women (1) know, intuitively, both when physical abuse is imminent and how brutal it will be; and (2) are psychologically incapable of leaving their abusers. Under these circumstances, a battered wife can potentially meet the criteria of self-defense: she knows that a potentially life-threatening beating is imminent (when the husband returns or, in some cases, awakes) but she is (psychologically) incapable of leaving. Justice Wilson, writing for the Court, accepted this argument and found Lavallée innocent. Lenore Walker, the advocacy scholar praised by Eberts, is the academic source of the BWS theory relied upon by Justice Wilson.

While most Canadians may be unfamiliar with Lenore Walker, many will remember the famous Super Bowl wife-beating hoax of January 1993. The day after a feminist press conference announced that Super Bowl Sunday is "the biggest day of the year for violence against women," Lenore Walker appeared on ABC's "Good Morning America" and claimed to "have compiled a ten year record showing a sharp increase in violent incidents against women on Super Bowl Sundays." In the weeks following, as the hoax unraveled for lack of any evidence, Walker was pressed to go public with her data. After several weeks of avoiding phone calls from the media, she finally announced that, "We don't use them [survey data] for public consumption.... We used them to guide us in advocacy projects."[61]

Similar problems exist with the BWS theory incorporated in Lavallée. Published in 1979, Walker's book on the subject does not restrict the definition of battery to physical violence, but extends it to include "forceful physical or *psychological behaviour* by a man" intended "to coerce [a woman] to do something he wants her to do." In one of her case-studies, Walker pronounces "Paul" guilty of battering his wife by "ignoring her and by working late, in order to move up the corporate ladder, for the entire five years of their marriage."[62] Given this expansive definition, it is hardly surprising that Walker's studies "found" that wife-battering occurs in 50 percent of all American families.[63]

From this finding, it is only a small step to Walker's next conclusion: that almost all women who kill their mates are victims of BWS. "Women don't kill men," she writes, "unless they've been pushed to a point of desperation."[64] This conclusion meshes neatly with Walker's broader "feminist political gender analysis ... of interpersonal violence ... as the socialized androcentric need for power." "The problem of violence against women," Walker theorizes, is the "misuse of power by men who have been socialized into believing they have the right to control the women in their lives, even through violent means."[65]

Armed with her BWS theory, Walker was much in demand as an expert witness in assault and murder trials during the 1980s. By 1991 she had testified in approximately 150 cases, collecting $170 an hour for her services. In 1993 she testified in the defense of Peggy Saiz, a Denver woman who shot and killed her sleeping husband after they had sex. Following the murder, Saiz made the house look like a robbery had occurred and then went disco-dancing with her sister. At trial, it was disclosed that at the time of the murder Saiz was having an affair with another man; that she purchased several thousand dollars of life insurance on her husband two weeks before the shooting; and that she had gone target shooting the day before she shot her husband. These uncontested facts notwithstanding, Walker testified that Peggy Saiz's behaviour was consistent with battered-wife syndrome.

More generally, the reliability of feminist advocacy research on male/female family violence has been widely challenged on both sides of the border. Several US studies found that "women assault their partners at about the same rate – for both severe and minor assaults – as men assault their partners."[66] The same results have been duplicated in Canada. Reena Sommer's 1994 Manitoba study found that the favourite feminist excuse for female-initiated violence – that it is almost always in self-defense – was true only 10 per cent of the time. In 1994, John Fekete observed that in the "strange world of family violence research," results have been ignored, explained away and even withheld because they contradict the "woman-as-victim" thesis.[67] Fekete's claim was confirmed in 1999 when it came to light that a 1989 study of domestic violence, which reported men as the sole aggressors, did not report half of its own data. This study was a major factor in a subsequent parliamentary study ("The War Against Women") and a $10 million dollar federal inquiry into violence against women. The 1999 re-analysis of the *original data* found that women were equally aggressive and actually more prone to initiate violence,[68] though male violence generally does more damage.

Christina Sommers has explained this syndrome: the purpose of feminist scholarship is not to understand the world but to transform it. Equality is more important than accuracy.[69] While this may not trouble the editors of feminist journals, it is certainly a suspect foundation for public policy decisions. Yet when judges make policy, they are often asked to rest it on precisely such foundations.

Advocacy scholarship is brought to the attention of judges through two primary sources. The first and most obvious is the factums of the interest group lawyers who appear before the courts. The ability to cite academic literature confers authority and legitimacy on an otherwise novel interpretive position. This is the central function of the influencing the influencers strategy: "The simultaneous appearance of numerous articles all supporting the same position puts judges and legal scholars on notice that there is support for the position advanced."[70] In *Lavallée*, for example, Justice Wilson relied not only on the work of Lenore Walker, but on three other law review articles.

Julie Blackman, "Ideas Toward the Representation of Battered Women Who Kill," *Women's Rights Law Reporter* 227 (1986).

Phyllis Crocker, "The Meaning of Equality for Battered Women Who Kill Men in Self-Defense," *Harvard Women's Law Journal* 121 (1985).

M.J. Willoughby, "Rendering Each Woman her Due: Can a Battered Woman Claim Self-Defense When She Kills Her Sleeping Batterer," *Kansas Law Review* 169 (1989).

Note not just the focus of these articles but the fact that two of the three were published in law reviews devoted exclusively to feminist issues.[71] The *Lavallée* case is an example of the feminist legal strategy of "flooding the market with women's stories."[72] Indeed, in this instance, the circle is closed: a feminist judge cites feminist authors published in feminist journals to acquit a woman charged with murdering her husband. *Lavallée* is symptomatic of the interaction of judicial activism and advocacy scholarship.

While factums come through the front door of the Court, advocacy scholarship also comes in the back door in the persons of the clerks. At times, the connection between clerks and the advocacy scholarship relevant to a particular case is direct and personal. As Ian Brodie notes, sometimes "the clerks have just finished taking law school classes taught by the very same activists who are intervening in the cases."[73] Lorne Sossin, a former clerk to Chief Justice Lamer, adds that "Clerks tend to have had their legal education more influenced by law reviews. They usually rely on the reviews more heavily when forming their opinions ... than do the Justices." He believes that the ability of clerks "to bring this other body of literature before the justice may well have an impact on the decision and the way in which it is justified." He adds that "this is especially important with respect to cases involving the Charter because [Charter issues] may hinge on arguments derived from unconventional legal sources." Sossin suggests that the clerks' penchant for using law reviews as authorities explains "the frequency with which law reviews are now cited in Supreme Court judgments."[74]

The role of clerks as conduits for law review commentary was indirectly confirmed by a 1983 comment by former Chief Justice Dickson. After observing that scholarship was an important source of interpretation, Dickson went on to complain that "one rarely finds reference to scholarly writing in the factums that counsel present to the courts."[75] How then does it find its way into judicial decisions? The "ghost-writing" role of Dickson's former clerk, Joel Bakan, has already been noted. This may explain the reference to several law review articles in the Chief Justice's opinion in Oakes, despite the fact that none were mentioned in the factums presented to the Court. This conjecture is consistent with Greene et al.'s speculation that the much higher incidence of citations to legal scholarship in the Supreme Court decisions than in the decisions of provincial courts of appeal is due to the greater number of clerks at the Supreme Court.[76]

Conclusion

University-based intellectuals are at the heart of the postmaterialist left in all western democracies. They diagnose our social ills – racism, sexism, heterosexism, etc. – and prescribe the cures. What distinguishes American and now Canadian politics is the extent to which this new knowledge class successfully pursues its agendas through litigation and the courts. The consequent politicization of legal scholarship in Canada parallels – indeed, emulates – post-war American practice. Peltason noted that "since 1937, changes in public policy first have been mentioned in the nation's law reviews."[77] The process has not been spontaneous and happenstance. In the US, "flooding the law reviews"[78] with favourable articles has been an established tactic of movement interest groups since it was first used by the NAACP in the 1950s. In Canada, it became part of an explicit strategy of influencing the influencers adopted at the outset of the Charter era. It has been an astoundingly successful strategy, in large part because it has been largely unopposed. The legal commentators are all singing from the same hymnbook.

The Court Party's transformation of Canada's appellate judiciary in one generation could not have been achieved without the active participation and support of the law schools and universities. Universities (and in Canada, this means another arm of the state) provide the personnel, the institutional support, and the ideas that have sustained Canada's rights revolution.

SEVEN

WHAT'S WRONG WITH THE CHARTER REVOLUTION AND THE COURT PARTY?

A majority, held in restraint by constitutional checks and limitations, and always chang-
ing easily, with deliberate changes in public opinions and sentiments, is the only true
sovereign of a free people. Whoever rejects it, does of necessity, fly to anarchy or to
despotism. Unanimity is impossible; the rule of a minority, as a permanent arrangement
is wholly inadmissable.

Abraham Lincoln, .
First Inaugural Address, 4 March 1861

In the course of describing and analyzing them, we have made no attempt
to hide our opposition to both the Charter Revolution and the Court Party.
In this final chapter we explain more systematically what, in our view, is
wrong with the Court Party's project of enhanced judicial power.[1]

Our primary objection to the Charter Revolution is that it is deeply and
fundamentally undemocratic, not just in the simple and obvious sense of
being anti-majoritarian, but also in the more serious sense of eroding the
habits and temperament of representative democracy. The growth of courtroom rights talk undermines perhaps the fundamental prerequisite of
decent liberal democratic politics: the willingness to engage those with
whom one disagrees in the ongoing attempt to combine diverse interests
into temporarily viable governing majorities. Liberal democracy works only
when majorities rather than minorities rule, and when it is obvious to all
that ruling majorities are themselves coalitions of minorities in a pluralistic
society. Partisan opponents, in short, must nevertheless be seen as fellow
citizens who might be future allies. Representative institutions facilitate this
fundamental democratic disposition; judicial power undermines it. The
kind of courtroom politics promoted by the Court Party, in short, is author-
itarian, not just in process but, more dangerously, in spirit.

Our concern is nicely framed by two quotations from the work of Peter
Russell, one from his analysis of Canada's mega-constitutional politics, the

other from his reflections on judicial policymaking. First, in *Constitutional Odyssey*, Russell infers from our constitutional history, especially from the mega-constitutional politics of recent decades, that "not all Canadians have consented to form a single people in which a majority or some special majority have, to use John Locke's phrase, 'a right to set and conclude the rest.'"[2] This willingness to be concluded by the majority is what defines a sovereign people, at least one that wishes to govern itself democratically. Although a sovereign democratic people will certainly exhibit partisan political division, such division remains subordinate to an overarching agreement to remain a single people. As a member of a sovereign people, in other words, one must agree to treat one's partisan opponents as fellow citizens, whose rule, should they form the majority, one is willing to accept. Because not all Canadians have agreed to treat each other in this way – because, in other words, what divides us often outweighs our common citizenship – we are not, in Russell's view, a sovereign people; the subtitle of *Constitutional Odyssey* asks whether we can become one.

Second, in an oft-quoted passage from an early article on the Charter of Rights and Freedoms, Russell worries about the "negative side" of "transferring the policymaking focus from the legislative to the judicial arena." This transfer, he says, "represents a further flight from politics, a deepening disillusionment with the procedures of representative government and government by discussion as means of resolving fundamental questions of political justice."[3] This second concern is connected to the first inasmuch as it suggests that the Charter, which the Court Party's unifiers believed would help Canadians become a sovereign people, may in fact hinder us from becoming one; indeed, it may make us even less of a sovereign people than we currently are. A people prepared to treat political opponents as legitimate surely needs to make government by discussion a leading means of settling political differences. To the extent that the Charter represents a flight from this kind of politics, it can be understood as threatening rather than promoting the unity necessary to a sovereign people.

There is a sense, of course, in which this conclusion is already a truism. As we have already noted, the Charter has done little to remedy the division that most obviously reflects the failure of Canadians to become a sovereign people; namely, the division between Quebec and the rest of Canada (ROC). Instead of ameliorating these tensions, as Pierre Trudeau hoped it would, the Charter has intensified them.[4]

However, the exacerbation of Quebec/ROC tensions is far from the only way in which the Charter threatens the capacity of Canadians to act as a sovereign people. While the Charter has clearly taken deeper root in the ROC, it is questionable even in this context whether it fortifies or threatens our existence as a sovereign people. Canadians in the ROC may indeed be more united by Charterphilia,[5] but the resulting flight from "the procedures of representative government and government by discussion" does little to maintain or strengthen the inclination to allow the majority "to set and conclude the rest." The Quebec/ROC divide, in other words, is not the only deepening gulf between Canadians. Contemporary identity politics and inflated political rhetoric are making ordinary democratic politics more difficult in many other respects. Even in the ROC, Canadians are arguably becoming less of a single people, and the Charter-enhanced flight from representative democracy is at least partly to blame.[6]

Many of liberal democracy's early constitutionalists in Britain and the United States might have predicted the corrosive effects of the Charter. They understood what we appear to have forgotten: that even a regime dedicated to the protection of rights does not necessarily benefit from institutionalizing rights talk too prominently in public life. These pioneers put little faith in judicially enforceable bills of rights – and for good reason. They believed that representative democracy, not judicialized politics, is mainly how a sovereign people should protect rights.

In fact, although one would never guess it from the current infatuation with bills of rights, it is remarkable just how recently such documents have become prominent features of modern constitutionalism. The protection of rights was certainly the chief end of early liberal theorists and statesmen, but constitutionally and judicially enforceable bills of rights as we know them were not their preferred means to this end. The first major bill of this kind is to be found not in the recommendations of Locke or Blackstone, but in the US Constitution.[7] There it appears as a series of amendments, insisted on by the anti-federalists as a way of constraining only the national government, not their preferred state governments. Although the federalist proponents of the constitution were willing to concede the bill of rights, they obviously did not think that it was necessary – not because they did not respect rights, but because they thought (and said) that the main constitution, the pre-bill-of-rights constitution, was itself the true and most effective bill of rights.[8]

Rights, in this view, were best protected by preventing the emergence of oppressive majority factions, not by preaching moral rectitude to majorities through such parchment barriers as bills of rights. Oppressive factions would be prevented by the so-called "new science of politics." At the heart of this new science was representative democracy, organized in a system of institutional checks and balances, and superimposed on a society sufficiently diverse to require the moderating aggregation of many factions into decent governing majorities. For the American founders, in short, the surest protection against majority tyranny was to undermine – that is, fragment – natural majorities. Properly structured representative democracy (as opposed to pure democracy) was to replace majority rule with minorities rule; that is, with majority coalitions of diverse minorities.[9]

Representation facilitated this strategy by permitting a territory large and diverse enough to forestall the emergence of natural majorities. But representation did more than extend the size and diversity of a political jurisdiction; it also served "to refine and to enlarge the public views by passing them through the medium of a chosen body of citizens." Members of the legislature, a "select and stable body," would have the opportunity to acquire a "due sense of national character," as opposed to being mere spokesmen for the parochial concerns of their constituents.[10] Thus deliberation or "government by discussion," not just representation of interests, was also considered a vital safeguard for rights.

It would be a mistake to exclude the courts from the ambit of the new science of politics. When Alexander Hamilton listed the components of that science in Federalist Paper No. 9, he explicitly included "the institution of courts composed of judges holding their offices during good behavior." But Hamilton was interested primarily in adjudicative independence, not in judicial enforcement of entrenched rights. True, he did believe that the judiciary would sometimes have to declare laws unconstitutional and thus void, but he saw this as a limited power to invalidate only "acts contrary to the manifest tenor of the Constitution";[11] that is, absolutely clear contraventions of the constitution. This is made clear by his only example: the passage of bills of attainder and ex post facto laws, which are explicitly prohibited.

There is nothing in Hamilton's defense of judicial review that suggests that he would have supported modern purposive analysis, which contemplates the invalidation of policy that contravenes no explicit textual command, so long as it contravenes the deeper "purposes" of the text, as discovered between its lines by judges.[12] In fact, in Federalist Paper No. 81, Hamilton suggests that such loosely grounded rulings would be "usurpations on the authority of the legislature" and grounds for "impeachment." More to our point, his limited defense of judicial review was part of his attempt to urge the ratification of a constitution that did not include a bill of rights. Indeed, it was Hamilton who in Federalist Paper No. 84 insisted that the proposed constitution – the pre-bill-of-rights version – was "itself, in every rational sense, and to every useful purpose, a bill of rights."[13]

According to recent scholarship, prominent theorists of the Westminster parliamentary tradition – Lord Durham and A.V. Dicey, for example – thought along similar lines. Janet Ajzenstat argues that Durham saw responsible government as contributing to constitutional "balance," which for him, as for other Whigs, meant just what "checks and balances" did to the Americans, and served precisely the same function.

Ajzenstat comes to similar conclusions about Dicey. Dicey believed that "the Westminster system's two great principles, parliamentary sovereignty and the rule of law, are ... mutually reinforcing." To be sure, Dicey believed that the security of rights depended primarily on judge-made law (that is, the common law and judicial interpretation of statutes) and thus required independent and impartial courts. Still, Ajzenstat contends, he thought that "in the absence of parliamentary sovereignty efforts by the judiciary will come to nothing."[14]

For Dicey, as for Durham, parliamentary sovereignty was the key to protecting rights, rather than the main threat to rights, as is now generally assumed, because the sovereign parliament embodied the principle of checks and balances. Parliamentary checks and balances were certainly different, and perhaps less elaborate, than those of the US congressional system, but they were no less effective for that. Their essence lay in the freedom of the opposition parties to criticize and expose government violations of the people's rights. Anticipation of such criticism and the prospect of being punished at the polls were expected to pre-empt any governmental proclivity to invade the rights of its citizens. Dicey and his generation had great confidence in the efficacy of partisan debate and public deliberation in producing sound public policy; i.e., policy that respects rights. Part of this confidence came from the Whig embrace of the natural-right tradition and of the power of reasoned debate to apply this tradition to the affairs of state. Ajzenstat laments that, with the advent of the Charter (and probably before), Canadians' "confidence in the power of public debate to resolve issues for the common good has taken a beating." If we lose it altogether, she warns, "we lose the essence of constitutional democracy."[15] In the Australian context, John Uhr has recently mounted a similar defense of partisan debate as the key to sustaining "deliberative democracy."[16]

In sum, early constitutionalists in both the American and English systems sought to protect rights more through representative democracy and checks and balances than through bills of rights. If these devices of the new science of politics were in good working order, a bill of rights would not be necessary; if they were not working well, the constitutional pronouncements of robed judges, wielding the power of neither sword nor purse, would make little difference.

As these early theorists would have predicted, the US Bill of Rights did in fact make *very* little difference, at least for most of US constitutional history. During the nineteenth century, only nine federal laws were voided for violating the Bill of Rights. As recently as 1925, the total was only 15. The most prominent judicial invalidation, moreover, was the infamous pro-slavery judgment in *Dred Scott v. Sanford*, "scarcely a monument to liberty."[17] As for the states, we have seen that the original Bill of Rights did not even apply to them. The origins of the modern emphasis on the Bill of Rights by Americans can be traced back *at best* to the *Gitlow* case in 1925, in which the Supreme Court began incorporating the Bill of Rights into the Fourteenth Amendment, thus making it applicable to the states. In fact, the modern infatuation with bills of rights is probably most accurately traced to *Brown v. Board of Education* in 1954 — less than 50 years ago. For most of its history, liberal-democratic constitutionalism has depended for the protection of rights mainly on properly constructed representative institutions and the government by discussion that they entail.

Recent decades, however, have witnessed a sustained and twofold challenge to representative democracy. In Canada, as elsewhere, it is manifested by the growing popularity of both populism and constitutionally entrenched rights. To adapt Russell's formulation slightly, if populism reflects a flight from representative government and government by discussion, the Charter represents a further flight in the same direction.

Populism and the Court Party differ in obvious ways.[18] Indeed, in contemporary Canadian politics, they inhabit opposite ends of the political spectrum, with right-wing populists launching some of the most vociferous attacks on judicial power, while the left-leaning Court Party fulminates about the tyranny of the majority entailed by populism. As important as the opposition between populists and Court Party interests, however, is their common challenge to representative democracy. When populists do not like what representatives have done, they generally do not wish to wait until a general election to "throw the rascals out"; they want to be able to recall them *now*. Similarly, if Court Party interests do not like legislative policies, they increasingly want courts, not elections, to reverse those policies. By the same token, populists advocate the use of initiatives and referenda to force their agenda on reluctant legislatures, just as rights advocates ask the courts to force their agenda on the legislature through such devices of positive activism as reading in. In our view, the pincer movement of populism and the Court Party against representative democracy is a problematic development. An analysis of the pros and cons posed by populism is beyond the scope of this book;[19] the rights-based challenge, we contend, is dangerous because it simultaneously leads to a moral inflation of policy claims and substitutes the coercion of court orders for the persuasion of parliamentary (and public) debate.

Because the other rights-protecting features of Canadian constitutionalism are in reasonably good repair (though we concede that they are far from perfect) policies challenged under the Charter cannot be honestly described as tyrannical deprivations of rights. As Russell observed in 1969, it is simply not plausible to claim that constitutionally entrenched rights prevent real tyranny and oppression by democratic majorities. "Do you feel menaced," he asked, "by the prospect of the great Canadian majority, acting through its elected representatives in Ottawa, steam-rolling over your basic rights and liberties in pursuit of its own interests? Are you comforted by [entrenched rights that enable] our judiciary to veto these strident majoritarian demands and secure your liberty? If you ask yourself these questions and can honestly answer them in the affirmative, what you surely need is a psychiatrist not a bill of rights."[20]

On a sane view of our legislative process, the pros and cons of the kinds of policies that actually issue from that process, and that come to be challenged under the Charter, are almost always matters of reasonable disagreement, as shown by the fact that they generally arouse disagreement even among judges. As we noted in chapter 2, if the core meaning of rights were to be violated by government policy, judicial review would almost never be effective. Concerted government attack on the core meaning of a fundamental right is the very definition of tyranny, and courts are normally too weak to oppose either the tyranny of the majority or the tyranny of a single despot.[21] The real effect of the Court Party project is thus not to protect rights in any fundamental sense, but to encourage rights claiming, a partisan exercise whose objective is not to protect the fundamental core of existing rights but to change public policy through the judicial creation of new rights. Rights claiming is driven by the need to infuse a policy claim with higher, indeed ultimate, moral status.

A generation ago Canadians understood the distinction between truly fundamental rights and rights claiming. Speaking against Pierre Trudeau's Charter project, Donald Smiley warned that, "When we are engaged in analysis rather than rhetoric we should perhaps do better to use the expression 'preferred human claims' ... rather than 'human right.'"[22] Even the late Chief Justice Bora Laskin, celebrated for his early defense of civil liberties, saw the difference: "Claims of interests which are labeled 'civil liberties' differ from other claims or interests that are the product of our society in the weight that is attached to them. Indeed, association of the label with a particular demand is a recognized technique for focusing attention upon it and for surrounding it with substance and respectability."[23]

More substance and respectability, one must add, than the demand would otherwise have had. Indeed, substance and respectability are terms much too tame to describe the weight that is added to a political demand by translating it into rights talk. Mary Ann Glendon has most clearly set out the ways in which rights talk acts as an uncompromising language of trumps that does not brook reasonable disagreement.[24] Rights claiming, in other words, inflates issues well beyond their true significance.

The inflationary character of rights claiming is well illustrated in a case reported a couple of years ago on the CBC's national news. A woman in Toronto had, for environmental reasons, replaced her lawn with a garden of weeds — a project likely to arouse the sympathy of anyone who, like us, hates the weekend chore of mowing lawns. Apparently the local by-law officers displayed no such sympathy. Instead of obeying the law, however, the woman went to court, arguing that the by-law infringed her freedom of expression — and she won! No doubt a higher court was more sensible, but that is beside the present point, which is that the Charter allowed an environmental activist to claim a fundamental right to grow weeds, a right that would trump the majority's desire for manicured lawns and its fear that unkempt weed gardens lower neighbouring property values. Perhaps the majority is misguided in these concerns, but to claim that its will is trumped by a right to grow weeds is an inflated policy claim if ever there was one.

Most claims brought under the Charter are not as trivial as this, but we would contend that, however important and controversial the issues raised by Charter jurisprudence might be, they almost always turn out to be matters of reasonable disagreement that are unnecessarily inflated through courtroom rights talk. Courtroom rights talk, in other words, is encouraging in Canadians the same bad political instinct that Alexander Bickel criticized the US Supreme Court for fostering in American society in the 1960s: moral oversensitivity. For a democracy, being morally oversensitive is as dangerous as being morally undersensitive. It unduly lowers the threshold at which citizens feel justified in abandoning the democratic process, be it through civil disobedience, appeal to the courts, or (in the extreme case) revolt and secession. Canada would do well to heed Bickel's plea that the "morality of rights" be balanced with the "morality of consent."[25]

We do not wish to be misunderstood. We are not suggesting that inflation of political rhetoric would disappear in the absence of a Charter of Rights and Freedoms. To the contrary, like James Madison, we believe that the tendency to rhetorical inflation is endemic to political life. Political zealotry, Madison argued, is rooted in human nature. People will fight, he suggested, not only because their interests differ, but because they love their own opinions and wish to see them prevail, so much so that "where no substantial occasion presents itself the most frivolous and fanciful distinctions have been sufficient to … excite [the] most violent conflicts."[26] In other words, the temptation to inflate objectively minor disagreements into major conflicts is simply part of the human condition. The constitutional task is not to eradicate this tendency, but to find institutional ways of checking and moderating it, so that political opponents come to see each other as fellow citizens, members of a single people prepared to let the majority set and conclude the rest. Courtroom rights talk, we believe, undermines this goal by amplifying rather than moderating the inflationary tendency.

The institutional transfer of power to the courts compounds the moral inflation of rights claiming. As a logical corollary of translating reasonable disagreements into uncompromising rights talk, in other words, the responsibility for concluding these agreements moves from legislatures to courts. Because opposition to the rights claim is presented as beyond the pale, it cannot be left to the decision of representative institutions, where opposition to virtually any policy able to make it onto the agenda is a fact of life. In other words, the policy issue cannot be left to be concluded by legislative majorities because the wrong side may form the majority.

Shifting power from the legislative to the judicial arena, in short, is a way of substituting coercion for government by discussion. To be sure, we should not exaggerate the distinction between the two institutional contexts. On the one hand, much debate takes place in the courtroom. On the other, no one should romanticize the nature of parliamentary (and public) debate. We all know that there is as much posturing and inflation of claims in legislative politics as there is in the courtroom. The symbolism of having legislative partisans separated by two swords' lengths underscores the intensity and uncompromising intransigence of much of their debate. Still, important differences between legislative and judicial debate must be kept in view.

For all its sound and fury, for all its raucous and uncompromising posturing, everything about legislative debate implies the *sine qua non* of a sovereign people: the willingness to abide by the rule of majorities with which one disagrees. Thus the rules of legislative debate require its participants to use civil and decorous language even as they insult their opponents. Insults are hurled not at that "SOB" over there, but at "the honourable member" opposite. Indeed, it is not even permitted to address a member directly or by name. Debate must not be personalized and *ad hominem*, so representatives address the Speaker and use the name of other members' constituencies or offices.

Such rules are suggested by the very nature of political debate among a sovereign people. As Walter Berns has said, democratic debate

> implies on the part of those participating in it a capacity and willingness to be persuaded, persuaded by another with an equal right to form the majority or to be part of it, with an equally legitimate interest, and, perhaps, with a superior argument. And it implies, and even encourages, the willingness to abide by the vote of the majority assembled. The importance of this cannot be exaggerated. Those who participate in this process are not permitted to overlook, because the rules require them to recognize, the right of every representative to be part of the majority, or to overlook the fact that the purpose of forming a majority is to govern.[27]

Judicialized politics, especially when it concerns constitutionally entrenched rights, carries a quite different set of implications. It has a much more closed and intolerant character. True, rules of decorum also govern in the court. Nevertheless, the point of the formalized courtroom combat about constitutional rights is to determine which side holds uncompromisable trumps. Courts do not always issue the trumps requested by rights claimants, of course. Sometimes, as in the *Morgentaler* case, for example, courts are more moderate than the litigants. Thus, the majority of Supreme Court justices struck down Canada's abortion law in *Morgentaler* not by explicitly siding with the pro-choice position but by emphasizing the procedural defects of the law. But this qualification is somewhat beside the point: the judicial arena encouraged extremists to claim constitutional trumps rather than to engage in government by discussion.

Moreover, the subtlety of the judicial reasons for invalidating the abortion law were lost on the media and the public, allowing the pro-choice side to claim that the constitution was more unambiguously on their side than it actually was. This was the predictable consequence both of the media's reliance for commentary on authorized knowers who were actually Court Party partisans, and the electronic media's natural attraction for black-and-white oppositions. As David Taras notes, in television news "the pro-con model is so rigidly adhered to ... that items are routinely dropped if spokespersons for opposing positions cannot be found."[28] The adversarial character of Charter litigation assures that this is never a problem. More importantly, the simplistic, pro-con format often legitimates or at least publicizes the misleading and often extreme assertions of authorized knowers, who in Charter cases are typically Court Party partisans from the law schools. Television viewers are presented with assertion and counter-assertion, usually with little contextual help to determine the truthfulness of either. This was certainly true of the *Morgentaler* case. The evening news on decision-day, 28 January 1988, was on the same level as locker-room interviews with the winning and losing teams after the Stanley Cup final. No substance, no information, just conflict – the thrill of victory, the agony of defeat.

In other words, even when judicial opinions are not clear-cut, the natural inclinations of the electronic media help winners in courtroom battles present themselves as having absolute right – or "rights" – on their side; the logical corollary, of course – and it is a corollary that winners typically go out of their way to emphasize – is that the losers are not only wrong but legally illegitimate. The losers, in other words, are beyond the pale; theirs is not an eligible policy position, and, if they form the majority, it is not a majority that can be allowed to set and conclude the rest.

A sovereign people's willingness to be concluded by the majority is implied by legislative politics and undermined by judicialized politics in yet another way. The assumption of legislative politics is that there are no permanent winners and losers. A majority that sets and concludes an issue is nevertheless not "conclusive" in its victory. As Janet Ajzenstat has written, the "boast" of liberal democracy

is that it does nothing to limit complaint and debate and nothing to prevent opposition groups and parties from organizing to plot the overthrow of particular laws and policies. As decrees of the executive branch, laws must be obeyed, but as measures emanating from the legislature, they may be endlessly contested. The fact of debate and popular participation does not undermine the requirement to obey;

and the fact that obedience is required enables continuing debate. No political loss is entirely without remedy. If interests remain unaggregated and the players retain their energy, the game can be virtually endless. Those who fall rise to fight again.[29]

This "boast" is logically entailed in liberal democracy's attempt to replace natural majorities with shifting coalitions of minorities. And it is essential to the agreement that forms a sovereign people – the agreement to abide by the will of the majority – that neither majorities nor minorities be permanent, that today's majority can become tomorrow's minority, and vice versa.

No such boast of policy flux issues from the realm of judicialized politics. To the contrary, victory in a courtroom rights battle carries the implication of permanence. The victor's policy is constitutionally entrenched, and the whole point of entrenchment is to guarantee a degree of permanence not possible in legislative politics. Certainly pro-choicers view *Morgentaler* in this light. Having exaggerated that decision's pro-choice implications, they then decry all proposals to re-regulate abortion as patently unconstitutional.[30]

But perhaps *Morgentaler* is the exception. Peter Hogg and Allison Thornton point to other cases in which legislatures, engaging in a more productive, moderating "dialogue" with courts, have enacted more moderate versions of invalidated legislation. When the Court struck down Quebec's signs law, for example, the province initially used the Charter's legislative override to resurrect it. Five years later, however, Quebec allowed the override to lapse and amended the law along the lines indicated by the Court; namely, allowing the reasonable use of other languages while still giving French preferential status. Here, surely, we have an example of how courts can moderate an emotional policy controversy.[31]

Or have we? Hogg and Thornton neglect the broader political context of this case. A significant segment of Quebec opinion, including francophone opinion, had reservations about the law in the period preceding the litigation. Indeed, the Bourassa government had gone so far as to promise during the 1985 election to relax the law. This proved to be a highly controversial promise, and thus one not easy to keep. Nevertheless, there was an ongoing debate about the matter in Quebec and no reason to suppose that the moderates could never carry the day.[32]

Unfortunately, opponents of the law were unwilling to continue the process of government by discussion and endure the rule of existing majorities in the meantime. The Charter encouraged them to think and act as if the existing policy was not only misguided, but wholly illegitimate and thus beyond the pale of ordinary democratic politics. They went to court, and by doing so they distorted and derailed the political debate among Quebeckers about signs policy. The debate was well and truly derailed when the Supreme Court of Canada ruled in 1988 that the law violated the "fundamental right" of freedom of expression and could not be "demonstrably justified" as a "reasonable limit" on that right.[33] This ruling entailed a serious and regrettable inflation of the issue. However misguided one considers the law to be – we certainly consider it a foolish and unnecessary law – it is going considerably over the top to characterize it as a tyrannical suppression of fundamental rights. Are people's lives put in danger when octagonal red signs at intersections say only *"Arrêt"*? Is it anything more than a minor inconvenience or irritation for an anglophone Montrealer to see well-known English establishments sporting French-only signs? Are we really to believe that anglophone visitors from elsewhere cannot recognize restaurants and department stores or find ones that will serve them in English? "Get real," one is inclined to say!

What is even more important, the Supreme Court ruling sent the following implicit message to members of the Quebec community. "The issue you have been debating is not one you are entitled to debate, and thus decide, for yourselves. In important respects, the issue has already been decided by the Charter. Those of you who have thus far been winning the political debate have done so illegitimately. Your opponents have been right all along." Paradoxically, this put Québécois opponents of the signs law in a difficult position. They had to choose between their opposition to the law and the right of the Quebec community to govern itself in this matter. Not surprisingly, the Bourassa government chose self-government, a choice it could make effective only by re-enacting the law with a notwithstanding clause. The ironic result was that a government that was on record as wanting to relax the law was put in the position of reinvigorating it.

By uniting the Québécois behind the signs law, moreover, the Supreme Court's ruling intensified tensions between Quebec and the ROC. As Russell aptly put it, the reaction in English Canada "was severe and ... tribal."[34] Coming at a crucial point in the debate about the Meech Lake Accord, the ruling helped undermine its ratification. English Canadians were not about to agree to the status of distinct society for a province that would trample the fundamental rights of fellow anglophones. We were not supporters of the Meech Lake Accord, but neither do we wish to celebrate the inflated rights rhetoric that helped defeat it. If the failure of Meech is the event of recent mega-constitutional politics that has most severely undermined the capacity of citizens of Quebec and the ROC to become a single, sovereign people, Charter litigation contributed significantly to this result.[35]

Hogg and Thornton's theory that judicial review constitutes dialogue rather than coercion – that it contributes to government by discussion rather than undermining it – is flawed by more than the use of an inapposite example. Their dialogue theory holds that a government unhappy with the judicial nullification of one of its policies has the means to reverse it either by enacting revised legislation or, more emphatically, by re-instating the old law through the use of the section 33 notwithstanding clause. "If the democratic will is there, the legislative objective will still be able to be accomplished," they declare.[36] If a government fails to use the tools at its disposal, that's the government's fault, not the court's.

While undoubtedly true in the abstract, this view is far too simplistic. It fails to recognize the staying power of a new, judicially created policy status quo (PSQ), especially when the issue cuts across the normal lines of partisan cleavage and divides a government caucus.[37] Again, *Morgentaler* provides a cogent example. Contrary to Chief Justice Lamer's beliefs, in 1988 the majority of Canadians were not opposed to the abortion policy that he voted to strike down. Under that policy, abortion was deemed wrong in theory but available in practice. (Dr. Morgentaler and his lawyers could not produce a single witness who had actually been prevented from getting an abortion.) This compromise accurately reflected Canadians' conflicting opinions on the abortion issue. In 1988, 24 per cent said that abortion should be legal under any circumstances, 14 per cent illegal under any circumstances, and 60 per cent legal under certain circumstances.[38]

A recently published study of abortion politics in Canada and the US found that from the late 1960s through the early 1990s "the contours of public opinion towards abortion have been generally unchanged. What exists is a situation where two intense minorities have polarized views of abortion policy that do not represent the feelings of a majority of Americans or Canadians. In both countries, the majority stands to the right of the strongest pro-choice position but left of the absolutist pro-life position."[39]

This pattern of support was replicated in House of Commons voting on the Mulroney government's efforts to enact a new abortion policy after the 1988 *Morgentaler* ruling. The new policy was designed to meet the procedural problems identified in the written judgment of Justices Dickson and Lamer. (The government mistakenly believed that these were the real reasons for Justice Lamer's vote.) It left abortion in the Criminal Code, but would have significantly widened access. In its final form, the policy would have abolished the requirement of committee approval, broadened the definition of health to include mental and psychological health, and lifted the "hospitals only" restriction.[40]

The government's compromise approach was opposed by both pro-choice and pro-life factions within Parliament, albeit for opposite reasons. Two pro-choice resolutions, which basically affirmed the new judicially-created PSQ of "no abortion law," were easily defeated in the House by votes of 191-29 and 198-20. A strong pro-life resolution, which would have created a more restrictive policy than the one struck down by the Court, received much more support but was narrowly defeated by a vote of 118-105. A paradoxical coalition of pro-choice and pro-life MPs then combined to defeat the government's own compromise proposal by a vote of 147-76.

In the following session, the government re-introduced a new compromise abortion policy, Bill C-43. To avoid a repeat of the earlier disaster, Mulroney invoked party discipline for his 40 cabinet ministers and warned pro-life MPs that this would be his last attempt. The House then approved the bill by a vote of 140-131. However, it was subsequently defeated by a tie vote (43-43) in the Senate. As in the House of Commons the year before, the pro-choice and pro-life minorities combined to vote against the policy compromise, but in the Senate there were no cabinet ministers to save it. The new judicially-created PSQ of no law thus continued by default, not because it commanded majority support in either Parliament or the public.[41]

The defeat of Bill C-43 illustrates a common dynamic between public opinion and Supreme Court decisions on contemporary rights issues. Contrary to the rhetoric of majority rule and minority rights, on most contemporary rights issues there is an unstable and unorganized majority or plurality opinion, bracketed by two opposing activist minorities. In terms of political process, Mary Ann Glendon's comparative study of abortion law in 20 Western democracies demonstrates that the legislative process usually plays to the moderating coalition of minorities necessary to create a legislative majority, while judicial politics plays to the minorities at the extremes of the policy continuum.[42] Thus, when the Supreme Court rules that a policy is unconstitutional, it typically displaces a compromise policy based on majority (or plurality) opinion with a new policy tailored to the demands of one of the two extremes.

In addition to transferring power from a majority coalition to a minority, a judicial ruling can also shift the considerable advantages of the policy status quo from one group of minority activists to the other. Depending on which of the two minority interests the Court sides with (e.g., pro-choice or pro-life), its ruling shifts the burden of mobilizing a new majority coalition (within voters, within a government caucus, and within a legislature) from the winning to the losing minority.

This transfer is a significant new advantage for the winning minority. Just as it was impossible for pro-choice activists to persuade either the Trudeau or Mulroney governments to amend parliament's compromise abortion law of 1969 prior to the Court's *Morgentaler* decision, so it has been equally impossible for pro-life activists to interest the Chrétien government in amending the new judicially-created PSQ of no abortion law. The reasons are the same: the issue is not a priority for the government, the opposition parties, or the majority of voters.

Indeed, the priority for most governments on such moral issues is to avoid them as much as possible. If the PSQ is minimally acceptable to the government, there is a strong incentive to leave it alone. Such issues cross-cut normal partisan cleavages and thus fracture party solidarity, from the cabinet to the caucus to the rank and file membership. Nor do they win any new supporters among the (indifferent) majority. To act risks losing support from the activist policy minority you abandon, without securing the support of the activists you help. (After all, the latter think you only did what was just.) In circumstances such as these, political self-interest favours government inaction over action.

A similar pattern occurred in Alberta after the Supreme Court's *Vriend* ruling in April 1998. The Klein Government and the Conservative Party of Alberta were deeply divided on whether to add sexual orientation to the Alberta Human Rights Act.[43] Two previous task forces had recommended against it, but with minority reports. Gay rights groups had lobbied aggressively for the reform. Social conservatives – a force to be reckoned with in Alberta politics – were just as strongly opposed. For the majority of Albertans, it was an issue of secondary importance.[44]

When the Supreme Court read in sexual orientation to the Alberta Human Rights Act, there was a strong public outcry, especially among the rural wing of the Alberta Tories, to invoke section 33. After a week of public debate, the cabinet was as divided as before. In the end, Premier Klein declared that his personal preference was not to invoke section 33, and a majority of the caucus fell into line.[45]

Describing the Alberta government's decision to live with the *Vriend* ruling, Hogg writes: "But because using the notwithstanding clause to override the decision had been an option, it is clear that this outcome was not forced on the government, but rather was its own choice."[46] Hogg is only half right in this assertion. He ignores the fact that the Court's ruling decisively changed the government's options. The government's preferred choice was not to act at all – to simply leave the old PSQ in place. The Court removed this option and, with the clever use of the reading in technique, created a new PSQ that extended the protection of the province's anti-discrimination act to gays.

Prior to the ruling, the Klein government could safely ignore this issue, upsetting only a small coalition of activists, few of whom were Tory supporters in any case. After it, the government had to choose between accepting the new, judicially created PSQ or invoking the notwithstanding clause, a decision that it knew would be strongly criticized in the national media and that risked creating a backlash among otherwise passive government supporters. The judicial ruling significantly raised the political costs of saying "no" to the winning minority. Before the judgment, saying no meant not giving something new; after, saying no (i.e., invoking section 33) meant taking away a constitutional right. For the same reason that the Klein government had refused to alter the old PSQ, it now accepted the new judicially created PSQ. In both instances, the safest thing was to do nothing.

Hogg and Thornton write that judicial nullification of a statute "rarely raises an absolute barrier to the wishes of democratic institutions."[47] The observation is right, but the conclusion they draw from it is wrong. It does not have to be an absolute barrier. Depending on the circumstances, a small barrier may suffice to sustain a long-term change in public policy.

In short, Hogg and Thornton's theory must be qualified to account for different circumstances. A government's ability to respond to judicial nullification of a policy depends on a variety of factors. When the policy is central to the government's program, the government should have little difficulty mustering the political will to respond effectively. Examples of this pattern of dialogue would include the Quebec government's use of notwithstanding in response to the *Quebec Public Signs Case* decision and Saskatchewan's preemptive use of section 33 to protect back-to-work legislation.

By contrast, when the issue cuts across partisan allegiances and divides the government caucus and when public opinion is fragmented between a relatively indifferent middle bracketed by two opposing groups of policy activists, the judicial creation of a new rights-based policy status quo may suffice to tip the balance in favour of the winning minority interest over that of their adversaries. Both *Morgentaler* and *Vriend* illustrate this pattern of non-response.

What Hogg and Thornton describe as a dialogue is usually a monologue, with judges doing most of the talking and legislatures most of the listening. According to the dialogue theory, the failure of a government to respond effectively to judicial activism is a matter of personal courage, or the lack thereof, on the part of government leaders. The fault, if there is any, rests with individuals. By contrast, we are suggesting that legislative paralysis is institutional in character: that legislative non-response in the face of judicial activism is the normal response in certain circumstances. When the issue in play cross-cuts and divides a government caucus, the political incentive structure invites government leaders to abdicate responsibility to the courts, perhaps even more so in a parliamentary than in a presidential system.[48]

Hogg and Thornton are not entirely mistaken, of course. Although dialogue is not the best way to characterize the process, it remains true that constitutional victories are not necessarily as permanent as their supporters want to make them appear. Although section 33 has become extremely difficult to use outside Quebec, its future revival cannot be entirely discounted. More to the point, we know that judicial rulings can and do change over time – sometimes a very long time – because of court bashing, court packing, or simply the generational changing of the judicial guard. Even if constitutional trumps are not as permanent as they appear, however, those who seek them want, and are encouraged to claim, such permanence. Even if constitutional victories cannot be made to stick in perpetuity, political partisans are nevertheless urged to speak and act as if they could, instead of being forced to live with the sobering thought that their policy preferences reflect no more than the will of a transient majority.

To transfer the resolution of reasonable disagreements from legislatures to courts inflates rhetoric to unwarranted levels and replaces negotiated, majoritarian compromise policies with the intensely held policy preferences of minorities. Rights-based judicial policymaking also grants the policy preferences of courtroom victors an aura of coercive force and permanence that they do not deserve. Issues that should be subject to the ongoing flux of government by discussion are presented as beyond legitimate debate, with the partisans claiming the right to permanent victory. As the morality of rights displaces the morality of consent, the politics of coercion replaces the politics of persuasion. The result is to embitter politics and decrease the inclination of political opponents to treat each other as fellow citizens – that is, as members of a sovereign people.

NOTES

Notes to Chapter One

1 Antonio Lamer, address, Canadian Bar Association, St. John's, Nfld., 23 August 1998.

2 Mary Dawson, "Oral Remarks," Round-table Conference on The Impact of the Charter on the Public Policy Process, Centre for Public Law and Public Policy, Toronto, 15-16 Nov. 1991 [unpublished].

3 See Peter H. Russell, "Canadian Constraints on Judicialization from Without," *International Political Science Review* 15:2 (1994): 165-75. Also see Martin Shapiro, "Juridicalization of Politics in the United States," *International Political Science Review* 15:2 (1994): 101-12.

4 Julie Jai, "Oral remarks," Round-table Conference [unpublished].

5 *The Queen v. Drybones*, [1970] S.C.R. 282.

6 Data provided by James Kelly, "Charter Activism and Canadian Federalism: Rebalancing Liberal Constitutionalism in Canada, 1982 to 1997," Ph.D. thesis, McGill University, 1998; and Patrick J. Monahan, "Constitutional Cases, 1991-1998," Professional Development Programme, 1998 Constitutional Cases: An Analysis of the 1998 Constitutional Decisions of the Supreme Court of Canada, Toronto, 16 April 1999. Our figures combine Kelly's data for 1982-97 with Monahan's data for 1998.

7 "Landmark gay ruling could affect 1,000 laws," *National Post*, 21 May 1999: A1.

8 Right-to-counsel warning: *Brownridge v. The Queen*, [1972] S.C.R. 926; exclusionary rule: *Hogan v. The Queen*, [1975] 2 S.C.R. 574; violation of rights of accused: *R. v. Collins*, [1987] 1 S.C.R. 265; questioning of suspects in absence of counsel: *R. v. Manninen*, [1987] 1 S.C.R. 1233; self-incrimination: *R. v. Hebert*, [1990] 2 S.C.R. 151; R. Harvie and Hamar Foster, "Ties that Bind? The Supreme Court of Canada, American Jurisprudence, and the Revision of Canadian Criminal Law under the Charter," *Osgoode Hall Law Journal* 28 (1990): 729; R. Harvie and Hamar Foster, "Different Drummers, Different Drums: The Supreme Court of Canada, American Jurisprudence, and the Continuing Revision of Criminal Law under the Charter," *Ottawa Law Review* 24 (1992): 39.

9 *Morgentaler v. The Queen*, [1988] 1 S.C.R. 30. Legal claims on behalf of the unborn include *Borowski v. Canada*, [1989] 1 S.C.R. 342; *Tremblay v. Daigle*, [1989] 2 S.C.R. 530; *R. v. Sullivan*, [1991] 1 S.C.R. 489. Restrictions on access to abortion services include *Moore v. British Columbia*, 50 D.L.R. (4th), 29.; *Ref. Re Freedom of Informed Choice (Abortions) Act*, 44 Saskatchewan Reports 104 (1985); *R. v. Morgentaler*, [1993] 3 S.C.R. 463; and the overruling of welfare agencies' efforts to protect the unborn occurred in *Winnipeg Child Services v. D.F.G.*, 138 D.L.R. (4th) 254 (Manitoba C.A., 1996).

10 Equality of the law for Native women: *Attorney-General of Canada v. Lavell and Bedard*, [1974]

S.C.R. 1349; "disparate impact": *Andrews v. Law Society of British Columbia*, [1989] 1 S.C.R. 143. While the US Supreme Court has read the Civil Rights Act as prohibiting systemic discrimination, it has not read the equal protection clause of the 14th Amendment to the Constitution as prohibiting such discrimination. See Rainer Knopff (with Thomas Flanagan), *Human Rights and Social Technology: The New War on Discrimination* (Ottawa: Carleton University Press, 1989) 58. Pay equity was considered in *Service Employees International Union, Local 204 v. Ontario (Attorney General)*, [1997] O.J. No. 3563.

11 In *Eldridge v. British Columbia (Attorney General)*, [1997] 3 S.C.R. 493., the Supreme Court ruled that a British Columbia hospital's decision not to provide sign-language interpreters for deaf patients violated the equality rights of the latter and ordered the hospital to provide such interpreters in the future. Minority language school rights were considered in *Mahé v. Alberta*, [1990] 1 S.C.R. 342; Judges salaries were addressed in *Reference Re Remuneration of Judges of the Provincial Court of PEI; Reference re: Independence and Impartiality of Judges of the Provincial Court of PEI*, [1997] 3 S.C.R. 3. Social benefit programs were widened by the judgements in *Schachter v. Canada*, (1992) 93 D.L.R. (4th) 1; *Haig and Birch v. Canada*, [1992] 57 O.A.C. 272; *Vriend v. Alberta*, [1998] 1 S.C.R. 493

12 Peter Russell, Rainer Knopff, and Ted Morton, *Federalism and the Charter: Leading Constitutional Decisions, A New Edition* (Ottawa: Carleton University Press, 1989) 19.

13 Nadine Strossen, *Defending Pornography: Free Speech, Sex, and the Fight for Women's Rights* (Toronto: Scribner, 1995) 229.

14 *Egan and Nesbitt v. Canada*, [1995] 2 S.C.R. 513.

15 As quoted by J. Sallot,"How the charter changes Justice," *The Globe and Mail* 17 April 1992: A11.

16 Interview with Stephen Bindman, "Thank God for the charter," *Ottawa Citizen*, 17 April 1997: A1.

17 Patrick Monahan, "Oral Remarks," Round-table Conference [unpublished]; Peter Hogg, "Oral Remarks" Round-table Conference [unpublished]; Jeffrey Simpson, "Remarks on the Impact of the Charter," Round-table Conference [unpublished].

18 Rory Leishman,"Robed dictators: a coup from the courtroom has usurped our democracy," *Next City* (Fall 1998): 34-41; "Benevolent Monarch: How the Charter has helped Antonio Lamer turn his dubious ideals into the Law of the land," *Alberta Report*, 21 Sept. 1998: 20-23. Also see Alex MacDonald, *Outrage: Canada's Justice System on Trial* (Vancouver: Raincoast Books, 1999).

19 Steve Chase,"Expert urges use of notwithstanding clause," *Calgary Herald*, 2 April 1998: A2; Steve Chase, "Notwithstanding clause: Klein ponders overruling courts on gay rights," *Calgary Herald*, 7 April 1998: A1; Brian Laghi, "Alberta's gay rights fight turns ugly: Tory caucus under pressure to override Supreme Court of Canada ruling," *The Globe and Mail*, 9 April 1998: A1; Peter Menzies, "Legislatures write laws; Let's keep it that way," *Calgary Herald*, 8 April 1998: A14; Christopher P. Manfredi, "Court's declaration of indepen-

dence should be tested," *Calgary Herald*, 28 April 1998: A17; Luiza Chwialkowska, "High court reopens battle between judges, politicians," *National Post*, 21 May 1999: A2; editorial, "Yellow-bellied politics," *National Post*, 21 May 1999: A19; Sheldon Alberts, "McLellan rejects calls to overturn child-porn ruling," *National Post*, 2 Feb. 1999: A1; Sheldon Alberts, "4 maverick MPs ignore Liberal line over porn motion," *National Post*, 3 Feb. 1999: A7; editorial, "Making Canada safe for child porn (again)," *National Post*, 2 July 1999: A19.

20 Robert Fife, "Ex-premiers call for use of Charter's 'safety-valve,'" *National Post*, 1 March 1999: A1.

21 Darcy Henton, "Province slams door on gay marriages," *Calgary Herald*, 19 March 1999: A1; Jill Mahoney, "Alberta government decides to say no to same sex marriages," *The Globe and Mail*, 19 March 1999: A4.

22 Jonathan Jenkins, "Alberta wants Supreme committee: Courting Justice," *Calgary Sun*, 28 March 1999: 13; Preston Manning, "Parliament, not judges, must make the laws of the land," *The Globe and Mail*, 16 June 1998: A23; Peter H. Russell, "Reform's Judicial Agenda," *Policy Options* (April 1999): 12-15; editorial,"A short reading from the book of Ruth," *The Globe and Mail*, 29 July 1993: A20; editorial,"A Supreme Court for a new age," *The Globe and Mail*, 28 Aug. 1997: A16; Anthony Keller, "Wanted: a public word with the would-be judges," *The Globe and Mail*, 1 Dec. 1997; William Thorsell, "What to look for, and guard against, in a Supreme Court judge," *The Globe and Mail*, 20 Dec. 1997: D6; editorial,"Judging the judges," *National Post*, 10 May 1999: A15; Andrew Coyne, "Appointment process undermines Supreme Court," *Calgary Herald*, 16 June 1998: A18; F.L. Morton, "Charter changed justices role: Their selection needs review," *The Financial Post*, 20 Feb. 1989: 16; F.L. Morton, "To bring judicial appointments out of the closet," *The Globe and Mail*, 22 Sept. 1997: A19; Jacob Ziegel, "Merit Selection and Democratization of Appointments to the Supreme Court of Canada," *Choices* 5:2 (1999); "La Forest favours US-style public review for Supreme Court Judges," *The Globe and Mail*, 3 Sept. 1997: A7; Cristin Schmitz, "A Supreme Challenge Met," *Lawyers Weekly*, 26 Sept. 1997: 1.

23 Joseph Fletcher and Paul Howe, "Canadian Attitudes Toward the Charter," Annual Meeting of the Canadian Political Science Association, Université de Sherbrooke, 8 June 1999: 4, 9.

24 Fletcher and Howe 16, 23.

25 Ian Greene, Carl Baar, Peter McCormick, George Szablowski, and Martin Thomas, *Final Appeal: Decision-Making in Canadian Courts of Appeal* (Halifax: James Lorimer and Co., 1998) 188.

26 Lamer, address, CBA.

27 See, for example, the Supreme Court's reply to critics in *Vriend v. Alberta*, [1998] 1 S.C.R. 493; 563-564.

28 Lorraine Weinrib, "The Activist Constitution," *Policy Options* (April 1999): 28.

29 Christin Schmitz, "McLachlin traces court 'activism' to lawmakers' 'inactivism,'" *The*

Lawyers Weekly, 30 April 1999: 3; Janice Tibbetts, "Politicians duck divisive issues, chief justice says," *National Post*, 12 July 1999: A1; "Holding Court," *National Post*, 14 July 1999: A14.

30 Janice Tibbetts, "Top court judges shy away from rewriting laws: study," *National Post*, 9 April 1999: A4.

31 Mary Eberts, "From Undue Deference to Principled Dialogue: Vriend Restores a Constitutional Perspective on Judicial Role in Charter Cases," Professional Development Programme.

32 Kelly 96, Table 6. Our figures combine Kelly's data for 1982-97 with Monahan's data for 1998.

33 Avril Allen and F.L. Morton, "Feminists in the Courts: Measuring Interest Group Success," *Canadian Journal of Political Science* (forthcoming).

Aboriginal rights cases have the highest success rate – 46 per cent – of all Charter litigation; Kelly 89, Table 5. Also see Hamar Foster, "Canadian Indians, Time and the Law: What Happened North of 49," Interim Meeting, Research Committee on Comparative Judicial Studies, Santa Fe, New Mexico, 1-4 August 1993; Peter H. Russell, "The Catalytic Role of Courts in Aboriginal Constitutional Politics: Canada in Comparative Perspective," IPSA Research Committee on Comparative Judicial Studies, Université de Sherbrooke, 21 August 1995.

Language and education rights cases have the second highest success rate – 41 per cent – in all Charter litigation; Kelly 89, Table 5. Also, see pages 4-6 in Kelly ch. 3, and Didi Herman, "The Good, the Bad and the Smugly: Sexual Orientation and Perspectives on the Charter," *Charting the Consequences: The Impact of the Charter of Rights on Canadian Law and Politics*, ed. David Schneiderman and Kate Sutherland (Toronto: University of Toronto Press, 1997); Jonathon Gatehouse, "Landmark gay ruling could affect 1,000 laws," *National Post*, 21 May 1999: A1.

34 Peter H. Russell, "The Supreme Court and Federal-Provincial Relations: The Political Use of Legal Resources," *Canadian Public Policy* 11 (1985): 161, 164. Such uncertainty has been increased by the Supreme Court's habit of qualifying its rulings with declarations that each case must be considered on its unique merits and facts. The Court's over reliance on section 1 in cases involving statutes also creates uncertainty, since each application of the *Oakes* test is case unique.

35 Deaf patients: *Eldridge v. British Columbia (Attorney General)*, [1997] 3 S.C.R. 493; spousal benefits: *M. v. H.*, [1999] 2 S.C.R. 3; topless women: *R. v. Jacob*, (1996) 31 O.R. (3d) 350; euthanasia: *Rodriguez v. British Columbia (Attorney General)*, [1993] 3 S.C.R. 519., *R. v. Latimer*, [1997] 1 S.C.R. 217; child pornography: *R. v. Sharpe*, [1999] B.C.C.A. 416.

36 Eugene Forsey, The Martland Lecture, University of Calgary, 1983.

37 R.I. Cheffins, "The Supreme Court of Canada: The Quiet Court in the Unquiet Country," *Osgoode Hall Law Journal* 4 (1966): 259-360; Kenneth McNaught, "Political Trials and the Canadian Political Tradition," *Courts and Trials: A Multidisciplinary Approach* ed. M.L. Fried-

land (Toronto: University of Toronto Press, 1975) 137; *Morgentaler v. The Queen* (1975) 20 C.C.C. (2d) 452, 461; Wayne MacKay, "Fairness after the Charter: A Rose by Any Other Name," *Queen's Law Journal* 10 (1985): 263.

38 J.R. Mallory, The Timlin Lecture. University of Saskatchewan, 1984: 8.

39 Berend Hovius and Robert Martin, "The Canadian Charter of Rights and Freedoms in the Supreme Court of Canada," *The Canadian Bar Review* 61: 1 (March 1983): 354.

40 *The Queen v. Therens*, [1985] 1 S.C.R. 613.

41 Bindman, "Thank God for the charter." See also Justice Lamer in *Reference re British Columbia Motor Vehicle Act*, [1985] 2 S.C.R. 486 (497): "[T]he historic decision to entrench the Charter in our Constitution was taken not by the courts but by the elected representatives of the people of Canada. It was those representatives who extended the scope of constitutional adjudication and entrusted the courts with this new and onerous responsibility."

42 This argument is the central thesis of Samuel Bottomley, "Implied Constitutional Rights," M.A. thesis, University of Calgary, 1997. All our examples are developed in Bottomley's analysis. Also, Joseph B. Board, "Judicial Activism in Sweden," *Judicial Activism in a Comparative Perspective*, ed. Kenneth Holland, (New York: St. Martin's Press, 1991).

43 Alec Stone, *The Birth of Judicial Politics in France* (Oxford: Oxford University Press, 1992); Martin Edelman, *Courts, Politics and Culture in Israel* (Charlottesville, VA: University Press of Virginia, 1994); Menachem Hofnung, "The Unintended Consequences of Unplanned Constitutional Reform: Constitutional Politics in Israel," *American Journal of Comparative Law* 44 (1996): 601; "The High Court's 1992 Free Speech decisions," *Australian Capital Televison Pty Ltd v. The Commonwealth*, 66 ALJR 695; *Nationwide News v. Wills*, 66 ALJR 658. For discussion, see Bottomley, 110-28.

44 See, for example, the civil liberties decisions of the Supreme Court of Canada during the 1950s: *Boucher v. The King*, [1951] 1 S.C.R. 265; *Saumur v. The City of Quebec*, [1953] 2 S.C.R.299; *Birks and Sons (Montreal) Ltd. v. Montreal*, [1955] 1 S.C.R. 799; *Chaput v. Romain*, [1955] S.C.R. 834; *Switzman v. Elbling and Attorney General of Quebec*, [1957] S.C.R. 285; *Roncarelli v. Duplessis*, [1959] 1 S.C.R. 121.

45 See Bottomley ch. 7.

46 Gregory Hein, "Post-Materialists in Court: The Consequence of Value Change in the Power of Institutions," Annual Conference, Canadian Political Science Association, Université de Sherbrooke and Bishop's University, June 1999: 39. This argument is developed more fully in Rainer Knopff and F.L. Morton, "The Charter Two-Step" *Charter Politics* (Toronto: Nelson Canada, 1992) ch. 3.

47 Mark Silverstein, *Judicious Choices: The New Politics of Supreme Court Confirmations* (New York: W.W. Norton and Co., 1994) 34.

48 Charles Epp, "Do Bills of Rights Matter? The Canadian Charter of Rights and Freedoms," *American Political Science Review* 90.4 (Dec. 1996): 765-79. Indeed, Epp provides persua-

sive evidence that those trends that other commentators (including ourselves) had attributed to the Charter pre-date 1982 and reflect the prior development of a SSLM in Canada.

49 See Troy Riddell and F. L. Morton, "Competition for Constitutional Advantage: Reasonable Limits, Distinct Society, and the Canada Clause," *Canadian Journal of Political Science* 31:3 (Sept. 1998): 467-93; Robert Sheppard, "Rights advocates hail changes; Epp says nothing done for West," *The Globe and Mail*, 13 Jan. 1981: 11; Ian Brodie, "Interest Groups and the Supreme Court of Canada," Ph.D. thesis, University of Calgary, 1997, ch.2.

50 Minutes of the Special Joint Committee 1980-81, v.9:58.

51 See Penney Kome, *The Taking of Twenty-Eight: Women Challenge the Constitution* (Toronto: The Women's Press, 1983).

52 M. Elizabeth Atcheson, Mary Eberts, and Beth Symes *Women and Legal Action: Precedents, Resources and Strategies for the Future* (Ottawa: Canadian Advisory Council on the Status of Women, 1984) 163; I. Brodie, "Interest Groups and the Supreme Court." Allen and Morton found that feminists won 70 per cent of the 47 appeal court rulings they studied; Allen and Morton, "Feminists in the Courts." Hein reports a 64 per cent success rate in 68 cases; Hein 29.

53 These are some of the groups that have received funding from the Court Challenges Program.

54 *Andrews v. Law Society of British Columbia*, [1989] 1 S.C.R. 143.

55 See Sherene Razack, *Canadian Feminism and the Law: The Women's Legal Education and Action Fund and the Pursuit of Equality* (Toronto: Second Story Press, 1991) 36-63; and Atcheson, Eberts, and Symes 172.

56 Alan C. Cairns, "The Charter: A Political Science Perspective," *The Impact of the Charter on the Public Policy Process*, ed. Patrick Monahan and Marie Finkelstein (Toronto: Centre for Public Law and Public Policy, York University, 1993) 158-59.

57 LEAF and the CCLA opposed each other in the rape shield case of *R. v. Seaboyer; R. v. Gayme*, [1991] 2 S.C.R. 577, and again in the Court's two main censorship cases, *The Queen v. Keegstra*, [1990] 3 S.C.R. 697 and *R. v. Butler*, [1992] 1 S.C.R. 452. The position favoured by LEAF won in both instances. The conflict between civil libertarians and feminists is the focus of chapter 2, A. Allan Borovoy, *The New Anti-Liberals* (Toronto: Canadian Scholars Press, Inc., 1999). See James Tully, "Diversity's Gambit Declined," *Constitutional Predicament: Canada After the Referendum of 1992*, ed. Curtis Cook (Montreal/Kingston: McGill-Queen's University Press, 1994) 193-95.

58 Deborah Coyne, "How to Escape the Meech Lake Morass and Other Misadventures," Annual Meeting of the Council of Canadians, Ottawa, 14 Oct. 1989: 3.

59 See Peter H. Russell, *Constitutional Odyssey: Can Canadians be A Sovereign People?* (Toronto: University of Toronto Press, 1992) 142-43.

60 The relationship between formal amendments and judge-made amendments is the

subject of Christopher P. Manfredi, "Institutional Design and the Politics of Constitutional Modification: Understanding Amendment Failure in the United States and Canada," *Law and Society Review* 31:1 (1997): 111-36.

61 Arthur M. Schlesinger, Jr., *The Imperial Presidency* (Toronto: Popular Library, 1974); Nathan Glazer, "Towards an Imperial Judiciary," *The Public Interest* 41 (1975); Allan Gotlieb, "The Republican Rules of the Game," *The Globe and Mail*, 1 Jan. 1995: A19.

62 Keith Archer et al., *Parameters of Power: Canada's Political Institutions* (Toronto: Nelson Canada, 1995).

63 Peter H. Russell, "The Effect of a Charter of Rights on the Policy-Making Role of Canadian Courts," *Canadian Public Administration* 25 (1982): 1-33.

64 Peter H. Russell, "The Supreme Court's Interpretation of the Constitution," *Politics Canada*, 5th ed., ed. Paul E. Fox (McGraw-Hill Ryerson Limited, 1982) 608.

65 Thomas and Mary Edsall, *Chain Reaction: The Impact of Race, Rights and Taxes on American Politics* (Norton, 1992); repr. *The Lanahan Readings in the American Polity*, ed. Ann G. Serow and Everett C. Ladd (Baltimore: Lanahan Publishers, Inc., 1997) 464.

66 Silverstein 88.

67 Theodore J. Lowi and Benjamin Ginsberg, *American Government: Freedom and Power*, 3rd ed. (New York: W.W. Norton and Co., 1994) 353.

68 For left-wing critics, see Michael Mandel, *The Charter of Rights and the Legalization of Politics in Canada*, rev. ed. (Toronto: Thompson Educational Publishing, 1994); Allan C. Hutchinson, *Waiting for Coraf: A Critique of Law and Rights* (Toronto: University of Toronto Press, 1995); and Joel Bakan, *Just Words: Constitutional Rights and Civil Wrongs* (Toronto: University of Toronto Press, 1997); for conservative critics, see notes 18-22, above.

Notes to Chapter Two

1 Felix Frankfurter letter cited in Louis Fisher, *Constitutional Dialogues: Interpretation as a Political Process* (Princeton, NJ: Princeton University Press, 1988) 244.

2 *Vriend v. Alberta*, [1998] 1 S.C.R. 493; 564.

3 See F.L. Morton, Peter H. Russell, and Troy Riddell, "The Canadian Charter of Rights and Freedoms: A Descriptive Analysis of the First Decade, 1982-1992," *National Journal of Constitutional Law* 5 (1994): 1-60; Monahan, "Constitutional Cases"; Greene, et al. 16, 141.

4 Paul M. Sniderman, Joseph F. Fletcher, Peter H. Russell, and Philip E. Tetlock, *The Clash of Rights: Liberty, Equality and Legitimacy in Pluralist Democracy* (Yale University Press, 1996) 52.

5 Peter H. Russell, "The Political Purposes of the Canadian Charter of Rights and Freedoms," *Canadian Bar Review* 61 (1983): 43-44. The "contestability of rights" is also a central theme of Sniderman, et al.

6 Knopff and Morton, *Charter Politics* 149.

7 For example, police officers could be disciplined directly for illegal procedure while still

admitting the reliable "fruits" of the tainted procedure. On the difficulty of controlling police misbehaviour indirectly by excluding evidence, see Donald L. Horowitz, *The Courts and Social Policy* (Washington, DC: Brookings Institution, 1977) ch. 6.

8 The judicial redefinition of "spouse" to include gay and lesbians is controversial even among those who agree with much else in the gay rights agenda. For example, when figure skater Brian Orser's estranged homosexual partner sued for support payments, William Thorsell, who has often supported gay rights, wrote in *The Globe and Mail* that it would be unjust for a court to retroactively change the law under which Orser had entered into his relationship; namely, that "a gay person did not risk prior sole ownership of his or her 'matrimonial home,' among other things, if the relationship broke up after a time." See Thorsell, "The new old rules of the game," *The Globe and Mail*, 28 Nov. 1998: D6. This, like most other Charter issues, is obviously a matter about which it is possible to have reasonable disagreements.

9 See Rainer Knopff, "Populism and the Politics of Rights: The Dual Attack on Representative Democracy," *Canadian Journal of Political Science* 31:4 (1998), and Rainer Knopff, "Courts Don't Make Good Compromises," *Policy Options* (April 1999).

10 Alexander Hamilton, James Madison, and John Jay, *The Federalist Papers*, ed. Clinton Rossiter (New York: New American Library, 1961) 465.

11 James Madison, "Letter" to Thomas Jefferson, 17 October 1788, *The Forging of American Federalism: Selected Writings of James Madison*, ed. Saul K. Padover (New York: Harper & Row, 1965) 254.

12 Mandel 459-60, n.4.

13 Robert G. McCloskey, *The American Supreme Court*, rev. ed. Sanford Levinson (University of Chicago Press, 1994) 132, 135; Robert Scigliano, *The Supreme Court and the Presidency* (New York: Free Press, 1971) 36-39.

14 *Attorney General of Canada v. Lavell and Bedard*, [1974] S.C.R. 1349; *Bliss v. A.-G. Canada*, [1979] 1 S.C.R. 183.

15 *Hogan v. The Queen*, [1975] 2 S.C.R. 574.

16 See Minutes of Proceedings, 46: 136-37.

17 *R. v. Hebert*, [1990] 2 S.C.R. 151; *R. v. Ross*, [1989] 1 S.C.R. 3 (pre-indictment line-ups); *R. v. Dyment*, [1988] 2 S.C.R. 417 (involuntary blood samples). For comparisons to US practice, see Harvie and Foster, "Different Drummers, Different Drums."

18 Peter Hogg said that the section 2 guarantees, including the guarantee of freedom of conscience and religion, "are more elaborately expressed than their counterparts in s. 1 of the Canadian Bill of Rights, but they probably do not make any substantive change." See Hogg, "A Comparison of the Canadian Charter of Rights and Freedoms with the Canadian Bill of Rights," *The Canadian Charter of Rights and Freedoms: Commentary* ed. Walter S. Tarnopolsky and Gérald-A. Beaudoin (Toronto: Carswell, 1982) 16.

19 *R. v. Big M Drug Mart, Ltd.*, [1985] 1 S.C.R. 295 overruling *Robertson and Rosetanni v. The Queen*,

[1963] 1 S.C.R. 651. The Supreme Court subsequently upheld a provincial version of Sunday closing legislation that was cast in secular language ("Retail Holidays Closing Act"). See *Edwards Books and Art Ltd. v. The Queen*, [1986] 2 S.C.R. 713. In the US the Supreme Court has upheld legislation that, like the Lord's Day Act, was originally enacted for religious purposes, on the grounds that it had acquired a secular purpose over time. *McGowan v. Maryland*, 366 U.S. 420 (1961); *Braunfeld v. Brown*, 366 U.S. 599 (1961); *Galagher v. Crownkosher Supermarkets of Massachusetts*, 366 U.S. 617 (1961); *Two Guys from Harrison-Allentown v. McGinley*, 366 U.S. 482 (1961).

20 *R. v. Therens*, [1985] 1 S.C.R. 613, overruling *Chromiak v. The Queen*, [1980] 1 S.C.R. 471.

21 Minutes of Proceedings, 48: 124.

22 *R. v. Collins*, [1987] 1 S.C.R. 265; Jody Ann Shugar, "Judicial Discretion and the Charter: A Qualitative and Quantitative Examination of the Exclusionary Rule," M.A. thesis, McGill University, 1995, 76, 111.

23 David M. Paciocco, "The Judicial Repeal of s.24(2) and the Development of the Canadian Exclusionary Rule," *The Criminal Law Quarterly* 32 (1989-90): 326.

24 Harvie and Foster, "Different Drummers" 59.

25 Factum of the Attorney-General of Canada, *Stillman v. The Queen*, Supreme Court of Canada (Court File No. 24631); *R. v. Stillman*, [1997] 1 S.C.R. 607.

26 See Justice Wilson's judgment in *Andrews v. Law Society of British Columbia*, [1989] 1 S.C.R. 143, 152; see also Justice Linden in *Schachtschneider v. The Queen*, 93 D.T.C. 5308-5313; Anthony A. Peacock, "Strange Brew: Tocqueville, Rights and the Technology of Equality," *Rethinking the Constitution: Perspectives on Canadian Constitutional Reform, Interpretation and Theory*, ed. Anthony A. Peacock (Toronto: Oxford University Press, 1996) 123.

27 An example of the former is *R. v. Seaboyer; R. v. Gayme*, [1991] 2 S.C.R. 577. Examples of the latter include *Eldridge v. British Columbia (Attorney General)*, [1997] 3 S.C.R. 493; *Vriend v. Alberta*, [1998] 1 S.C.R. 493.; *Mahé v. Alberta*, [1990] 1 S.C.R. 342; *Reference re Renumeration of Judges of the Provincial Court of PEI; Reference re: Independence and Impartiality of Judges of the Provincial Court of PEI*, [1997] 3 S.C.R. 3.

28 An important and obvious exception is the section 23 minority language education rights.

29 For details, see Morton, *Morgentaler v. Borowski: Abortion, The Charter, and the Courts* (Toronto: McClelland and Stewart, 1992) 111-116, 239-242; *Morgentaler v. The Queen*, [1988] 1 S.C.R. 30., 143-146.

30 Romanow, Whyte, and Leeson 214; Sanders 321; Hogg 82-83.

31 "It'll be 'a day of mourning' for Indians," *Vancouver Sun*, 15 April 1982: B8, as cited by Sanders 324.

32 *R. v. Sparrow*, [1990] 1 S.C.R. 1075.

33 Foster, "Canadian Indians, Time, and the Law" 46-47.

34 Part IV, Section A (41) of the Charlottetown Accord outlined an aboriginal inherent

right to self-government. See McRoberts and Monahan 301.

35 *Egan and Nesbitt v. Canada,* [1995] 2 S.C.R. 513.

36 Monahan, *Politics and the Constitution* 78-79.

37 *Reference re British Columbia Motor Vehicle Act,* [1985] 2 S.C.R. 486, 497.

38 Bindman, "Thank God for the Charter." Also see Chief Justice Lamer's comments in his judgment in the *Reference re British Columbia Motor Vehicle Act,* [1985] S.C.R. 486.

39 *Vriend v. Alberta,* [1998] 1 S.C.R. 493; 563.

40 Wilson 9.

41 Weinrib, "The Activist Constitution" 28.

42 Morton, *Morgentaler v. Borowski* 115; Monahan, *Politics and the Constitution* 76.

43 *Reference re British Columbia Motor Vehicle Act,* [1985] 2 S.C.R. 486, 509.

44 See Walter Berns, *The First Amendment and the Future of American Democracy* (New York: Basic Books, 1976) ch. 1.

45 Ronald Dworkin, *Taking Rights Seriously* (Cambridge, MA: Harvard University Press, 1977) 135-37. See also Knopff and Morton, *Charter Politics* 119-25.

46 *Dubois v. The Queen,* [1985] 2 S.C.R. 350, 384.

47 Most Canadian legislatures have voluntarily added sexual orientation to their human rights laws. See Donald D. Carter, "Employment Benefits for Same Sex Couples: The Expanding Entitlement," *Canadian Public Policy* 24:1 (1998).

48 Christopher Wolfe, *The Rise of Modern Judicial Review: From Constitutional Interpretation to Judge-Made Law* (New York: Basic Books, 1986) 323; Christopher Manfredi, "The Use of United States Decisions by the Supreme Court of Canada Under the Charter of Rights and Freedoms," *Canadian Journal of Political Science* 23 (1990): 513.

49 For a fuller discussion, see F. L. Morton and Rainer Knopff, "Permanence and Change in a Written Constitution: The 'Living Tree' Doctrine and the Charter of Rights," *Supreme Court Law Review* 1 (1990): 533-46.

50 *Attorney-General of Quebec v. Quebec Association of Protestant School Boards,* [1984] 2 S.C.R. 66.

51 *Daigle v. Tremblay,* (1989) 59 D.L.R. (4th) 609 (Que. C.A.)

52 *Tremblay v. Daigle,* [1989] 2 S.C.R. 530, 555.

53 For a fuller discussion of these issues, see Morton, *Morgentaler v. Borowski* 282, 287, 289.

54 See *Hunter (Director of Investigation and Research) v. Southam Inc.,* [1984] 2 S.C.R 145; and *R. v. Big M Drug Mart, Ltd,* [1985] 1 S.C.R 295.

55 Knopff and Morton, *Charter Politics* 131.

56 Peter H. Russell, "Canada's Charter of Rights and Freedoms: A Political Report," *Public Law* (Autumn 1988): 389. Also Manfredi, "The Use of United States Decisions" 513; Pierre Trudeau, *Federalism and the French Canadians* (Toronto: Macmillan, 1968) 18; For a fuller discussion, see Knopff and Morton, *Charter Politics* 114-19.

57 Bindman, "Thank God for the Charter."

58 Tibbetts, "Politicians duck divisive issues."

59 Raymond Tatalovich, *Abortion in the United States and Canada: A Comparative Study* (Armonk, NY: M.E. Sharpe, 1997) 110. In the 1960s, surveys indicated that three-quarters of both Americans and Canadians approved of abortions for therapeutic health reasons, while two-thirds opposed the legalization of "life-style" abortions. By the 1990s, 57 per cent of Canadians still approved "some regulation"; 10 per cent supported "prohibition"; and 31 per cent favoured "no regulation." US figures for the 1990s were comparable.

60 Stephen Bindman, "Door opens: Supreme Court lets groups intervene in cases," *Ottawa Citizen*, 9 March 1991: B8.

61 Jeff Sallot, "How the Charter changes justice," *The Globe and Mail*, 17 April 1992: A11.

62 Greene, et al. 126, 187, 188.

63 Tibbetts, "Politicians duck divisive issues" A1.

64 See, for example, Archer, et al. 309-12; Christopher P. Manfredi, *Canada and the Paradox of Liberal Constitutionalism: Judicial Power and the Charter* (Toronto: McClelland and Stewart, 1993); Knopff and Morton, *Charter Politics* 231-32; Monahan, *Politics and the Constitution* 7.

65 Ian Hunter, "Taking the law in vain," *National Post*, 29 July 1999.

66 See Carl and Ellen Baar, "Diagnostic Adjudication in Appellate Courts: The Supreme Court of Canada and the Charter of Rights," *Osgoode Hall Law Journal* 27 (1989): 1-25.

67 Alexis de Tocqueville, *Democracy in America*, ed. J.P. Mayer, trans. George Lawrence (Garden City, NY: Anchor, 1969) 103.

68 Interest groups who have directly litigated Charter claims before the Supreme Court of Canada include: the Quebec Association of Protestant Schools, Operation Dismantle, Société des Acadiens, Public Service Alliance of Canada, the Toronto Public School Board, B.C. Government Employees Union, and the Committee for the Commonwealth of Canada. There are of course many more whose cases did not reach the Supreme Court. The Canadian Abortion Rights Action League (CARAL) covered most of the legal expenses incurred by Henry Morgentaler in his successful challenge to the abortion law. Campaign Life financially backed Joe Borowski's pro-life Charter case. The National Citizens' Coalition (NCC) financially backed the successful Charter challenge to restrictions on third-party ("PAC") election expenditures and also Merv Lavigne's unsuccessful challenge to labour union expenditures for political causes. The Canadian Council of Churches has sustained an ongoing litigation campaign against the government's refugee determination policies.

69 *Minister of Justice v. Borowski*, [1981] 2 S.C.R. 575, 578-579.

70 See Morton, *Morgentaler v. Borowski*, ch. 10.

71 *Skapinker v. Law Society of Upper Canada*, [1984] 1 S.C.R. 357; *Mercure v. Saskatchewan*, [1988] 1 S.C.R. 234; *M. v. H.*, [1999] 2 S.C.R. 3; *Minister of Justice v. Borowski*, [1989] 1 S.C.R. 342.

72 This campaign is recounted in I. Brodie "Interest Groups and the Supreme Court" 50-55.

73 This development parallels American experience, where interest group intervention in constitutional cases has become the norm not the exception. For example, *amicus curiae*

(the equivalent of interveners) were present in 53 per cent of the non-commercial cases before the US Supreme Court between 1970 and 1980 and in over two-thirds of the cases when criminal cases are also excluded. Karen O'Connor and Lee Epstein, "Amicus Curiae Participation in U.S. Supreme Court Litigation: An Appraisal of Hakman's 'Folklore,'" *Law and Society Review* 16 (1981-82): 311-18.

74 I. Brodie, "Interest Groups and the Supreme Court" 55-71.

75 See Knopff and Morton, *Charter Politics* 185-86. Mandel, *The Charter of Rights* 233-34.

76 *R. v. Smith*, [1987] 1 S.C.R. 1045; for details about the overturning of mandatory sentencing, see Knopff and Morton, *Charter Politics* 186.

77 Lorraine Weinrib, Letter "Re: An itch for the scratching," *National Post*, 3 June 1999.

78 *R. v. Sellars*, [1980] 1 S.C.R. 527.

79 Carl Baar, "Criminal Court Delay and the Charter: The Use and Misuse of Social Facts in Judicial Policy Making," *Canadian Bar Review*, (1993): 305-336, 319.

80 See Alexander M. Bickel, *The Least Dangerous Branch: the Supreme Court at the Bar of Politics* (New Haven, CT: Yale University Press, 1986) 58.

81 Silverstein 58, 59.

82 Laurence Tribe, *American Constitutional Law*, 2nd ed. (Mineola, NY: Foundation Press, 1988) 68; as cited in Silverstein 58.

83 Silverstein 58.

Notes to Chapter Three

1 Charles R. Epp, *The Rights Revolution: Lawyers, Activists, and Supreme Courts in Comparative Perspective* (Chicago: University of Chicago Press, 1998) 13.

2 The first three categories are adopted from Peter Russell's analysis, in "The Political Purposes of the Charter: Have They Been Fulfilled? An Agnostic's Report Card," *Protecting Rights & Freedoms: Essays on the Charter's Place in Canada's Political, Legal, and Intellectual Life*, Philip Bryden, Steven Davis, and John Russell, eds. (Toronto: University of Toronto Press, 1994) 37.

3 Pierre Elliott Trudeau, *Federalism and the French Canadians*, (Toronto: Macmillan, 1968) xxiii.

4 Russell, "The Political Purposes of the Canadian Charter of Rights and Freedoms"; Rainer Knopff and F.L Morton, "Nation-Building and the Canadian Charter of Rights and Freedoms," *Constitutionalism, State and Society in Canada*, ed. Alan Cairns and Cynthia Williams (Toronto: University of Toronto Press, 1985); Knopff and Morton, *Charter and Politics* 1992.

5 Pierre Trudeau, "A Constitutional Declaration of Rights," address, Canadian Bar Association, 4 Sept. 1967, Trudeau, *Federalism and the French Canadians* 54.

6 As quoted in Russell, "The Political Purposes of the Charter" 34.

7 Kenneth McRoberts, *Misconceiving Canada: The Struggle for National Unity* (Oxford University Press, 1997) ch.4.

8 Romanow, Whyte, and Leeson 94, 197, 199, 234, 258; Mandel, *The Charter of Rights*, 17, 29, 111; Trudeau, *Federalism and the French Canadians* 5.

9 For more detailed account of federal funding of language rights groups, cf. ch. 4; and also Leslie A. Pal, *Interests of State: The Politics of Language, Multiculturalism and Feminism in Canada*. (Montreal/Kingston: McGill-Queen's Press, 1993) chs. 5 and 7.

10 Christopher P. Manfredi, "Constitutional Rights and Interest Advocacy: Litigating Educational Reform in Canada and the United States," *Equity and Community: The Charter, Interest Advocacy and Representation*, ed. F. Leslie Seidle (Montreal: Institute for Research on Public Policy, 1993) 91-117.

11 Mary Catherine Courtright, "Language Rights and the Courts: Advancing Minority Language Rights through Litigation," University of Calgary, 1997 [unpublished].

12 *Association des parents francophones (Columbie Brittanique) v. British Columbia*, [1996] 27 B.C.L.R. (3d), 83; *Mahé v. Alberta*, [1990] 1 S.C.R. 342; *Reference re Public Schools Act, Manitoba*, (1990) 67 D.L.R. (4th) 491; *Marchand v. Simcoe Board of Education*, (1986) 29 D.L.R. (4th) 596 (Ont. H.C.J.); *Reference re Education Act, Ontario*, (1984) 10 D.L.R. (4th) 491; *Lavoie v. Nova Scotia*, (1989) 58 D.L.R. (4th) 293 (N.S.S.C.A.D.); *Reference re School Act, PEI*, (1988) 49 D.L.R. (4th) 499; *Forest v. Manitoba*, [1979] 2 S.C.R. 1032.; *Reference re Language Rights under the Manitoba Act, 1870*, [1985] 2 S.C.R. 347; *R. v. Mercure*, [1988] 1 S.C.R. 234.

13 Alliance Quebec was officially formed in 1982, replacing the Council of Quebec Minorities, which had been formed out of several preceding Anglophone-rights groups: Participation Quebec, Positive Action Committee, and the Townshippers' Association. All had been funded by Ottawa.

14 *A.-G. Quebec v. Blaikie*, [1979] 2 S.C.R. 1016; *A.-G. Quebec v. Quebec Association of Protestant School Boards*, [1985] 2 S.C.R. 66; *Quebec v. Ford et al.*, [1988] 2 S.C.R. 712.

15 In the landmark case of *Mahé v. Alberta*, [1990] 1 S.C.R. 342, for example, the following OLMG groups intervened to support the section 23 claims of Alberta Francophones: the Association canadienne-française de l'Alberta, Alliance Quebec, Alliance for Language Communities in Quebec, the Association canadienne-française de l'Ontario, the Association des conseils scolaires de l'Ontario, the Association des enseignantes et des enseignants franco-ontariens.

16 Manfredi, "Constitutional Rights and Interest Advocacy." Also Matthew Hennigar, "Litigating Pan-Canadianism: The Constitutional Litigation Strategy of the Canadian Federal Government in Charter Cases, 1982-1993," M.A. thesis, University of Calgary, 1996.

17 For details, cf. McRoberts, *Misconceiving Canada* 110-16.

18 Guy LaForest, *Trudeau and the End of a Canadian Dream* (Montreal/Kingston: McGill-Queen's University Press, 1995); For a Charter patriot's view of the Meech Lake Accord, see Deborah Coyne, "Commentary," *After Meech Lake: Lessons for the Future*, ed. David E. Smith, Peter MacKinnon, and John C. Courtney (Calgary: Fifth House Publishers, 1991) 139-45.

For an academic perspective, see Alan C. Cairns, "The Charter, Interest Groups, Executive Federalism and Constitutional Reform," Smith, et al. 13-31; and Alan C. Cairns, "Citizens (Outsiders) and Governments (Insiders) in Constitution Making: The Case of Meech Lake," *Canadian Public Policy* 14 (Sept. 1988): 121-45.

19 See F.L. Morton, "The Charter in the Rest of Canada," *Beyond Quebec: Taking Stock of Canada*, ed. Kenneth McRoberts (McGill-Queen's University Press, 1995) 93-114.

20 Sniderman et al.; and Fletcher and Howe, "Canadian Attitudes Toward the Charter and the Court." Sniderman et al.'s claim has been challenged based on a different analysis of the same survey data. See Richard Vengroff and F.L. Morton, "Regional Perspectives on Canada's Charter of Rights: A Reexamination of Democratic Elitism," *Canadian Journal of Political Science* (forthcoming).

21 The Supreme Court has always exercised a unifying effect on provincial laws because it has the final interpretive authority for provincial as well as federal law. But provincial legislatures always had the freedom to enact new legislation that overruled the Court's interpretation. Moreover, the Court has in recent decades devoted itself to federal and constitutional public law, leaving provincial courts of appeal with the *de facto* final word on most provincial law. See Archer et al. 332-33.

22 The Federalists and their celebrated Chief Justice, John Marshall (1800-1835), were the first. The New Deal Courts, especially the Warren Court (1953-1968), were the most recent. An important exception were the Republican dominated courts from the Civil War to the New Deal (1865-1930).

23 Jennifer Smith, "The Origins of Judicial Review in Canada," *Canadian Journal of Political Science* 16 (1983) 115; André Bzdera, "Comparative Analysis of Federal High Courts: A Political Theory of Judicial Review," *Canadian Journal of Political Science* 26 (1993): 1-29.

24 Russell, "The Political Purposes of the Canadian Charter" 37.

25 This, of course, is the central thesis of Hobbes' *Leviathan*. See also, Walter Berns, *Freedom, Virtue and the First Amendment* (New York: Greenwood Press, 1969) 153-56, 174-75.

26 John Stuart Mill, *On Liberty*, ed. Currin V. Shields (Indianapolis: Bobbs-Merrill, 1956) 4, 5-7.

27 For a different account of how best to protect rights, see Rainer Knopff, "Populism and the Politics of Rights."

28 For the US, see *Lochner v. New York*, 198 U.S. 45 (1905), and *Adkins v. Children's Hospital*, 261 U.S. 525 (1923). For Canada, see *Attorney-General of Canada v. Attorney-General of Ontario* (Labour Conventions Case), [1937] A.C. 327.

29 J.R. Mallory, "The Courts and the Sovereignty of the Canadian Parliament," *Canadian Journal of Economics and Political Science* 10 (1944): 169.

30 Doug Owram, *The Government Generation: Canadian Intellectuals and the State, 1900-1945* (Toronto: University of Toronto Press, 1986).

31 See Paul Weiler, *In the Last Resort: A Critical Study of the Supreme Court of Canada* (Toronto: Car-

swell Methuen, 1974). Also J.A. Corry, *Law and Policy* (Toronto: Clark, Irwin, 1962) 62; Alan Cairns, "The Past and Future of the Canadian Administrative State," *University of Toronto Law Journal* 40 (1990): 319-61. So strong was elite belief in parliamentary supremacy that even when the Supreme Court was given the opportunity to enforce rights against the government – by the 1960 Bill of Rights – it turned it down. See, J. Pigeon's dissent in *Drybones v. the Queen*, [1970] S.C.R. 282: "In the traditional British system that is our own by virtue of the BNA Act, the responsibility for updating the statutes in this changing world rests exclusively upon Parliament. If the Parliament of Canada intended to depart from that principle in enacting the Bill, one would expect to find clear language expressing that intention." *Drybones* was the only pre-1982 case in which the 1960 Bill of Rights was used to invalidate a law, and Pigeon's dissent thus quickly became the *de facto* majority view. In 1975 in the first *Morgentaler* case, [1976] 1 S.C.R. 616, Chief Justice Laskin wrote what in effect was a funeral oration for the Bill of Rights:

> It cannot be forgotten that it is a statutory instrument, illustrative of Parliament's primacy within the limits of its assigned legislative authority, and this is a relative consideration in determining how far the language of the *Canadian Bill of Rights* should be taken in assessing the quality of federal enactments which are challenged under s.1(a).

Not even Laskin, the most activist member of the Court, was willing to accept Henry Morgentaler's invitation to follow *Roe v. Wade* and the reformist political role it implied for the courts.

32 Silverstein 47.

33 See *R. v. P (M.B.)*, [1994] 1 S.C.R. 555; *R. v. Underwood*, [1998] 1 S.C.R. 77; *Singh v. Canada (Minister of Employment and Immigration)*, [1985] 1 S.C.R. 177.

34 Calculated from list provided to the authors by Alan Borovoy, Executive Director of the CCLA, 20 Oct. 1997. Between 1984 and 1993, the CCLA had 10 interventions in the Supreme Court while LEAF had 11. I. Brodie, "Interest Groups and the Supreme Court of Canada" 66, Table 2.7.

35 *Zylberberg v. Sudbury Board of Education*, (1989), 52 D.L.R (4th) 577; Borovoy, 16; *R. v. Butler*, [1992] 1 S.C.R. 452; *R. v. Keegstra*, [1990] 3 S.C.R. 697.

36 Russell, "The Political Purposes of the Charter" 40.

37 Joel Bakan and David Schneiderman, eds., *Social Justice and the Constitution: Perspectives on a Social Union for Canada* (Carleton University Press, 1992); Hutchinson, *Waiting for CORAF*; Bakan, *Just Words*; Mandel, *Charter of Rights*.

38 Mandel, *Charter of Rights*, 460.

39 Feminists have won important policy and/or legal changes in the fields of abortion, family law, anti-discrimination law, immigration, and criminal law. See Allen and Morton, "Feminists in the Courts."

40 See Women's Legal Education and Action Fund, *Equality and the Charter: Ten Years of Feminist*

Advocacy Before the Supreme Court of Canada (Edmond Montgomery, 1996) xv-xxvi; Anne F. Bayefsky and Mary Eberts, eds. *Equality Rights and the Canadian Charter of Rights and Freedoms* (Toronto: Carswell, 1985); Rainer Knopff, "What Do Equality Rights Protect Canadians Against?" *Canadian Journal of Political Science* 20:2 (1987): 265-86.

41 Justice Rosalie Abella, Speech, Edmonton International Human Rights Conference, 28 Nov. 1998.

42 See Bayefsky and Eberts, *Equality Rights and the Charter*; and also Rainer Knopff, "What do Equality Rights Protect Canadians Against?" Knopff's article illustrates that the primary effect of a jurisprudence of systemic discrimination is an institutional transfer of policy-making authority to the courts and that the inconsistent application of the equal effects principle discloses the left-wing ideological motivation of this transfer.

43 See "Aggressive challenges to discrimination urged," *The National*, Feb. 1989: 7.

44 *Andrews v. Law Society of British Columbia*, [1989] 1 S.C.R. 143.

45 *Egan v. Canada*, [1995] 2 S.C.R. 513; *Andrews v. Law Society of British Columbia*, [1989] 1 S.C.R. 143.

46 Coyne, "How to Escape the Meech Lake Morass."

47 I. Brodie, "Interest Groups and the Supreme Court of Canada," 86-113; Michael Grange, "Rights group seeks to join fight against welfare rule," *The Globe and Mail* 22 Jan. 1996: A4; Donn Downey, "Welfare not a court issue, ministry says," *The Globe and Mail* 15 Nov. 1995: A9; Sean Fine, "Activists tackle shackles of the poor," *The Globe and Mail* 25 Nov. 1992: A1, A7. Also: "BC welfare recipients protected by Charter s.15, may challenge statute," *Lawyers' Weekly* 5 July 1991; *R. v. Sparrow*, [1990] 1 S.C.R. 1075; *R. v. Sioui*, [1990]; *Native Women's Association of Canada v. Canada*, [1994] 3 S.C.R. 627; *R. v. Badger*, [1996] 1 S.C.R. 771.

48 Mary Ellen Turpel, "Aboriginal Peoples' Struggle for Fundamental Political Change," McRoberts and Monahan 134-38.

49 *Mahé v. Alberta*, [1990] 1 S.C.R. 342.

50 Brodie's examples include "universal and affordable childcare, income security for single mothers and elderly women, the protection of women from male violence, affirmative action, and pay equity." Janine Brodie, "The Women's Movement outside Quebec: Shifting Relations with the Canadian State," McRoberts, *Beyond Quebec*, 344.

51 Abella.

52 Section 32 covers the "application of the Charter." It applies the Charter to "the Parliament and government of Canada" and "the legislature and government of each province." Section 52 of the Constitution Act, 1982, says that "any law that is inconsistent with the provisions of the Constitution is, to the extent of the inconsistency, of no force or effect"; Dianne Pothier, "The Sounds of Silence: Charter Application when the Legislature Declines to Speak," *Constitutional Forum* 7:4 (1996): 113-19.

53 Dale Gibson, "Distinguishing the Governors from the Governed: The meaning of "Government" under Section 32(1) of the Charter," *Manitoba Law Journal* 13:4 (1983): 514.

54 Dale Gibson, "The Charter of Rights and the Private Sector," *Manitoba Law Journal* 12

(1982): 218: "... every aspect of life falls within the law's embrace, in the sense that every act a person may commit is either prohibited or permitted by law. It has long been one of our most fundamental bulwarks of freedom that the law permits whatever it does not clearly proscribe. Viewed against this notion of the law's plentitude, it is possible to regard all private conduct as subject to law, and therefore to the Charter."

55 *Dolphin Delivery Ltd. v. R.W.D.S.U., Local 580,* [1986] 2 S.C.R. 573. Also, *McKinney v. University of Guelph,* [1990] 2 S.C.R. 229.

56 *Blainey v. Ontario Hockey Association,* (1986) 54 O.R. (2d) 177; *Haig v. Canada,* (1991) 5 O.R. (3d) 245; *Vriend v. Alberta,* [1998] 1 S.C.R. 493.

57 See Thomas E. Flanagan, "The Staying Power of the Status Quo: Collective Choice After Morgentaler," *Canadian Journal of Political Science,* 30 (March 1997): 31-53; and F.L. Morton, "Dialogue or Monologue?" *Policy Options* 20:3 (April 1999): 23-26.

58 *Schachter v. Canada,* Factum of the Respondent/Intervenor, the Women's Legal Education and Action Fund, in the Supreme Court of Canada, File 21889, 29.

59 *Schachter v. Canada,* [1992] 2 S.C.R. 679.

60 Kelly Toughill, "Women take aim at civil liberties group," *Toronto Star,* 30 Aug. 1992: A1, A6. Also, Borovoy 13.

61 See Borovoy 143-49.

62 Borovoy began his career of political activism working for the Jewish Labour Committee and the Labour Committee for Human Rights. See Borovoy x.

63 *Lavigne v. Ontario Public Service Employees Union,* [1991] 2 S.C.R. 211.

64 See Thomas Sowell, *A Conflict of Visions: Ideological Origins of Political Struggles* (New York: William Morrow, 1987), 146-51; ch. 2.

65 Cf. Knopff, *Human Rights and Social Technology* and Rainer Knopff, "Rights, Power-Knowledge, and Social Technology," *George Grant and the Future of Canada,* ed. Yusuf K. Umar (Calgary: University of Calgary Press, 1992).

66 James Q. Wilson, *The Moral Sense* (Toronto: Macmillan, 1993); Frans de Waal, *Good Natured: The Origins of Right and Wrong in Humans and Other Animals* (Cambridge, MA: Harvard University Press, 1996). Knopff, *Human Rights and Social Technology* chs. 1, 8.

67 Hamilton, et al. 322.

68 This is the memorable first sentence of the first chapter of Jean Jacques Rousseau's famous treatise, *The Social Contract.*

69 David Greener, "Deconstructing Family: A Case Study of Legal Advocacy Scholarship," M.A. thesis, University of Calgary, 1997, 59-69; Hein, "Post-Materialists in Court" 4, 32.

70 Janet Ajzenstat, *The Political Thought of Lord Durham* (Montreal/Kingston: McGill-Queen's University Press, 1988) 69.

71 Ward Elliot, *The Rise of Guardian Democracy: The Supreme Court's Role in Voting Rights Disputes, 1845-1969* (Harvard University Press, 1974).

72 George Radwanski, *Trudeau* (Toronto: Macmillan, 1978) 192, as quoted by I. Brodie, "Interest Groups and the Supreme Court of Canada" 161.

73 Pal ch. 5.

74 I. Brodie, "Interest Groups and the Supreme Court of Canada" 162.

75 J.R. Mallory, *Social Credit and the Federal Power in Canada* (Toronto: University of Toronto Press, 1954) 182, as quoted in I. Brodie, "Interest Groups and the Supreme Court of Canada" 67.

76 Seymour Martin Lipset, "The Industrial Proletariat and the Intelligentsia in a Comparative Perspective," *Consensus and Conflict* (New Brunswick and Oxford: Transaction Books, 1985) 187, 196.

77 Khayyam Z. Paltiel, "The Changing Environment and Role of Special Interest Groups," *Canadian Public Administration* 25:2 (1982): 198-210.

78 Jack L. Walker, "The Origins and Maintenance of Interest Groups in America," *American Political Science Review* 77:2 (1983): 390-406; Jack L. Walker, "Interest groups, Iron Triangles, and Representative Institutions in American National Government," *British Journal of Political Science* 14 (1984): 161-85. The growth of postmaterialist value change in Canada has been well documented. See Neil Nevitte, *The Decline of Deference* (Peterborough, ON: Broadview, 1996). In addition to our own work, the link between postmaterialism and Charter politics has been developed by Ian Brodie and Neil Nevitte "Evaluating the Citizens' Constitution Theory," *Canadian Journal of Political Science* 26:2 (1993): 235-60; and by Vengroff and Morton, "Regional Perspectives on Canada's Charter of Rights"; and Hein, "Post-Materialists in Court."

79 Lipset 196, 194.

80 Ronald Inglehart, *Culture Shift in Advanced Industrial Nations* (Princeton: Princeton University Press, 1990) 325; 321; 331.

81 Unlike the feminists, environmentalists' success rate did not increase after 1982, but has remained steady at about 40 per cent. Hein, "Post-Materialists in Court" 8, 12, 29. The Public Interest Advocacy Centre, the West Coast Environmental Law Association, and the Canadian Environmental Law Association were followed by the Canadian Environmental Defense Fund, the Quebec Environmental Law Centre, the Sierra Legal Defense Fund, the East Coast Environmental Law Association, and the B.C. Public Interest Advocacy Centre.

82 Hein, "Post-Materialists in Court" 31; *Minister of Finance of Canada v. Finlay*, [1986] 2 S.C.R. 607.

83 Silverstein 64.

84 Silverstein 71.

85 Sherene Razack's personal interview with Marilou McPhedran, February 1988, as reported in Gregory Hein, "Social Movements and the Expansion of Judicial Power: Feminists and Environmentalists in Canada from 1970 to 1995," Ph.D. thesis, University of Toronto, 1997, 226.

86 The policies promoted by these elites often benefit mainly them. As Christopher Lasch argues, feminism's "commitment to the two-career family" is of particular interest to

the "professional and managerial class" and largely explains the prominence of feminism in that class. Lasch, *The Revolt of the Elites and the Betrayal of Democracy* (New York: W.W. Norton, 1995) 33. Similarly, Thomas Sowell has gathered a wealth of international evidence showing how affirmative action programs typically benefit the already-better-off segments of the disadvantaged groups in whose name they are undertaken. Thomas Sowell, *Preferential Policies: An International Perspective* (New York: William Morrow & Co., 1990).

87 Thomas Sowell, *Conflict of Visions* 40-41.

88 Sowell, *Conflict of Visions* 43, 44.

89 Richard J. Herrnstein and Charles Murray, *The Bell Curve: Intelligence and Class Structure in American Life* (New York: The Free Press, 1994) Part I.

90 Lasch 20, 28, 26.

91 Sowell, *Conflict of Visions* 46, quoting Condorcet.

92 For further discussion see Knopff, "Rights, Power-Knowledge, and Social Technology" 66-70.

93 Knopff, "Rights, Power-Knowledge, and Social Technology" 70.

94 See Gregory Hein, "Interest Group Litigation in Canada, 1988-1998," *Choices* (forthcoming).

95 This is one of the principal conclusions of Gregory Hein's Ph.D. thesis, "Social Movements and the Expansion of Judicial Power: Feminists and Environmentalists in Canada from 1970 to 1995" (cited above, note 85).

96 Cf. Russell, *Constitutional Odyssey* 34: "... history shapes constitutional meaning more than framers' intent."

Notes to Chapter Four

1 Quoted in Stephen Wasby, *Race Relations Litigation in an Age of Complexity* (Charlottesville, VA: University Press of Virginia, 1995) 96.

2 Mancur Olson, *The Logic of Collective Action: Public Goods and the Theory of Groups.* (Cambridge, MA: Harvard University Press, 1965).

3 Jack L. Walker Jr., *Mobilizing Interest Groups in America: Patrons, Professions and Social Movements* (Ann Arbor: University of Michigan Press, 1991); Pal 23.

4 Alan Cairns, "The Embedded State: State-Society Relations in Canada," *State and Society: Canada in a Comparative Perspective*, ed. K. Banting (Toronto: University of Toronto Press, 1986) 58. See also, Alan Cairns, "The Past and Future of the Canadian Administrative State," *University of Toronto Law Journal* 40 (1990): 319-361.

5 It also creates incentives for the "service providers" to organize, and they typically organize first; cf. Walker, *Mobilizing Interest Groups* 29-30.

6 Walker, *Mobilizing Interest Groups* 13, 30.

7 Pal 102, 103.

8 In 1990, the FFHQ was renamed the Fédération des communautés francophones et aca-
   diennes du Canada. Pal ch. 7.

9 Pal 102, 114, ch.8.

10 Its initial title was the "Ad Hoc Committee on the Status of Women."

11 Pal ch. 9.

12 Pal 108-109; James S. Frideres, *Native Peoples in Canada: Contemporary Conflicts*, 4th ed. (Scarborough: Prentice Hall Canada, 1993) 296, 310; also, Sanders, "The Indian Lobby," and the
   discussion of native legal victories in Chapter 2.

13 See Frederick Zemans, "Legal Aid and Advice in Canada," *Osgoode Hall Law Journal* 16, 663-
   693 (1978): 667.

14 Law Reform Commission Act, R.S.C. 1970, c. 23 (1st Supp).

15 See Brenda Ann Long, "Judicial Reform of the Criminal Law Under the Charter of
   Rights and Freedoms," M.A. thesis, University of Calgary, 1996.

16 Knopff, *Human Rights and Social Technology*.

17 Special Joint Committee on the Constitution (1980-81) 5:5-28; 5A:1-4; for submission of
   the New Brunswick Human Rights Commission see Joint Committee, 11:27-45; for submission of the Saskatchewan Human Rights Commission see Joint Committee, 20:5-27.
       Commenting on the Supreme Court's embrace of the concept of "substantive"
   rather than "formal" equality, Reva Devins notes: "In the context of human rights law,
   the concepts of constructive discrimination, accommodation, employment equity or
   special programmes, were earlier manifestations of this more sophisticated notion of
   equality." Reva Devins, "A Perspective From the Ontario Human Rights Commission,"
   Monahan and Finkelstein 145, 153.

18 Kome 100. Also see Kome, 50.

19 Pal 112.

20 Pal 155; 196; 221. The National Action Committee (NAC) alone received a $500,000 grant.
   The Canadian Research Institute for the Advancement of Women (CRIAW) received
   $361,200. In 1987-88, LEAF received $269,770 from the Women's Program.

21 Walker, "The Origins and Maintenance of Interest Groups in America" 398; Walker,
   "Interest Groups, Iron Triangles, and Representative Institutions" 169.

22 For Canada, see Paltiel. For the US, cf. Walker, "The Origins and Maintenance of Interest Groups in America" and "Interest Groups, Iron Triangles, and Representative Institutions in American National Government."

23 Pal 8; 171; 179.

24 Hein, "Social Movements and the Expansion of Judicial Power" 226.

25 Pal 204; 237-38.

26 Patrick A. McCartney, "Government Sponsorship of Voluntary Associations in Canada:
   Research and Reflections," Canadian Political Science Association, Kingston, Ontario,
   1991: 15, Table 3. Cited in I. Brodie, "Interest Groups and the Supreme Court" 85.

27 I. Brodie, "Interest Groups and the Supreme Court" 90, Table 3.1.

28 A more complete account of the CCP is provided by I. Brodie, "The Court Challenges Program" *Law, Politics and the Judicial Process in Canada*, ed. F.L. Morton (Calgary: University of Calgary Press, 1992) 251-55.

29 *A.G. Quebec v. Blaikie*, [1979] 2 S.C.R. 1016; *A.G. Quebec v. Quebec Association of Protestant School Boards*, [1984] 2 S.C.R. 66; *Lavoie v. Nova Scotia*, (1988) 47 D.L.R. (4th) 586 (N.S.S.C.T.D.); (1989) 58 D.L.R. (4th) 293 (N.S.S.C.A.D.); *Société des Acadiens v. Association of Parents for Fairness in Education*, (1986) 27 D.L.R. (4th) 406; *Marchand v. Simcoe Board of Education*, (1986) 29 D.L.R. (4th) 596 (Ont.H.C.J.); *Forest v. Manitoba*, [1979] 2.S.C.R. 1032; *Reference re Language Rights under the Manitoba Act, 1870*, [1985] 2 S.C.R. 347; *Reference re Public School Act* (Man.) S.79 (3), (4), and (7), [1993] 1 S.C.R. 839; *Mercure v. A.G. Saskatchewan*, [1988] 1 S.C.R. 234; *Mahé v. Alberta*, (1990) 68 D.L.R. (4th) 69.

30 *MacDonald v. City of Montreal*, [1986] 1 S.C.R. 460; *R. v. Bilodeau*, [1986] S.C.R. 449; *Société des Acadiens v. Association of Parents*, [1986] 1 S.C.R. 549.

31 Mary Catherine Courtright, "Language Rights and the Courts." "Success" is here defined simply as the Charter claimant winning the outcome of the case. Several different statistical studies – Morton, et al; Monahan; Kelly – of the Supreme Court's Charter decisions have all discovered the same success rate of roughly 33 per cent.

32 See Smith, "Origins of Judicial Review."

33 *Mahé v. Alberta*, [1990] 1 S.C.R. 342.

34 I. Brodie, "Interest Groups and the Supreme Court" 113.

35 "Ministers announce extension of Court Challenges Program," Government of Canada official news release, 25 Sept. 1985; Court Challenges Program Annual Report, 1991-91 (Ottawa, 1992).

36 I. Brodie, "Interest Groups and the Supreme Court" 100.

37 Ian Brodie, "The Court Challenges Program," 254; Bureau of Management Consulting, "Court Challenges Program Administration Review, Project No. 4-7645," (Ottawa: Department of Supply and Services, 1989) 12; as quoted in I. Brodie, "Interest Groups and the Supreme Court" 100.

38 Court Challenges Program of Canada, Annual Report 1986-87: 5.

39 I. Brodie, "Interest Groups and the Supreme Court" 112, Table 3.3; Court Challenges Program (CCP), Equality Rights Panel, Annual Report 1986-87. 19; Guide to the Charter, 1988, p.24; CCP Annual Report 1988-89. 11,16,17,18; CCP Annual Report 1989-90. 32; CCP Annual Report 1990-91.9; Broadside, Oct. 1988.

40 *Symes v. Canada*, [1994] 3 S.c.R. 695; I. Brodie, "Interest Groups and the Supreme Court" 112, Table 3.3.

41 I. Brodie, "Interest Groups and the Supreme Court" 109, Table 3.2.

42 J. Brodie, "The Women's Movement Outside Quebec" 346.

43 I. Brodie, "Interest Groups and the Supreme Court" 101-03.

44 Monahan, "The Charter Then and Now" 15.

45 For CCP funding, see I. Brodie, "Interest Groups and the Supreme Court" 108-13. For LEAF success in the courts, cf. Allen and Morton, "Feminists and the Courts."

46 Court Challenges Program of Canada, Annual Report 1994-95. Document prepared by François Boileau.

47 CCP Annual Report 1994-95. The new board of directors consisted of: Fernand Landry, Chair, Former Dean of the University of Moncton Faculty of Law; Avvy Go, Vice-Chair, Director of Metro-Toronto Chinese and South-East Asian Legal Clinic, former member of the CCP's Equality Rights Panel, and board member of the Chinese Canadian National Council (Toronto Chapter); Paul Charbonneau, Treasurer, former Executive Director, Fédération des francophones de Terre-Neuve et du Labrador and former Executive Director of the Commission nationale des parents francophones; André Paradis, Executive Director of La Ligue des droits et libertés; and Victoria Percival-Hilton, former Director of Legal Affairs and Government Services and Interim Executive Director of Alliance Quebec. The Chair of the Language Rights Panel was Marc Godbout, and the Chair of the Equality Panel was Shelagh Day.

48 Shelagh Day, Co-Chair. Ken Norman, Co-Chair, Professor of Law, University of Saskatchewan since 1969; Chief Commissioner of the Saskatchewan Human Rights Commission (1978-83); member of the Equality Rights Panel of the CCP (1988-92). Daniel Dortélus, lawyer; member of federal Immigration Advisory Council (1990-92); member of the Quebec Human Rights Tribunal since 1990; past Vice-President of the Congress of Black Lawyers of Quebec; Board member of the Ligue des droits et libertés and the Centre for Research Action on Race Relations in Montreal. Avvy Go, social worker; Chair and past President of the Chinese Canadian National Council; former Director of Metro-Toronto Chinese and South-East Asian Legal Clinic; former member of the CCP's Equality Rights Panel; former President and member of the Ontario Advisory Council onWomen's Issues and the Minister's Advisory Group on Employment Equity and Social Assistance Legislation; currently Director of Senior Services at the Woodgreen Community Centre and and a member of the Coalition of Women for Employment Equity. Sharon McIvor, lawyer and currently professor of Aboriginal law at Queen's University; member of Lower Nicola Indian Band; Justice Coordinator for Native Womens' Association of Canada (1992-95); member of the National Aboriginal Advisory Commitee to the Commissioner of Correctional Services Canada; past member of the Equality Rights Panel of the CCP.

49 1999-2000 Department of Canadian Heritage Estimates (Part III), 50.

50 *Evaluation of the Test Case Funding Program*. Prepared for the Department of Indian and Northern Affairs, Milligan and Company, Inc. (Jan. 1989): i.

51 Individuals can also apply, but rarely receive the grants. By 1989, the Program had only made four grants to counsel for individuals. Legal Liaison and Support Study, *Test Case Funding Program*, Prepared for the Department of Indian Affairs and Northern Development by E.L. Oscapella and Associates Consulting, Ltd. (Nov. 1988): 16, 17, 37.

52 "A network for feminist socio-legal research" and "Canadian network on social policy and environmental law." Information provided by Brian Biggar, Communications Division, Social Sciences and Humanities Research Council; fax, 26 July 1996.

53 Alan C. Cairns, "Ritual, Taboo, and Bias in Constitutional Controversies, or Constitutional Talk Canadian Style," *Disruptions: Constitutional Struggles from the Charter to Meech Lake*, ed. Douglas E. Williams (Toronto: McClelland and Stewart, 1991) 199-222.

54 Author's conversation with John P. Petch, a lawyer with the Calgary firm Howard Mackie.

55 The 1994-95 budget was $200 million, but within a year the Plan had already run up a $70 million deficit. (Kirk Makin, "Funding woes put legal aid on trial," *The Globe and Mail* 14 Nov. 1995: A6.) The earlier figures come from the Ontario Legal Aid Plan's Annual Reports, published by The Law Society of Upper Canada, 1968 to the present.

56 From 1985 to 1995, 11.6 per cent annual growth in legal aid budget, adjusting for inflation. During the same time-frame, Ontario's population grew by only 1.7 per cent; its crime rate by 1.7 per cent; and its economy by 2.7 per cent. (Editorial, "Reforming legal aid as guide for future," *The Globe and Mail* 27 Dec. 1996: A16; "Crime-fighting costs near $10B," *The Calgary Sun* 29 Nov. 1994. The figure for 1988 was $300 million.

57 Michael Valpy "Legal-aid system is an easy political target" (*The Globe and Mail* 12 Sept. 1995): A22. Of the $263.4 million total, $118.7 goes for criminal cases, $95.1 million for family law matters (child custody and support orders) and $20.2 on other miscellaneous civil matters; "Legal Aid Assists Over 400,000 in 1990-91," Law Society of Upper Canada press release, 25 March 1992; *Singh v. Canada (Minister of Employment and Immigration)*, [1985] 2 S.C.R. 177.

58 Epp "Do Bills of Rights Matter?" 765, 776.

59 Ontario Legal Aid Annual Reports show that from 1980 to 1985 – the year that Charter appeals began to reach the Supreme Court – expenditures for appeals to the SCC averaged less than $100,000 annually. By 1990, this expenditure category reached $250,000.

60 "Poor parents must be given legal aid," *Calgary Herald* (11 Sept. 1999): A6; *New Brunswick v. G. (J.)*, Supreme Court of Canada (10 Sept. 1999), unreported.

61 Janice Tibbetts, "High Court expands legal aid's limit again," *National Post* 16 Sept. 1999: A8; *Winters v. Legal Services Society*, Supreme Court of Canada (15 Sept. 1999), unreported.

62 The Law Foundation of British Columbia, 1995 Annual Report.

63 B.C. Public Advocacy Centre, *Ten Year Report* (1991).

64 The Law Foundation of British Columbia, 1995 Annual Report.

65 Its Law Foundation aside, Ontario has provided the Court Party with a variety of other resources. Cf. discussion in ch. 5, p. 116, 119, 120, 122.

66 Pal 45.

67 While not as explicit as here, this is an important theme in Pal, ch.6.

Notes to chapter five

1   Pal 23.

2   Pal 42.

3   "Lobbying on the Internet," *The Globe and Mail*, 22 Sept. 1997: A19.

4   Paul Brantingham and Stephen T. Easton, "The Crime Bill: Who Pays and How Much?" *Fraser Forum* (Feb. 1996); "Court reform: safe for democracy," editorial, *The Globe and Mail*, 19 Sept. 1996: A22.

5   Owen Lippert, "Law and Markets," 10 Sept. 1997 [unpublished].

6   *Reference re Remuneration of Judges of the Provincial Court of PEI; Reference re: Independence and Impartiality of the Provincial Court of PEI*, [1997] 3 S.C.R. 3 at 109.

7   *Re Renumeration of Judges of the Provincial Court*, 184, 191, 195-96; Section 11(d) reads: "Any person charged with an offense has the right ... to be presumed innocent until proven guilty according to law in a fair and public hearing by an *independent and impartial tribunal*" (emphasis added).

8   Campbell Clark, "Judges taking Quebec to court," *National Post*, 13 May 1999: A4.

9   Bob Beatty and Darcy Henton, "Province fights judges' pay hike," *Calgary Herald*, 26 Jan. 1999: A1; Ted Morton, "Judging the judges," *Calgary Herald*, 6 Feb. 1999: I-15; Daryl Slade and Darcy Henton, "Court orders pay raise for judges," *Calgary Herald*, 23 July 1999: A1.

10 Campbell Clark, "Judges taking Quebec to court," *National Post*, 13 May 1999: A4.

11 According to a 1996 Statistics Canada report, the average salary of Canada's 1,765 judges (a figure that includes both provincial and superior court judges) was $126,246. Specialist physicians came in second at $123,976, then dentists at $102,433, and senior managers of manufacturing, transportation or utility companies at $99,360. Lawyers made an average of $81,617 and engineers $72,543. The average salary for university professors was $68,195. "1996 Census," Sources of Income, Earnings and Total Income, and Family Income (Stats Can. Cat. No. 11-001E, ISSN 0827-0465) 13.

12 The "filter" metaphor is used by Lorne Sossin, "The Sounds of Silence: Law Clerks, Policy-Making and the Supreme Court of Canada," *University of British Columbia Law Review* 30 (1996): 279, 292, 308.

13 Donald J. Savoie, *Governing From the Centre: The Concentration of Power in Canadian Politics* (Toronto: University of Toronto Press, 1999) 7.

14 Neil Seeman, "Who runs Canada," *National Post*, 24 July 1999: B3.

15 Seeman.

16 Those who praise the section 1/Oakes Test as a distinctively Canadian approach to rights litigation will be disappointed to learn that Bakan sees it as a distillation of the various balancing tests developed by the US Supreme Court, something that Bakan had studied as a graduate student at Harvard. Independent anonymous sources.

17 Brian Dickson, "The Public Responsibilities of Lawyers," *Manitoba Law Journal* 13 (1983): 186.

18 Independent anonymous sources. Bakan was not completely without influence in this case. Unlike the majority, Dickson did interpret freedom of association to include the right to strike, but then upheld the Alberta statute on section 1 reasonable limits grounds.

19 Edward Lazarus, *Closed Chambers: The First Eyewitness Account of the Epic Struggles Inside the Supreme Court* (New York: Times Books, 1998) 271.

20 Lazarus 273.

21 Robert Bork, *The Tempting of America: The Political Seduction of the Law* (New York: Simon and Schuster, 1990) 136.

22 These connections were first pointed out by Troy Q. Riddell, "The Development of Section 1 of the Charter of Rights: A Study in Constitutional Politics," M.A. thesis, University of Calgary, 1994: 68, fn. 125.

23 Sossin 303.

24 Lazarus 263.

25 Mary Eberts, Lecture, Faculty of Law, University of Calgary, 7 Dec. 1988. For details of the case, see Morton, *Morgentaler v. Borowski* 252-56.

26 Sossin 302; 303, fn. 68.

27 For France, see Stone; for Germany, see Donald Kommers, "The Federal Constitutional Court in the German Political System," *Comparative Political Studies* 26: 4 (Jan. 1994): 470-491; and for the UK, see Kate Malleson, "A British Bill of Rights: Incorporating the European Convention on Human Rights," in "Judicial Power in Canada and Britain," *Choices* 5:1 (1999): 21-36.

28 Julia Gulej, "Tribunal rewrites rights code to give gays 'spousal' benefits," *The Lawyers' Weekly* 11 Sept. 1992: 1. The case is *Leshner v. Ontario*, [1992] 16 C.H.R.R. 184; also "Employers must offer equal benefits to same-sex couples, OHRC decides," *The Lawyers Weekly* 20 Aug. 1993: 11. The case is *Clinton v. Ontario Blue Cross*, O.H.R.C. [unreported]. The Public Service Staff Relations arbitrator ruled that Ottawa violated human rights law by not allowing a gay public servant a family-related leave to attend his ailing partner; cf. Margaret Philp, "Gay employee wins family leaves," *The Globe and Mail*, 2 Oct. 1993: A3; Estanislao Ozlewicz, "Refugee delays ruled unlawful," *The Globe and Mail*, 10 Oct. 1991: A1; *Singh v. Minister of Employment and Immigration*, (1985) 17 D.L.R. (4th) 422.

29 *Cooper v. Canada (Human Rights Commission)*, [1996] 3 S.C.R. 854 at 869, 870, 878-880.

30 See the profiles of selected Court Party activists in chapter 6.

31 Reva Devins, "A Perspective From the Ontario Human Rights Commission," Monahan and Finkelstein 145, 152.

32 Devins 153.

33 Devins 150-151; *The Lawyers' Weekly* 11 Sept. 1992: 1. The case is *Leshner v. Ministry of the Attorney-General*, [1992] 16 C.H.R.R. 184.

34 Knopff, *Human Rights and Social Technology*.

35 *Haig and Birch v. Canada*, (1992) 95 D.L.R. (4th) 1.

36 Herman 203.

37 See Graham Haig, "Legal recognition," *The Globe and Mail*, 8 May 1997: A22.

38 For details of this whole issue, see Brodie, "Interest Groups and the Supreme Court of Canada" 167-73.

39 *Rosenberg v. Canada (Attorney General)*, (1998) 38 O.R. (3d) 577.

40 Edward Greenspan, "Reform seeks curbs on judicial activism," *The Globe and Mail*, 9 June 1998: A4; Sheldon Alberts, "Calgary Reform MP stirs up political storm over same-sex ruling," *Calgary Herald*, 9 June 1998: A7.

41 These included: Canadian AIDS Society; Canadian Association of Elizabeth Fry Societies; Charter Committee on Poverty Issues; Chinese Canadian National Council; Coalition for Lesbian and Gay Rights in Ontario; DisAbled Women's Network; End Legislated Poverty; EGALE; Minority Advocacy Rights Council; National Action Committee on the Status of Women; National Association of Women and the Law; Table feministe francophone; Metro Toronto Chinese and Southeast Asian Legal Clinic.

42 *Reference re Education Act of Ontario and Minority Language Education Rights*, (1984) 10 D.L.R. (4th) 491; *Blainey v. Ontario Hockey Association*, (1985) 52 O.R. (2d) 225 (Ont. H.C.); Ian Scott, "Law, Policy and the Role of the Attorney General: Constancy and Change in the 1980s," *University of Toronto Law Journal* 39 (1989): 109-126.

43 Sean Fine, "Courts lead politicians on gay rights," *The Globe and Mail* 12 May 1995: A4; Virginia Galt, "Lesbian pairs allowed to adopt," *The Globe and Mail* 11 May 1995: A1.

44 Thomas Claridge, "Ontario backtracks on legal definition of spouse," *The Globe and Mail* 13 Sept. 1995: A2.

45 *M. v. H.*, (1996) O.R. (3d) 593; 608.

46 Manfredi, "Constitutional Rights and Interest Advocacy" 91-117.

47 Monahan and Finkelstein 1-48; 16-24; 10.

48 Monahan and Finkelstein 43; Brodie, "The Charter and the Policy Process" 234.

49 Monahan and Finkelstein 6, 7, 37.

50 David Lepofsky, personal interview, Toronto, 14 Dec. 1994.

51 Monahan and Finkelstein 13, 16.

52 Standing Committee on Justice and Human Rights, 17 Feb. 1998, http://www.parl.gc.ca/InfoComDoc/JURI/Meetings/Evidence/juriev28-e.htm#T1540.

53 *R. v. Stillman* (1997), 113 C.C.C. (3d) 321.

54 I. Brodie, "Interest Groups and The Supreme Court" ch. 5.

55 Canada, Department of Justice, *Toward Equality* (Ottawa: Ministry of Supply and Services, 1986) 3-4, 13, 49-56.

56 Helene Goulet and Jim Hendry, "Systemic Discrimination," Fourth Annual Conference on Human Rights and the Charter, Department of Justice, Human Rights Law Section, 16-17 Nov. 1992; National Symposium on Women, Law, and the Administration of Justice, Vancouver, B.C., 1991 (Ottawa: Department of Justice, 1992); "Lawyers win concessions from Ottawa on rape bill," *The Toronto Star* 3 June 1992: A3.

57 Shawn W. Ho, "The Macro- and Micro-Constitutional Strategies of Provincial Govern-ments in Charter Politics: A Study of Alberta, Saskatchewan and Ontario 1982-1992," M.A. thesis, University of Calgary, 1995.

58 Lauri Hausegger, "The Effectiveness of Interest Group Litigation: An Assessment of LEAF's Participation in Supreme Court Cases," M.A. thesis, University of Calgary, 1994.

59 I. Brodie "Interest Groups and The Supreme Court" ch. 5.

60 No systematic study has been done of the Harris government's Charter factums. How-ever, Harris's outspoken political opposition to employment equity and wage equity clearly put him at odds with the feminists and the Court Party. There is also the one well-publicized incident involving the *M. v. H.* lesbian palimony case in which Harris's Attorney-General switched positions completely. See Thomas Claridge, "Ontario back-tracks on legal definition of spouse," *The Globe and Mail* 13 Sept. 1995: A2.

61 For a more elaborate account, see I. Brodie, "Interest Groups and the Supreme Court of Canada" ch. 5.

62 Mary Dawson, "The Impact of the Charter on the Public Policy Process and the Depart-ment of Justice," Monahan and Finkelstein 61.

63 Monahan and Finkelstein 12; Dawson 52.

64 Allan Linden, former LRC Commissioner, personal interview 1 June 1995.

65 See Harvie and Foster, "Different Drummers, Different Drums" and "Ties that Bind"; also Manfredi, *Judicial Power and the Charter* ch. 4.

66 This thesis and the following evidence are drawn from Long.

67 Law Reform Commission of Canada, *Twentieth Annual Report* (Ottawa: Minister of Supply and Services, 1991) 4.

68 *Hunter (Director of Investigation and Research) v. Southam Inc.*, [1984] 2 S.C.R. 145; *R. v. Duarte*, [1990] 1 S.C.R. 30. and *R. v. Wiggins*, [1990] 1 S.C.R. 62; *R. v. Therens*, [1985] 1 S.C.R. 613; *R. v. Manninen*, [1987] 1 S.C.R. 1233; *R. v. Dersch*, [1990] 2 S.C.R. 1505 and *R. v. Garafoli*, [1990] 2 S.C.R. 1421; *R. v. Stinchcombe*, [1991] 3 S.C.R. 326; *R. v. Askov*, [1990] 2 S.C.R. 1199 and *R. v. Morin*, [1992] 1 S.C.R. 771; *R. v. Collins*, [1987] 1 S.C.R. 265; *Reference re Section 94(2) of the Motor Vehicle Act (British Columbia)*, [1985] 2 S.C.R. 486; *R. v. Vaillancourt*, [1987] 2 S.C.R. 636; *R. v. Martineau*, [1990] 2 S.C.R. 633; *R. v. Daviault* [1994] 3 S.C.R. 63; *R. v. Chaulk*, [1990] 3 S.C.R. 1303; *R. v. Landry*, [1991] 1 S.C.R. 99.

69 Long 130.

70 *R. v. Manninen*, [1987] 1 S.C.R. 1233; *R. v. Ross*, [1989] 1 S.C.R. 3; *R. v. Brydges* [1990] 1 S.C.R 190; *R. v. Bartle*, [1994] 3 S.C.R. 173; *R. v. Mills* [1986] 1 S.C.R. 863; *R. v. Collins*, [1987] 1 S.C.R. 265; *Reference re B.C. Motor Vehicle Act*, [1985] 2 S.C.R. 486; *R. v. Vaillancourt*, [1987] 2 S.C.R. 636; *R. v. Martineau*, [1990] 2 S.C.R. 633; *R. v. Daviault*, [1994] 3 S.C.R. 63; *R. v. Chaulk*, [1990] 3 S.C.R. 1303; *R. v. Landry*, [1991] 1 S.C.R. 99.

71 Long 5.

72 Dale Gibson, "Judges as Legislators: Not Whether but How," *Alberta Law Review* 25 (1987): 263.

73 It was founded as the Canadian Judicial Centre in 1988, but changed its title to National Judicial Institute in 1990.

74 Canada, Library of Parliament, *Hansard* (House of Commons Debates) 15 Sept. 1992: 13185.

75 "Mandatory gender 'sensitivity training' soon for judges?" *The Lawyers' Weekly* 27 Sept. 1991: 16.

76 *The Lawyers' Weekly* 27 Sept. 1991: 16.

77 Atcheson, Eberts, and Symes 172.

78 Judge Gerald Seniuk, "Training centre for judges tackles sensitive social issues," *National*, Oct. 1993: 8.

79 Judge John Maher, as quoted in *National*, Oct. 1993.

80 *National*, Oct. 1993: 8.

81 Canada, Canadian Advisory Council of the Status of Women, *1986-87 Annual Report* (Ottawa: Ministry of Supply and Services).

82 "Canada's judges go back to school," *National,* Sept. 1991: 30.

83 *The Lawyers Weekly* 27 Sept. 1991: 16; *National*, Sept. 1991: 30.

84 Sheilah Martin and Kathleen Mahoney, eds., *Equality and Judicial Neutrality* (Scarborough: Carswell, 1987).

85 David Vienneau, "Some judges balking at anti-sexism training," *The Toronto Star* 10 Dec. 1991: B1, B8.

86 Letter from C. Gwendolyn Landolt, National Vice-President of REAL Women, to David Marshall, Executive Director, Canadian Judicial Institute, 4 March 1991.

87 T. David Marshall, *Judicial Conduct and Accountability* (Scarborough: Carswell, 1995) 58.

88 See Janice Tibbetts and Shawn Ohler, "Sex-assault ruling sparks judicial war of words," *National Post* 26 Feb. 1999: A1; Shawn Ohler, "Judge reiterates belief that that teen wasn't assaulted," *National Post* 27 Feb. 1999: A1; Shawn Ohler, "Judge apologizes for 'cruel' attack on senior justice," *National Post* 2 March 1999: A1; Shawn Ohler, "Groundswell of support rises for embattled McClung," *National Post* 3 March 1999: A6; Robert Fife, "McClung reprimanded for critical remarks made at L'Heureux-Dubé," *National Post* 22 May 1999: A4.

89 Fife.

Notes to Chapter Six

1 James C. MacPherson, "Working Within the Dickson Court," *Manitoba Law Journal* 20 (1991): 519, 523.

2 Glendon 218.

3 Russell, "The Political Purposes of the Charter" 37.

4 Walter S. Tarnopolsky, "The Charter and the Supreme Court of Canada," *The Charter Ten Years Later* ed. Gerald-A. Beaudoin (Les Editions Yvon Blais, Inc., 1992) 63-70 at 63.

Tarnopolsky specifically identifies Professor Dale Gibson and the other academics who conducted a cross-country "Charter Tour" in early 1982. This group met with judges and encouraged them to adopt a more activist approach to the Charter than they had to the 1960 Bill of Rights.

5 Marc Gold, "The Mask of Objectivity: Politics and Rhetoric in the Supreme Court of Canada," *Supreme Court Law Review* 7 (1985): 460.

6 Foster 780.

7 Justice l'Heureux-Dubé, Lecture, University of Calgary Faculty of Law, 23 Oct. 1996, as quoted by Greener 3.

8 Alec Stone, review of *The Constitutional Jurisprudence of the Federal Republic of Germany* by Donald P. Kommers (Durham, NC: Duke University Press, 1994) and *La politique saisie par le droit* (Paris: Economica, 1988) by Louis Favoreau, *Comparative Political Studies* (Oct. 1990): 413. See also Stone 104.

9 Michael Keren, *Professionals Against Populism: The Peres Government and Democracy* (New York: State University of New York Press, 1995) 10.

10 Bora Laskin, "The Supreme Court of Canada: A Final Court of and for Canadians," *Canadian Bar Review* 29 (1951): 1038-1079 at 1046.

11 David A.A. Stager and Harry W. Arthurs, *Lawyers in Canada* (Toronto: University of Toronto Press, 1990) 302; 303.

12 Stager and Arthurs 84-91; 304.

13 Louis Fisher, *Constitutional Dialogues: Interpretation as a Political Process* (Princeton University Press, 1988) 17.

14 Robert Martin, "Reconstituting Democracy: Orthodoxy and Research in Law and Social Science," Peacock 249.

15 Stager and Arthurs, Chapters 8, 9.

16 John Fekete, *Moral Panic: Biopolitics Rising* (Montreal/Toronto: Robert Davies Publishing: 1994) 204.

17 Borovoy.

18 Russell "The Political Purposes of the Charter" 38.

19 See J. Mark Tushnet, "Critical Legal Studies: A Political History," 100 *Yale Law Review* 115 (1991); Eleanor Kerlow, *Poisoned Ivy: How Egos, Ideology, and Power Politics Almost Ruined Harvard Law School* (New York: St. Martin's Press, 1994); and Charles Sellers, *The Market Revolution: Jacksonian America, 1815-1846* (New York and Oxford: Oxford University Press, 1991) 47.

20 "When Jurors Ignore the Law," *New York Times* 27 May 1997: A24.

21 "For black scholars wedded to prism of race, new and separate goals," *New York Times* 5 May 1997: A14.

22 Martin Loney, "Prejudice in the law schools," *National Post*, 21 April 1999: A18; Martin Loney, "Some more equal than others," *National Post*, 22 Sept. 1999: A18.

23 As of June 1996, the NAWL national office in Ottawa reported having caucuses at the

following university law schools: Victoria, Alberta, Calgary, Saskatchewan, Osgoode Hall, Toronto, Queen's, Western, Montreal, McGill, and Dalhousie.

24 NAWL, "General Information Package," April 1995.

25 Russell, "The Effect of the Charter of Rights" 16.

26 Walter S. Tarnopolsky, *The Canadian Bill of Rights*, 2nd ed. (Toronto: McClelland and Stewart, 1975); Walter S. Tarnopolsky, *Discrimination and the Law in Canada* (Toronto: Richard De Boo, 1982).

27 "Time magazine recognizes Saskatchewan judge as leader," *National Post*, 23 Sept. 1999: A10.

28 The term comes from Tuchman (1978), as reported by Miljan, "Courts and the Media," 10.

29 See Morton, *Morgentaler v. Borowski* 233.

30 See discussion of clerks in chapter 5, pp. 110-13.

31 Greene et al., 150.

32 Dawson, "Oral remarks," Round-table Conference.

33 Martin Shapiro, "Public Law and Judicial Politics," *The State of the Discipline II*, ed. A.W. Finifter, (Washington, DC: APSA, 1993): 373.

34 Atcheson, Eberts, and Symes 172, emphasis added.

35 Marilou McPhedran, address, "Critical Perspectives on the Constitution," University of Western Ontario, March 1983; as recounted in Mandel, *The Charter of Rights* 40.

36 Razack 37; Sheilah McIntyre, "Journey throughout uncharted territory," *Broadside* (March 1983), as cited in Hein, "Social Movements and the Expansion of Judicial Power" 228.

37 Thomas E. Flanagan, review of, *Equality Rights and the Canadian Charter of Rights and Freedoms* by Anne F. Bayefsky and Mary Eberts, eds. (Toronto: Carswell, 1985), *Canadian Journal of Law and Society* 1 (1986): 174-76.

38 Postmaterialist is here defined as journals/reporters whose primary focus or content involves one or more of the following: rights, minorities, justice or equality issues, environment, feminism, law and society. The journals are: *Supreme Court Law Review; Intervenor; Educational Law Journal, Law Now, Environmental Law Alert, Environmental Policy and Law*, and *Journal of Environmental Law and Practice; Canadian Rights Reporter, Canadian Human Rights Yearbook, Canadian Human Rights Advocate, Canadian Journal of Women and the Law, Windsor Yearbook of Access to Justice, Droit et Libertés, Actualités-Justice, Canadian Journal of Law and Society, Focus on Canadian Employment and Equality Rights, Constitutional Forum, Windsor Review of Legal and Social Issues, National Journal of Constitutional Law, Review of Constitutional Studies, IR/HR Legal Review*.

39 Cairns, "Ritual, Taboo, and Bias in Constitutional Controversies" 281.

40 See David Schneiderman, ed., "Conversations Among Friends," Proceedings of an interdisciplinary conference on Women and Constitutional Reform, Centre for Constitutional Studies, University of Alberta, 1992.

41 V.O. Key, *Politics, Parties and Pressure Groups* (New York: Thomas Y. Crowell, 1958) 154.

42 Monahan and Finkelstein 46.

43 Shapiro "Public Law and Judicial Politics" 374.

44 The major exceptions to this are feminists who write in support of censorship of obscenity and against the rights of male defendants in sexual assault cases, and Quebec nationalists who support narrow interpretations of the language rights of the anglophone minority.

45 Riddell.

46 Dickson 186.

47 The original wording of Section 1 was an attempt to appease the opponents of judicial power – the eight provincial governments who opposed Trudeau's Charter project. When this original wording was sharply criticized by feminists and civil libertarians, the Trudeau government responded by adopting the current wording. Cf. Riddell 6-16.

48 Riddell 42-46; 46-50; 50-53.

49 *R. v. Oakes*, [1986] 1 S.C.R. 103.

50 See Bernard M. Dickens, "A Canadian Development: Non-Party Intervention," *Modern Law Review* 40 (1977): 666-676; James V. West, "Public Interest Groups and the Judicial Process in Canada: The Need for a More Realistic Jurisprudence," *Occasional Paper no. 5* (Carleton University: Department of Political Studies, 1979); J. Welch, "No Room at the Top: Interest Group Intervenors and Charter Litigation in the Supreme Court of Canada," *University of Toronto Law Journal* 43 (1985): 204; Kenneth P. Swan, "Intervention and Amicus Curiae Status in Charter Litigation," *Charter Litigation* ed. Robert Sharpe, (Toronto: Butterworths, 1986): 27-44; Phillip L. Bryden, "Public Interest Intervention in the Courts," *Canadian Bar Review* 66 (1987): 491-527; I. Brodie, "Interest Groups and the Supreme Court of Canada," 181-85.

51 Jody Freeman, "Defining Family In *Mossop v. DSS*: The Challenge of Anti-Essentialism and Interactive Discrimination for Human Rights Legislation." *University of Toronto Law Journal* 44 (1994): 95 as cited in Greener 59.

52 Didi Herman, "Are We Family? Lesbian Rights and Women's Liberation," *Osgoode Hall Law Journal* 28.4 (Winter 1990): 803 as cited by Greener 54.

53 Herman, "The Good, the Bad, and the Smugly" 203.

54 Greener 9, 51.

55 Greener 7.

56 Freeman 73 as cited in Greener.

57 *Egan and Nesbitt v. Canada*, [1995] 2 S.C.R. 513; *M. v. H.*, [1999] 2 S.C.R. 3.

58 Carl Baar, "Court Delay Data as Social Science Evidence: The Supreme Court of Canada and 'Trial Within a Reasonable Time'" [unpublished] 18. Also see Baar, "Criminal Court Delay."

59 Eberts, Lecture, Faculty of Law, University of Calgary, 12 Jan. 1996.

60 Norberg v. Wynrib, [1992] 2 S.C.R. 226; Moge v. Moge, [1992] 3 S.C.R. 853. For LEAF's factum on both these cases see Women's Legal Education and Action Fund 223-44; 321-44. Noted in Hein, "Post-Materialists in Court" 22. R. v. Lavallée, [1990] 1 S.C.R. 853.

61 Christina Hoff Sommers, Who Stole Feminism: How Women Have Betrayed Women (New York: Touchstone Books, 1994) 189, 191.

62 Lenore Walker, The Battered Woman (New York: Harper Collins, 1979), xv, 98; cited in Michael Weiss and Cathy Young, "Feminist Jurisprudence or Neo-Paternalism?" Cato Policy Analysis No. 256 (June 19, 1996) fn. 216, 218 emphasis added; Walker 98, cited in Weiss and Young.

63 Doug Brown, "Wife-Battering: Normal for Many," Los Angeles Times, 20 June 1985: View Section, 1 (quoting and discussing a speech by Lenore Walker); cited in Weiss and Young, fn. 219.

64 Quoted in Brown; cited in Weiss and Young, fn. 225.

65 Lenore Walker, "Psychology and Violence Against Women," American Psychologist (April 1989): 695; cited in Weiss and Young, fn. 215.

66 Sommers 194.

67 Fekete 89; 76-78.

68 Brad Evenson and Carol Milstone, "Women emerge as aggressors in Alberta survey," National Post, 10 July 1999: A1, A2. The original research article was by Leslie Kennedy and Donald Dutton, "The Incidence of Wife Assault in Alberta," Canadian Journal of Behavioural Sciences 21: 1 (1989): 40-54. The follow-up study is by Marilyn J. Kwong, Kim Bartholomew, and Donald G. Dutton, "Gender Differences in Patterns of Relationship Violence in Alberta," Canadian Journal of Behavioural Science 31: 3 (July 1999): 150-160.

69 Sommers 51, 62.

70 Karen O'Connor, Women's Organizations' Use of the Courts (Toronto: Lexington Books, 1980) 26.

71 Weiss and Young 3.

72 Razack 81.

73 Quoted in Seeman B3.

74 Sossin 299, 300.

75 Dickson 179, 180.

76 Greene et al. 150.

77 Jack W. Peltason, Federal Courts in the Judicial Process (New York: Random House, 1995) 52.

78 O'Connor 26.

Notes to Chapter Seven

1 A corollary criticism, which we do not develop here, is that the Charter Revolution is also bad for the courts because it is eroding judicial independence. While the adoption of the Charter made it inevitable that the Supreme Court would be invited to take

sides in what would otherwise be ordinary political disputes, it need not have accepted this invitation. There was an alternative route. Circumscribed by traditional restrictions on access and animated by a search for neutral principles that are indifferent to parties and specific outcomes, the Court's decisions would have been less glamorous but more prudent. By rejecting this more modest role and accepting the invitation of the Court Party to take sides, the Court has attained short-term power, but at the expense of its longer-term independence. American experience with judicial review demonstrates (repeatedly) that judicial over-reaching inevitably incites a political reaction. In time, political majorities re-establish a balance between elected governments and unelected judges. The Canadian Supreme Court's embrace of the Court Party agenda ensures that control of the court – mainly via appointments – will become an object of partisan competition. Judicial independence will suffer, as will the quality of the judges being appointed. It remains to be seen how serious the damage will be.

2 Russell, *Constitutional Odyssey* 5.

3 Russell, "The Effect of a Charter of Rights on the Policy-Making Role of Canadian Courts" 32.

4 Russell, "The Political Purposes of the Charter" 33-44.

5 Charterphilia should be distinguished from rights consciousness. As Russell and other commentators have pointed out, Quebecers are just as rights conscious as other Canadians. It is the imposed Charter, not rights, that they do not like.

6 See F.L. Morton, "The Charter and Canada outside Quebec," McRoberts, *Beyond Quebec* 93-116.

7 Some of the original 13 states had bills of rights prior to the present US Constitution. However, by comparison with the US Bill of Rights, which has become the model for modern bills of rights generally, they were quite limited in scope. Only two, for example, guaranteed freedom of speech. Many permitted religious establishments. And protections now considered routine, such as freedom of assembly, right to counsel, and protection against double jeopardy, were far from common. See Michael J. Sandel, *Democracy's Discontent* (Cambridge, MA: Harvard University Press, 1996) 35.

8 See Walter Berns, "The Constitution as a Bill of Rights," and Herbert Storing, "The Constitution and the Bill of Rights," *How Does the Constitution Secure Rights?*, ed. Robert A. Goldwin and William A. Schambra (Washington, DC: American Enterprise Institute, 1985); Thomas L. Pangle, *The Spirit of Modern Republicanism: The Moral Vision of the American Founders and the Philosophy of Locke* (Chicago: University of Chicago Press, 1988) 71-2, 125; Judith A. Best, "Fundamental Rights and the Structure of Government," and Robert A. Goldwin, "Congressman Madison Proposes Amendments to the Constitution," *The Framers and Fundamental Rights*, ed. Robert A. Licht (Washington, DC: AEI Press, 1993); Knopff and Morton, *Charter Politics* 173-5; Joseph M. Bessette, "Guarding the Constitution from Legislative Tyranny," *Is the Supreme Court the Guardian of the Constitution?*, ed. Robert A. Licht (Washington, DC: AEI Press, 1993); Manfredi, *Judicial Power and the Charter* 23-5;

Bradley C. S. Watson, "The Language of Rights and the Crisis of the Liberal Imagination," Peacock 88-91; Sandel 33-9.

9   See *Federalist Papers* Nos. 9, 10, and 51.

10 *Federalist Papers* Nos. 10, 63. These terms were used in reference to the Senate but apply with lesser force to the House as well.

11 *Federalist Papers* No. 78.

12 See Knopff and Morton, *Charter Politics* chap. 5.

13 Janet Ajzenstat, *The Political Thought of Lord Durham* (Montreal/Kingston: McGill-Queen's University Press, 1988) 71.

14 Janet Ajzenstat, "Reconciling Parliament and Rights: A.V. Dicey Reads the Canadian Charter of Rights and Freedoms," Annual Meeting of the Canadian Political Science Association (June 1996) 1, 2.

15 Ajzenstat, "Reconciling Parliament" 8, 16-17, 18, 19, 23-4, 25.

16 John Uhr, *Deliberative Democracy in Australia: The Changing Place of Parliament* (Cambridge: Cambridge University Press, 1998).

17 Walter Berns, *Taking the Constitution Seriously* (New York: Madison Books, 1987) 127.

18 See H.D. Forbes, "Trudeau's Moral Vision," Peacock 23.

19 See Knopff, "Populism and the Politics of Rights."

20 Peter H. Russell, "A Democratic Approach to Civil Liberties," *University of Toronto Law Journal* (1969): 107.

21 In the US, consider the Supreme Court's unwillingness to oppose Japanese-American relocations during World War II. In Uganda, when the Supreme Court began to intervene to stop Idi Amin's persecution of his political opponents, he ordered his secret police to shoot the judges. They did.

22 Donald Smiley, "The Case Against the Canadian Charter of Human Rights," *Canadian Journal of Political Science* 2 (1969): 277-91.

23 Bora Laskin, "An Inquiry into the Diefenbaker Bill of Rights," *Canadian Bar Review* 37 (1959): 79.

24 Mary Ann Glendon, *Rights Talk: The Impoverishment of Political Discourse* (New York: Free Press, 1991).

25 Alexander Bickel, *The Morality of Consent* (New Haven, CT: Yale University Press 1974).

26 *Federalist Papers* No. 10.

27 Berns 143.

28 David Taras, "Television and Public Policy: The CBC's Coverage of the Meech Lake Accord," *Canadian Public Policy* 15:3 (1989): 326.

29 Janet Ajzenstat, "The Decline of Procedural Liberalism," *Is Quebec Nationalism Just?*, ed. Joseph H. Carens (Montreal/Kingston: McGill-Queen's University Press, 1995) 130.

30 See Morton, *Morgentaler v. Borowski* 292.

31 Peter W. Hogg and Allison A. Bushell, "The Charter Dialogue between Courts and Leg-

islatures," *Osgoode Hall Law Journal* 35:1 (1997): 75-105. For a summary version of this argument, see Peter W. Hogg and Allison A. Thornton, "The Charter Dialogue between Courts and Legislatures," *Policy Options* 20:3 (1999): 19-23.

32 Eventually moderates did carry the day. See Scott Reid, "Penumbras for the People: Placing Judicial Supremacy Under Popular Control," Peacock 208. Nevertheless, the victory of moderation in this policy area was almost certainly delayed by the Signs Case.

33 *Ford v. Quebec (A.G.)*, [1988] 2 S.C.R. 712.

34 Russell, *Constitutional Odyssey* 146.

35 See Troy Riddell and F.L. Morton, "Competition for Constitutional Advantage: Reasonable Limits, Distinct Society, and the Canada Clause," *Canadian Journal of Political Science* 31:3 (1998): 467-493.

36 Hogg and Bushell 105.

37 Thomas Flanagan, "The Staying Power of the Legislative Status Quo: Collective Choice in Canada's Parliament after *Morgentaler*," *Canadian Journal of Political Science* 30:1 (1997).

38 Raymond Tatalovich, *The Politics of Abortion in the United States and Canada: A Comparative Study* (Armonk, NY: M.E. Sharpe, 1997) Table 4.1, 111.

39 Tatalovich 109 and ch. 4.

40 For details, see Morton, *Morgentaler v. Borowski* ch. 23.

41 For details, see Flanagan, ""The Staying Power of the Legislative Status Quo."

42 Glendon found that when "the legislative process is allowed to operate" the result is likely to be a middle-ground, policy compromise "that is apt to be distasteful to pro-life and pro-choice activists alike." Mary Ann Glendon, *Abortion and Divorce in Western Law* (Cambridge, MA: Harvard University Press, 1987) 40.

43 See "Klein ponders overruling courts on gay rights," *Calgary Herald*, 7 April 1998: A1; "Klein urged to nix gay rights," *Calgary Sun*, 13 April 1998: 4; George Koch, "How Klein ignored his supporters," *The Globe and Mail*, 16 April 1998: A23. On a different but related issue, see Rainer Knopff and Fred Wall, "Same-sex marriage issue drives a wedge among the right," *Calgary Herald*, 13 April 1999: H5.

44 The Klein Government's own surveys after the Supreme Court's ruling in *Vriend* indicated that only 1 per cent of Albertans identified "human rights" or "gay rights" as a "main issue of concern" in response to an open-ended question. See "Report of the Ministerial Task Force," 3 March 1999: 5 [unpublished].

45 Don Martin, "In rare move, Klein imposes his will on caucus," *Calgary Herald*, 10 April 1998: A15.

46 Hogg and Thornton 21.

47 Hogg and Bushell 81.

48 The lack of party discipline in a presidential system allows, even encourages, dissident members of the president's own party to challenge his leadership on issues such as abortion and gay rights.

LIST OF CASES CITED

Adkins v. Children's Hospital, 261 U.S. 525 (1923).

Andrews v. Law Society of British Columbia, [1989] 1 S.C.R. 143.

Association des Parents Francophones (Columbie Brittanique) v. British Columbia, [1996] 27 B.C.L.R. (3d) 83.

Attorney General of Canada v. Attorney General of Ontario (Labour Conventions Case), [1937] A.C. 327.

Attorney General of Canada v. Lavell and Bedard, [1974] S.C.R. 1349.

Attorney General of Canada v. Mossop, (1993) 100 D.L.R. (4th) 658.

Attorney General of Quebec v. Blaikie, [1979] 2 S.C.R. 1016.

Attorney General of Quebec v. Quebec Association of Protestant School Boards, [1984] 2 S.C.R. 66.

Australian Capital Television Pty Ltd. v. The Commonwealth, 66 ALJR 695.

Bilodeau v. Attorney General (Manitoba), [1986] 1 S.C.R. 449.

Birks and Sons (Montreal) Ltd. v. Montreal, [1955] 1 S.C.R. 799.

Blainey v. Ontario Hockey Association, (1985) 52 O.R. (2d) 225 (Ont H.C.); (1986) 54 O.R. (2d) 177.

Bliss v. Canada (Attorney General), [1979] 1 S.C.R. 183.

Boucher v. The King, [1951] 1 S.C.R. 265.

Borowski v. Canada, [1989] 1 S.C.R. 342.

Braunfield v. Brown, 366 U.S. 599 (1961).

Brownridge v. The Queen, [1972] S.C.R. 926.

Chaput v. Romain, [1955] S.C.R. 834.

Chromiak v. The Queen, [1980] 1 S.C.R. 471.

Cooper v. Canada (Human Rights Commission), [1986] 3 S.C.R. 854.

Cuddy Chicks Ltd. v. Ontario Labour Board, (1991) 81 D.L.R. (4th) 121.

Daigle v. Tremblay, (1989) 59 D.L.R. (4th) 609 (Que. C.A.).

Dersch v. Canada (Attorney General), [1990] 2 S.C.R. 1505.

Dolphin Delivery Ltd. v. R.W.D.S.U. Local 580, [1986] 2 S.C.R. 573.

Drybones v. The Queen, [1970] S.C.R. 282.

Dubois v. The Queen, [1985] 2 S.C.R. 350.

Edwards Books and Art Ltd. v. The Queen, [1986] 2 S.C.R. 713.

Egan and Nesbitt v. Canada, [1995] 2 S.C.R. 513.

Eldridge v. British Columbia (Attorney General), [1997] 3 S.C.R. 493.

Finlay v. Canada (Minister of Finance), [1986] 2 S.C.R. 607.

Forest v. Manitoba, [1979] 2 S.C.R. 1032.

Galagher v. Crownkosher Supermarkets of Massachussetts, 366 U.S. 617 (1961).

Haig v. Canada, (1991) 5 O.R. (3d) 245.

Haig and Birch v. Canada, [1992] 57 O.A.C. 272.

Haig and Birch v. Canada, (1992) 95 D.L.R. (4th) 1.

Hogan v. The Queen, [1975] 2 S.C.R. 574.

Hunter (Director of Investigation and Research). v. Southam Inc., [1984] 2 S.C.R. 145.

Lavigne v. Ontario Public Service Employees Union, [1991] 2 S.C.R. 211.

Lavoie v. Nova Scotia, (1988) 47 D.L.R. (4th) 586 (N.S.S.C.T.D.); (1989) 58 D.L.R. (4th) 293 (N.S.S.C.A.D.).

Leshner v. Ontario, [1992] 16 C.H.R.R. 184.

Lochner v. New York, 198 U.S. 45 (1905).

M. v. H., [1999] 2 S.C.R. 3; (1996) O.R. (3d) 593.

MacDonald v.City of Montreal, [1986] 1 S.C.R. 549.

Mahé v. Alberta, (1990) 68 D.L.R. (4th) 69.

Mahé v. Alberta, [1990] 1 S.C.R. 342.

Marchand v. Simcoe Board of Education, (1986) 29 D.L.R. (4th) 596 (Ont. H.C.J.).

McGowan v. Maryland, 366 U.S. 420 (1961).

McKinney v. University of Guelph, [1990] 2 S.C.R. 229.

Mercure v. Saskatchewan, [1988] 1 S.C.R. 234.

Minister of Justice v. Borowski, [1981] 2 S.C.R. 575.

Moge v. Moge, (1992) 99 D.L.R. (4th) 456.

Moore v. British Columbia, (1988) 50 D.L.R. (4th), 29.

Morgentaler v. The Queen, (1975) 20 C.C.C. (2d) 452.

Morgentaler v. The Queen, [1976] 1 S.C.R. 616.

Morgentaler v. The Queen, [1988] 1 S.C.R. 3.

Nationwide News v. Wills, [1992] 66 ALJR 658.

Native Women's Association of Canada v. Canada, [1994] 3 S.C.R. 627.

New Brunswick v. G.(J.), Supreme Court of Canada (Sept. 10, 1999), unreported.

Norberg v. Wynrib, [1992] 2 S.C.R. 226.

Quebec v. Ford et al., [1988] 2 S.C.R. 712.

R. v. Askov, [1990] 2 S.C.R. 1199.

R. v. Badger, [1996] 1 S.C.R. 771.

R. v. Bartle, [1994] 3 S.C.R. 173.

R. v. Big M Drug Mart, Ltd., [1985] 1 S.C.R. 295.

R. v. Brydges, [1990] 1 S.C.R. 190.

R. v. Butler, [1992] 1 S.C.R. 452.

R. v. Chaulk, [1990] 3 S.C.R. 1303.

R. v. Collins, [1987] 1 S.C.R. 265.

R. v. Daviault, [1994] 3 S.C.R. 63.

R. v. Dersch, [1990] 2 S.C.R. 1505.

R. v. Duarte, [1990] 1 S.C.R. 30.

R. v. Dyment, [1988] 2 S.C.R. 417.

R. v. Garafoli, [1990] 2 S.C.R. 1421.

R. v. Hebert, [1990] 2 S.C.R. 151.

R. v. Jacob, (1996) 31 O.R. (3d) 350.

R. v. Keegstra, [1990] 3 S.C.R. 697.

R. v. Landry, [1991] 1 S.C.R. 99.

R. v. Latimer, [1997] 1 S.C.R. 217.

R. v. Lavallee, [1990] 1 S.C.R. 853.

R. v. Manninen, [1987] 1 S.C.R. 1233.

R. v. Martineau, [1990] 2 S.C.R. 633.

R. v. Mercure, [1988] 1 S.C.R. 234.

R. v. Mills, [1986] 1 S.C.R. 863.

R. v. Morgentaler, [1993] 3 S.C.R. 463.

R. v. Morin, [1992] 1 S.C.R. 771.

R. v. Oakes, [1986] 1 S.C.R. 103.

R. v. P. (M.B.), [1994] 1 S.C.R. 555.

R. v. Ross, [1989] 1 S.C.R. 3.

R. v. Seaboyer; R. v. Gayme, [1991] 2 S.C.R. 577.

R. v. Sellars, [1980] 1 S.C.R. 527.

R. v. Sharpe, [1999] B.C.C.A. 416.

R. v. Sioui, [1990] 1 S.C.R. 1025.

R. v. Smith, [1987] 1 S.C.R. 1045.

R. v. Sparrow, [1990] 1 S.C.R. 1075.

R. v. Stillman, (1997) 113 C.C.C. (3d) 321.

R. v. Stillman, [1997] 1 S.C.R. 607.

R. v. Stinchcombe, [1991] 3 S.C.R. 326.

R. v. Sullivan, [1991] 1 S.C.R. 489.

R. v. Therens, [1985] 1 S.C.R. 613.

R. v. Underwood, [1998] 1 S.C.R. 77.

R. v. Vaillancourt, [1987] 2 S.C.R. 636.

R. v. Wiggins, [1990] 1 S.C.R. 62.

Reference re British Columbia Motor Vehicle Act, [1985] 2 S.C.R. 486.

Reference re Education Act, Ontario and Minority Language Education Rights, (1984), 10
    D.L.R. (4th) 491.

Ref. re Freedom of Informed Choice (Abortions) Act, 44 Saskatchewan Reports 104 (1985).

Reference re Language Rights under the Manitoba Act, 1870, [1985] 2 S.C.R. 347.

Reference re Public Schools Act, Manitoba, (1990) 67 D.L.R. (4th) 491.

Reference re Public Schools Act, Manitoba, s. 79 (3), (4) and (7), [1993] 1 S.C.R. 839.

Reference re Renumeration of Judges of the Provincial Court of PEI: Reference re Independence and Impartiality of the Provinicial Court of PEI, [1997] 3 S.C.R. 3.

Reference re School Act, PEI, (1988) 49 D.L.R. (4th) 499.

Regina v. Mercure, [1988] 1 S.C.R. 234.

Rodriguez v. British Columbia (Attorney General), [1993] 3 S.C.R. 519.

Roncarelli v. Duplessis, [1959] 1 S.C.R. 121.

Rosenberg v. Canada (Attorney General), (1998) 38 O.R. (3d) 577.

Rosetanni v. The Queen, [1963] 1 S.C.R. 651.

Saumur v. Quebec, [1953] 2 S.C.R. 299.

Schachter v. Canada, (1992) 93 D.L.R. (4th) 1.

Schacter v. Canada, [1992] 2 S.C.R. 679.

Schachtschneider v. The Queen, 93 D.T.C. 5308-5313.

Service Employees International Union, Local 204 v. Ontario (Attorney General), [1997] O.J.
No. 3563.

Singh v. Minister of Employment and Immigration, (1985) 17 D.L.R. (4th) 422.

Singh v. Canada (Minister of Employment and Immigration), [1985] 1 S.C.R. 177.

Skapinker v. Law Society of Upper Canada, [1984] 1 S.C.R. 357.

Société des Acadiens v. Association of Parents for Fairness in Education, (1986) 27 D.L.R. (4th)
406.

Société des Acadiens v. Association of Parents, [1986] 1 S.C.R. 549.

Stillman v. The Queen, Supeme Court of Canada (Court File No. 24631).

Switzman v. Elbling and Attorney-General of Quebec, [1957] S.C.R. 285.

Symes v. Canada, [1994] 3 S.C.R. 695.

The Queen v. Drybones, [1970] S.C.R. 282.

The Queen v. Keegstra, [1990] 3 S.C.R. 697.

The Queen v. Therens, [1985] 1 S.C.R. 613.

Thibaudeau v. Canada, [1995] 2 S.C.R.627.

Tremblay v. Daigle, [1989] 2 S.C.R. 530.

Vriend v. Alberta, [1998] 1 S.C.R. 493.

Winnipeg Child Services v. D.F.G., 138 D.L.R. (4th) 254 (Manitoba C.A. 1996).

Winters v. Legal Services Society, Supreme Court of Canada (Sept. 15, 1999), unreported.

Zylberberg v. Sudbury Board of Education, (1989) 52 D.L.R. (4th) 577.

SELECT BIBLIOGRAPHY

Ajzenstadt, Janet. *The Political Thought of Lord Durham*. Montreal/Kingston: McGill-Queen's University Press, 1988.

—. "The Decline of Procedural Liberalism." *Is Quebec Nationalism Just?* Ed. Joseph H. Carens. Montreal/Kingston: McGill-Queen's University Press, 1995.

Allen, Avril and F.L. Morton. "Feminists and the Courts: Measuring Success of Interest Group Litigation." Canadian Journal of Political Science (forthcoming).

Archer, Keith, Roger Gibbins, Rainer Knopff, and Leslie A. Pal. *Parameters of Power: Canada's Political Institutions*. 2nd ed. Toronto: ITP Nelson, 1999.

Atcheson, Elizabeth M., Mary Eberts, and Beth Symes. *Women and Legal Action: Precedents, Resources and Strategies for the Future*. Ottawa: Canadian Advisory Council on the Status of Women, 1984.

Baar, Carl. "Criminal Court Delay and the Charter: The Use and Misuse of Facts in Judicial Policy Making." *Canadian Bar Review* 72 (1993): 305-36.

Baar, Carl and Ellen Baar. "Diagnostic Adjudication in Appellate Courts: The Supreme Court of Canada and the Charter of Rights." *Osgoode Hall Law Journal* (1989): 1-25.

Bakan, Joel. *Just Words: Constitutional Rights and Civil Wrongs*. Toronto: University of Toronto Press, 1997.

Bakan, Joel and David Schneiderman, eds. *Social Justice and the Constitution: Perspectives on a Social Union for Canada*. Ottawa: Carleton University Press, 1992.

Banting, K. ed. *State and Society: Canada in a Comparative Perspective*. Toronto: University of Toronto Press, 1986.

Banting, Keith and Richard Simeon. *And No One Cheered: Federalism, Democracy and the Constitution Act*. Toronto: Methuen/Carswell, 1983.

Bayefsky, Anne F. and Mary Eberts, eds. *Equality Rights and the Charter of Rights and Freedoms*. Toronto: Carswell, 1985.

Berns, Walter. *The First Amendment and the Future of American Democracy*. New York: Basic Books, 1976.

—. "The Constitution as a Bill of Rights." *How Does the Constitution Secure Rights?* Ed. Robert A. Goldwin and William A. Schambra (Washington, DC: American Enterprise Institute, 1985), 50-73.

—. *Freedom, Virtue and the First Amendment*. New York: Greenwood Press, 1969.

—. *Taking the Constitution Seriously*. New York: Madison Books, 1997.

Bessette, Joseph M. "Guarding the Constitution from Legislative Tyranny." *Is the Supreme Court the Guardian of the Constitution?* Ed. Robert A. Licht. Washington, DC: AEI Press, 1993.

Best, Judith A. "Fundamental Rights and the Structure of Government," *The Framers and Fundamental Rights*. Ed. Robert A. Licht. Washington, DC: AEI Press 1993.

Bickel, Alexander M. *The Least Dangerous Branch: The Supreme Court at the Bar of Politics*. Indianapolis and New York: Bobbs-Merrill Co., 1962.

——. *The Morality of Consent*. New Haven, CT: Yale University Press, 1974.

Board, Joseph B. "Judicial Activism in Sweden." *Judicial Activism in a Comparative Perspective*. Ed. Kenneth Holland. New York: St. Martin's Press, 1991. 174-87.

Bork, Robert. *The Tempting of America: The Political Seduction of the Law*. New York: Free Press, 1990.

Borovoy, A. Allan. *The New Anti Liberals*. Toronto: Canadian Scholars Press, Inc., 1999.

Bottomley, Samuel. "Implied Constitutional Rights." M.A. thesis. University of Calgary, 1997.

Brantingham, Paul and Stephen T. Easton. "The Crime Bill: Who Pays and How Much?" *Fraser Forum* (Feb. 1996).

Brodie, Ian. "The Court Challenges Program." *Law, Politics and the Judicial Process in Canada*. Ed. F.L. Morton. Calgary: University of Calgary Press, 1992. 224-26.

——. "Interest Groups and the Supreme Court of Canada." Ph.D. thesis. University of Calgary, 1997.

Brodie, Ian and Neil Nevitte. "Evaluating the Citizens' Constitution Theory." *Canadian Journal of Political Science* 26:2 (1993): 235-360.

Brodie, Janine. "The Women's Movement Outside Quebec: Shifting Relations with the Canadian State." *Beyond Quebec: Taking Stock of Canada*. Ed. Kenneth McRoberts. Montreal/Kingston: McGill-Queen's University Press, 1995. 333-57.

Bryden, Philip L. "Public Interest Intervention in the Courts." *Canadian Bar Review* 66 (1987): 491-527.

Bryden, Philip, Steven Davis, and John Russell, eds. *Protecting Rights & Freedoms: Essays on the Charter's Place in Canada's Political, Legal, and Intellectual Life*. Toronto: University of Toronto Press, 1994.

Bzdera, André. "Comparative Analysis of Federal High Courts: A Political Theory of Judicial Review." *Canadian Journal of Political Science* 26 (1993): 1-29.

Cairns, Alan C. "The Charter: A Political Science Perspective." *The Impact of the Charter on the Public Policy Process*. Ed. Patrick Monahan and Marie Finkelstein. Toronto: Centre for Public Law and Public Policy, York University, 1993. 157-68.

——. "The Charter, Interest Groups, Executive Federalism and Constitutional Reform." *After Meech Lake: Lessons for the Future*. Ed. David E. Smith, Peter MacKinnon, and John C. Courtney. Saskatoon, SK: Fifth House Publishers, 1991. 13-31.

——. "Citizens (Outsiders) and Governments (Insiders) in Constitution Making: The Case of Meech Lake." *Canadian Public Policy* 14 (September, 1988): 121-45.

——. "The Embedded State: State-Society Relations in Canada." *State and Society: Canada in a Comparative Perspective*. Ed. K. Banting. Toronto: University of Toronto Press, 1986. 53-86.

——. "The Past and Future of the Canadian Administrative State" *University of Toronto Law Journal* 10 (1990): 319-61.

——. "Ritual, Taboo, and Bias in Constitutional Controversies, or Constitutional Talk Canadian Style." *Disruptions: Constitutional Struggles from the Charter to Meech Lake*. Ed. Douglas E. Williams. Toronto: McClelland and Stewart, 1991. 199-222.

Canada. Department of Justice. *Toward Equality*. Ottawa: Ministry of Supply and Services, 1986.

Carter, Donald D. "Employment Benefits and Same Sex Couples: The Expanding Entitlement." *Canadian Public Policy* 24:1 (1998).

Cheffins, R.I. "The Supreme Court of Canada: The Quiet Court in the Unquiet Country." *Osgoode Hall Law Journal* 4 (1966): 259-360.

Corry, J.A. *Law and Policy*. Toronto: Clark, Irwin, 1962.

Coyne, Deborah. "Commentary." Smith et al. 139-145.

Dawson, Mary. "The Impact of the Charter on the Public Policy Process and the Department of Justice." Monahan and Finkelstein 51-60.

de Tocqueville, Alexis. *Democarcy in America*. Trans. George Lawrence. Ed. J.P. Mayer. Garden City, NY: Anchor, 1969.

de Waal, Frans. *Good Natured: The Origins of Right and Wrong in Humans and Other Animals*. Cambridge, MA: Harvard University Press, 1996.

Devins, Reva. "A Perspective From the Ontario Human Rights Commission." Monahan and Finkelstein 145-54.

Dickens, Bernard M. "A Canadian Development: Non-Party Intervention." *Modern Law Review* 40 (1977): 666-76.

Dickson, Brian. "The Public Responsibilities of Lawyers." *Manitoba Law Journal* 13 (1983): 175-88.

Dworkin, Ronald. *Taking Rights Seriously*. Cambridge, MA: Harvard University Press, 1977.

Edelman, Martin. *Courts, Politics and Culture in Israel*. Charlottesville, VA: University Press of Virginia, 1994.

Edsall, Thomas and Mary Edsall. *Chain Reaction: The Impact of Race, Rights and Taxes on American Politics*. Toronto: Norton, 1992. Reprinted from *The Lanahan Readings in the American Polity*. Ed. Ann G. Serow and Everett C. Ladd. Baltimore: Lanahan Publishing, 1997.

Elliot, Ward. *The Rise of Guardian Democracy: The Supreme Court's Role in Voting Rights Disputes, 1845-1969*. Cambridge, MA: Harvard University Press, 1974.

Epp, Charles R. "Do Bills of Rights Matter? The Canadian Charter of Rights and Freedoms." *American Political Science Review* 90.4 (Dec. 1996): 765-79.

——. *The Rights Revolution: Lawyers, Activists, and Supreme Courts in Comparative Perspective*. Chicago: University of Chicago Press, 1998.

Fekete, John. *Moral Panick: Biopolitics Rising*. Montreal: Robert Davies Publishing, 1994.

Fisher, Louis. *Constitutional Dialogues: Interpretation as a Political Process*. Princeton: Princeton University Press, 1988.

Flanagan, Thomas E. "The Staying Power of the Status Quo: Collective Choice After Morgentaler." *Canadian Journal of Political Science* 30 (1997): 31-53.

——. Rev. of *Equality Rights and the Canadian Charter of Rights and Freedoms*, edited by Anne F. Bayefsky and Mary Eberts. *Canadian Journal of Law and Society* 1 (1986): 174-76.

Fletcher, Joseph and Paul Howe. "Canadian Attitudes Toward the Charter and the Court:
Results of a Recent IRPP Survey in a Comparative Perspective." Annual Meeting of the
Canadian Political Science Association, Université de Sherbrooke, 8 June 1999.

Freeman, Jody. "Defining Family In Mossop v. DSS: The Challenge of Anti-Essentialism and
Interactive Discrimination for Human Rights Legislation." *University of Toronto Law Journal* 44
(1994).

Frideres, James S. *Native Peoples in Canada: Contemporary Conflicts.* 4th ed. Scarborough: Prentice
Hall Canada, 1993.

Gibson, Dale. "The Charter of Rights and the Private Sector." *Manitoba Law Journal* 12 (1982).

——. "Distinguishing the Governors form the Governed: The Meaning of 'Government'
Under Section 32(1) of the Charter." *Manitoba Law Journal* 13:4 (1983): 505-22.

——. "Judges as Legislators: Not Whether But How." *Alberta Law Review* 25 (1987): 214-63.

Glazer, Nathan. "Towards an Imperial Judiciary." *The Public Interest* 41 (1975): 104-23.

Glendon, Mary Ann. *Abortion and Divorce in Western Law.* Cambridge, MA: Harvard University
Press, 1987.

——. *A Nation Under Lawyers: The Legal Profession and the Democratic Experiment.* New York: Farrar,
Straus and Giroux, 1994.

——. *Rights Talk: The Impoverishment of Political Discourse.* New York: Free Press, 1991.

Gold, Marc. "The Mask of Objectivity: Politics and Rhetoric in the Supreme Court of
Canada." *Supreme Court Law Review* 7 (1985): 457-510.

Goldwin, Robert A. "Congressman Madison Proposes Amendments to the Constitution."
The Framers and Fundamental Rights. Ed. Robert A. Licht. Washington, DC: AEI Press, 1993.

Goldwin, Robert A. and William A. Schambra, ed. *How Does the Constitution Secure Rights?* Washington, DC: American Enterprise Institute, 1985.

Greene, Ian, Carl Baar, Peter McCormick, and George Szablowski. *Final Appeal: Decision Making
in Canadian Courts of Appeal.* Halifax: J. Lorimer, 1997.

Greener, David Raymond. "Deconstructing Family: A Case Study of Legal Advocacy Scholarship." M.A. thesis, University of Calgary, 1997.

Hamilton, Alexander, James Madison, and John Jay. *The Federalist Papers.* Ed. Clinton Rossiter.
New York: New American Library, 1961.

Harvie, R. and Hamar Foster. "Different Drummers, Different Drums: The Supreme Court
of Canada, American Jurisprudence and the Continuing Revision of Criminal Law under
the Charter." *Ottawa Law Review* 24 (1992): 39-115.

——. "Ties that Bind? The Supreme Court of Canada, American Jurisprudence, and the Revision of Canadian Criminal Law under the Charter." *Osgoode Hall Law Journal* 28 (1990): 730-88.

Hausseger, Lori. "The Effectiveness of Interest Group Litigation: An Assessment of LEAF's Participation in Supreme Court Cases." M.A. thesis, University of Calgary, 1994.

Hein, Gregory. "Interest Group Litigation in Canada, 1988-1998." *Choices* (forthcoming).

—. "Post-Materialists in Court: The Consequence of Value Change and the Power of Institutions." Annual Conference of the Canadian Political Science Association, Université de Sherbrooke and Bishop's University, June 1999.

—. "Social Movements and the Expansion of Judicial Power: Feminists and Environmentalists in Canada from 1970 to 1995." Ph.D. thesis, University of Toronto, 1997.

Hennigar, Matthew. "Litigating Pan-Canadianism: The Constitutional Litigation Strategy of the Canadian Federal Government in Charter Cases, 1982-1993." M.A. thesis, University of Calgary, 1996.

Herman, Didi. "Are We Family? Lesbian Rights and Women's Liberation." *Osgoode Hall Law Journal* 28:4 (Winter 1990).

—. "The Good, the Bad and the Smugly: Sexual Orientation and Perspectives on the Charter." *Charting the Consequences: The Impact of the Charter of Rights on Canadian Law and Politics.* Ed. David Schneiderman and Kate Sutherland. Toronto: University of Toronto Press, 1997. 200-17.

Hernstein, Richard J. and Charles Murray. *The Bell Curve: Intelligence and Class Structure in American Life.* New York: The Free Press, 1994.

Ho, Shawn W. "The Macro- and Micro- Constitutional Strategies of Provincial Governments in Charter Politics: A Study of Alberta, Saskatchewan and Ontario, 1982-1992." M.A. thesis, University of Calgary, 1995.

Hofnung, Menachem. "The Unintended Consequences of Unplanned Constitutional Reform: Constitutional Politics in Israel." *American Journal of Comparative Law* 44 (1996): 585-604.

Hogg, Peter. *Canada Act 1982 Annotated.* Toronto: Carswell, 1982.

—. "A Comparison of the Canadian Charter of Rights and Freedoms with the Canadian Bill of Rights," Tarnopolsky and Beaudoin 2-22.

Hogg, Peter and Allison A. Bushell. "The Charter Dialogue Between Courts and Legislatures." *Osgoode Hall Law Journal* 35:1 (1997): 75-105.

—. "The Charter Dialogue Between Courts and Legislatures." *Policy Options* 20:3 (1999): 19-23.

Horowitz, Donald L. *The Courts and Social Policy.* Washington, DC: Brookings Institution, 1977.

Hutchinson, Allan C. *Waiting for Coraf: A Critique of Law and Rights.* Toronto: University of Toronto Press, 1995.

Inglehart, Ronald. *Culture Shift in Advanced Industrial Nations.* Princeton, NJ: Princeton University Press, 1990.

Kelly, James. "Charter Activism and Canadian Federalism: Rebalancing Liberal Constitutionalism in Canada, 1982 to 1997." Ph.D. thesis, McGill University, 1998.

Kennedy, Leslie and Donald Dutton. "The Incidence of Wife Assault in Alberta." *Canadian Journal of Behavioural Science* 21:1 (1989): 40-54.

Kerlow, Eleanor. *Poisoned Ivy: How Egos, Ideology, and Power Politics Almost Ruined Harvard Law School.* New York: St Martin's Press, 1994.

Keren, Michael. *Professionals Against Populism: The Peres Government and Democracy.* New York: State University of New York Press, 1995.

Key, V.O. *Politics, Parties and Pressure Groups.* New York: Thomas Y. Crowell, 1958.

Knopff, Rainer. "Courts Don't Make Good Compromises." *Policy Options* (April 1999): 31-34.

——. "Populism and the Politics of Rights: The Dual Attack on Representative Democracy." *Canadian Journal of Political Science* 31:4, (1998): 683-706.

——. "Rights, Power-Knowledge, and Social Technology." *George Grant and the Future of Canada.* Ed. Yusuf K. Umar. Calgary: University of Calgary Press, 1992.

——. "What Do Equality Rights Protect Canadians Against?" *Canadian Journal of Political Science* 20:2 (1987): 265-86.

Knopff, Rainer (with Thomas Flanagan). *Human Rights and Social Technology: The New War on Discrimination.* Ottawa: Carleton University Press, 1989.

Knopff, Rainer and F.L. Morton. *Charter Politics.* Toronto: Nelson Canada, 1992.

——. "Nation-Building and the Canadian Charter of Rights and Freedoms." Report of the Royal Commission on the Economic Union and Development Prospects for Canada 1985. Vol. 33, *Constitutionalism, Citizenship and Society in Canada.* Ed. Alan Cairns and Cynthia Williams.Toronto: University of Toronto Press, 1985. 133-182.

Kome, Penney. *The Taking of the Twenty-Eight: Women Challenge the Constitution.* Toronto: The Women's Press, 1983.

Kommers, Donald. "The Federal Constitutional Court in the German Political System." *Comparative Political Studies* 26:4 (1994): 470-91.

Kwong, Marilyn, Him Bartholomew, and Donald G. Dutton, "Gender Differences in Patterns of Relationship Violence in Alberta." *Canadian Journal of Behavioural Science* 31:3 (1999): 150-60.

LaForest, Guy. *Trudeau and the End of a Canadian Dream.* Montreal/Kingston: McGill-Queen's University Press, 1995.

Lasch, Christopher. *The Revolt of the Elites and the Betrayal of Democracy.* New York: W.W. Norton, 1995.

Laskin, Bora. "The Supreme Court of Canada: A Final Court of and for Canadians." *Canadian Bar Review* 29 (1951): 1038-79.

——. "An Inquiry into the Diefenbaker Bill of Rights." *Canadian Bar Review* 37 (1959).

Law Reform Commission of Canada. *Twentieth Annual Report.* Ottawa: Supply and Services, 1991.

Lazarus, Edward. *Closed Chambers: The First Eyewitness Account of the Epic Struggles Inside the Supreme Court.* Time Books, 1998.

Legal Liaison and Support Study. Test Case Funding Program. Prepared for the Department of Indian
Affairs and Northern Development by E.L. Oscapella and Associates Consulting Ltd.,
November 1998.

Leishman, Rory. "Robed dictators: a coup from the courtroom has usurped our democracy." *Next City* (Fall 1998): 34-41.

Licht, Robert A., ed. *Is the Supreme Court the Guardian of the Constitution?* Washington, DC: AEI Press,
1993.

Lipset, Seymour Martin. "The Industrial Proletariat and the Intelligentsia in a Comparative
Perspective." *Consensus and Conflict.* New Brunswick: Transaction Books, 1985.

Long, Brenda Ann. "Judicial Reform of the Criminal Law Under the Charter of Rights and
Freedoms." M.A. thesis, University of Calgary, 1996.

Lowi, Theodore J. and Benjamin Ginsberg. *American Government: Freedom and Power.* 3rd ed. New
York: W.W. Norton, 1994.

MacDonald, Alex. *Outrage: Canda's Justice System on Trial.* Vancouver: Raincoast Books, 1999.

MacKay, Wayne. "Fairness after the Charter: A Rose by Any Other Name." *Queen's Law Journal*
10 (1985): 263-335.

MacPherson, James C. "Working with the Dickson Court." *Manitoba Law Journal* 20 (1991).

Madison, James. "Letter to Thomas Jefferson, October 17, 1788." *The Forging of American Federalism:
Selected Writings of James Madison.* Ed. Saul K. Padover. New York: Harper & Row, 1965.

Malleson, Kate. "A British Bill of Rights: Incorporating the European Convention on Human
Rights." *Choices* 5:1 (1999): 21-36.

Mallory, J.R. "The Courts and the Sovereignty of the Canadian Parliament." *Canadian Journal of
Economics and Political Science* 10 (1944): 165-78.

——. *Social Credit and the Federal Power in Canada.* Toronto: University of Toronto Press, 1954.

——. *The Timlin Lecture,* University of Saskatchewan, 1984.

Mandel, Michael. *The Charter of Rights and the Legalization of Politics in Canada.* Rev. ed. Toronto:
Thompson Educational Publishing, 1994.

Manfredi, Christopher P. *Judicial Power and the Charter: Canada and the Paradox of Liberal Constitutionalism.* Toronto: McClelland and Stewart Inc., 1993.

——. "Constitutional Rights and Interest Advocacy: Litigating Educational Reform in Canada
and the United States." *Equity and Community: The Charter, Interest Advocacy and Representation.* Ed.
F. Leslie Seidle. Montreal: Institute for Research on Public Policy, 1993. 91-117.

——. "Institutional Design and the Politics of Constitutional Modification: Understanding
Amendment Failure in the United States and Canada." *Law and Society Review* 31:1 (1997): 111-
36.

——. "The Use of United States Decisions by the Supreme Court of Canada Under the Charter of Rights and Freedoms." *Canadian Journal of Political Science* 23 (1990): 499-518.

Marshall, T. David, *Judicial Conduct and Accountability,* Scarborough: Carswell, 1995.

Martin, Robert. "Reconstituting Democracy: Orthodoxy and Research in Law and Social Science." Peacock 249-70.

Martin, Sheilah and Kathleen Mahoney, eds. *Equality and Judicial Neutrality*. Scarborough: Carswell, 1987.

McCartney, Patrick A. "Government Sponsorship of Voluntary Associations in Canada: Research and Reflections." Annual Meeting of the Canadian Political Science Association, Kingston, Ontario, 1991.

McCloskey, Robert G. *The American Supreme Court*. 2nd ed. Rev. Sanford Levinson. Chicago: University of Chicago Press, 1994.

McNaught, Kenneth, "Political Trials and the Canadian Political Tradition." *Courts and Trials: A Multidisciplinary Approach*. Ed. M.L. Freidland. Toronto: University of Toronto Press, 1975. 137-61.

McRoberts, Kenneth. *Misconceiving Canada: The Struggle for National Unity*. Don Mills, ON: Oxford University Press, 1997.

McRoberts, Kenneth, ed. *Beyond Quebec: Taking Stock of Canada*. Montreal/Kingston: McGill-Queen's University Press, 1995.

McRoberts, Kenneth and Patrick Monahan, eds. *The Charlottetown Accord, the Referendum, and the Future of Canada*. Toronto: University of Toronto Press, 1993.

Miljan, Lydia and Barry Cooper. "Courts and the Media: Providing a Climate for Social Change." Annual Meeting of the Canadian Political Science Association, St. John's Nfld., June 8-10, 1997.

Mill, John Stuart. *On Liberty*. Ed. Currin V. Shields. Indianapolis, IN: Bobbs-Merrill, 1956.

Monahan, Patrick J. "Constitutional Cases, 1991-1998." Professional Development Programme, "1998 Constitutional Cases: An Analysis of the 1998 Constitutional Decisions of the Supreme Court of Canada," Toronto, 16 April 1999.

——. *Politics and the Constitution: The Charter, Federalism and the Supreme Court of Canada*. Toronto: Carswell/Methuen, 1987.

Monahan, Patrick and Marie Finkelstein. "The Charter of Rights and Public Policy in Canada," Monahan and Finkelstein 1-48.

—— . Ed. *The Impact of the Charter on the Public Policy Process*. Toronto: Centre for Public Law and Public Policy, York University, 1993.

Morton, F.L. "The Charter in the Rest of Canada," McRoberts 93-114.

——. *Morgentaler v. Borowski: Abortion, The Charter and The Courts*. Toronto: McClelland and Stewart, 1992.

——. "Dialogue or Monologue?" *Policy Options* 20:3 (April 1999): 23-26.

Morton, F.L. and Rainer Knopff, Ed. "Permanence and Change in a Written Constitution: The 'Living Tree' Doctrine and the Charter of Rights." *Supreme Court Law Review*, 2nd series, 1 (1990): 533-546.

Morton, F.L., Peter H. Russell, and Troy Riddell. "The Canadian Charter of Rights and Freedoms: A Descriptive Analysis of the First Decade, 1982-1992." *National Journal of Constitutional
Law* 5 (1994): 1-60.

Nevitte, Neil. *The Decline of Deference*. Peterborough, ON: Broadview Press, 1996.

O'Connor, Karen. *Women's Organizations' Use of the Courts*. Toronto: Lexington Books, 1980.

O'Connor, Karen and Lee Epstein, "Amicus Curiae Participation in U.S. Supreme Court Litigation: An Appraisal of Hakman's 'Folklore'." *Law and Society Review* 16 (1981-82): 311-18.

Olson, Mancur. *The Logic of Collective Action: Public Goods and the Theory of Groups*. Cambridge, MA:
Harvard University Press, 1965.

Owram, Doug. *The Government Generation: Canadian Intellectuals and the State, 1900-1945*. Toronto: University of Toronto Press, 1986.

Paciocco, David M. "The Judicial Repeal of s.24(2) and the Development of the Canadian
Exclusionary Rule." *The Criminal Law Quarterly* 32 (1989-90): 326-65.

Pal, Leslie A. *Interests of State: The Politics of Language, Multiculturalism and Feminism in Canada*. Mon-
treal/Kingston: McGill-Queen's Press, 1993.

Pangle, Thomas L. *The Spirit of Modern Republicanism: The Moral Vision of the American Founders and the
Philosophy of Locke*. Chicago: University of Chicago Press, 1988.

Paltiel, Khayyam Z. "The Changing Environment and Role of Special Interest Groups." *Canadian Public Administration* 25:2 (1982): 198-210.

Peacock, Anthony A. "Strange Brew: Tocqueville, Rights and the Technology of Equality."
Peacock 122-60.

—. Ed., *Rethinking the Constitution: Perspectives on Canadian Constitutional Reform, Interpretation and Theory*.
Toronto: Oxford University Press, 1996.

Peltason, Jack W. *Federal Courts in the Judicial Process*. New York: Doubleday, 1995.

Pothier, Dianne. "The Sounds of Silence: Charter Application when the Legislature Declines
to Speak." *Constitutional Forum* 7:4 (1996): 514.

Radwanski, George. *Trudeau*. Toronto: Macmillan, 1978.

Razack, Sharene, *Canadian Feminism and the Law: The Women's Legal Education and Action Fund and the
Pursuit of Equality*. Toronto: Second Story Press, 1991.

Riddell, Troy, "The Development of Section 1 of the Charter of Rights: A Study in Constitutional Politics." M.A. thesis, University of Calgary, 1994.

Riddell, Troy and F.L. Morton. "Competition for Constitutional Advantage: Reasonable
Limits, Distinct Society and the Canada Clause." *Canadian Journal of Political Science* 31:3
(September 1998): 467-93.

Romanow, Roy, John Whyte, and Howard Leeson. *Canada Notwithstanding: The Making of the Constitution 1976-1982*. Toronto: Carswell/Methuen, 1984.

Russell, Peter H. "Canada's Charter of Rights and Freedoms: A Political Report." *Public Law*
(Autumn 1988), 385-401.

——. "Canadian Constraints on Judicialization from Without." *International Political Science Review* 15:2 (1994): 165-75.

——. *Constitutional Odyssey.* 2nd ed. Toronto: University of Toronto Press, 1993.

——. "A Democratic Approach to Civil Liberties." *University of Toronto Law Journal* 19 (1969): 109-31.

——. "The Effect of a Charter or Rights on the Policy-Making Role of Canadian Courts." *Canadian Public Administration* 25 (1982): 1-33.

——. "The Political Purposes of the Canadian Charter of Rights and Freedoms," *Canadian Bar Review* 61 (1983): 30-54.

——. "The Political Purposes of the Charter: Have They Been Fulfilled? An Agnostic's Report Card." Bryden et al. 33-44.

——. "Reform's Judicial Agenda." *Policy Options* (April 1999): 12-15.

——. "The Supreme Court and Federal-Provincial Relations: The Political Use of Legal Resources." *Canadian Public Policy* (1985): 161-70.

——. "The Supreme Court's Interpretation of the Constitution." *Politics Canada.* 5th ed. Ed. Paul W. Fox. Toronto: McGraw-Hill Ryerson Limited, 1992.

Russell, Peter H., Rainer Knopff and Ted Morton. *Federalism and the Charter: Leading Constitutional Decision, A New Edition.* Ottawa: Carleton University Press, 1989.

Sanders, Douglas E. "The Indian Lobby." Banting and Simeon 301-32.

Savoie, Donald. *Governing From the Centre: The Concentration of Power in Canadian Politics.* Toronto: University of Toronto Press, 1999.

Schneiderman, David and Kate Sutherland, eds. *Charting the Consequences: The Impact of the Charter of Rights on Canadian Law and Politics.* Toronto: University of Toronto Press, 1997.

Schlesinger, Jr., Arthur M. *The Imperial Presidency.* Toronto: Popular Library, 1974.

Scigliano, Robert. *The Supreme Court and the Presidency.* New York: Free Press, 1971.

Scott, Ian. "Law, Policy and the Role of the Attorney General: Constancy and Change in the 1980s." *University of Toronto Law Journal* 39 (1989): 109-26.

Sellars, Charles. *The Market Revolution: Jacksonian America, 1815-1846.* New York: Oxford University Press, 1991.

Shapiro, Martin. "Juridicalization of Politics in the United States." *International Political Science Review* 15:2 (1994): 101-12.

——. "Public Law and Judicial Politics." *The State of the Discipline II.* Ed. A.W. Finifter. Washington, DC: APSA, 1993. 365-81.

Shugar, Jody Ann. "Judicial Discretion and the Charter: A Qualitative and Quantitative Examination of the Exclusionary Rule." M.A. thesis, McGill University, Montreal, 1995.

Silverstein, Mark. *Judicious Choices: The New Politics of Supreme Court Confirmations.* New York: W.W. Norton and Co., 1994.

Smiley, Donald. "The Case Against the Canadian Charter of Human Rights." *Canadian Journal of Political Science* 2 (1969): 277-91.

Smith, David E., Peter MacKinnon, and John C. Courtney, eds. *After Meech Lake: Lessons for the Future*. Saskatoon, SK: Fifth House Publishers, 1991.

Smith, Jennifer. "The Origins of Judicial Review in Canada." *Canadian Journal of Political Science* 16 (1983): 115-34.

Sniderman, Paul M., Joseph F. Fletcher, Peter H. Russell, and Philip E. Tetlock. *The Clash of Rights: Liberty, Equality and Legitimacy in Pluralist Democracy*. New Haven, CT: Yale University Press, 1996.

Sommers, Christina Hoff. *Who Stole Feminism: How Women Have Betrayed Women*. New York: Simon & Schuster, 1994.

Sossin, Lorne. "The Sounds of Silence: Law Clerks, Policy Making and the Supreme Court of Canada. *U.B.C. Law Review* 30:2 (1996): 279-308.

Sowell, Thomas. *A Conflict of Visions: Ideological Origins of Political Struggles*. New York: Morrow & Co., 1987.

———. *Preferential Policies: An International Perspective*. New York: William Morrow & Co., 1990.

Stager, David A. and Harry W. Arthurs. *Lawyers in Canada*. Toronto: University of Toronto Press, 1990.

Stone, Alec. *The Birth of Judicial Politics in France*. Oxford: Oxford University Press, 1992.

———. Rev. of *The Constitutional Jurisprudence of the Federal Republic of Germany* by Donald P. Kommers and *La politique saisie par le droit* by Louis Favoreau. *Comparative Political Studies* (October 1990): 413.

Storing, Herbert. "The Constitution and the Bill of Rights." Goldwin and Schambra, 15-36.

Strossen, Nadine. *Defending Pornography: Free Speech, Sex, and the Fight for Women's Rights*. Toronto: Scribner, 1995.

Schneiderman, David and Kate Sutherland, eds. *Charting the Consequences: The Impact of the Charter of Rights on Canadian Law and Politics*. Toronto: University of Toronto Press, 1997.

Swan, Kenneth P. "Intervention and the Amicus Curiae Status in Charter Litigation." *Charter Litigation*. Ed. Robert Sharpe. Toronto: Butterworths, 1986. 27-44.

Taras, David, "Television and Public Policy: The CBC's Coverage of the Meech Lake Accord." *Canadian Public Policy* 15:3 (1989): 322.

Tarnopolsky, Walter S. *The Canadian Bill of Rights*. 2nd ed. Toronto: McClelland and Stewart, 1975.

———. "The Charter and the Supreme Court of Canada." *The Charter Ten Years Later*. Ed. Gerald A. Beaudoin. Les Editions Yvon Blais, Inc., 1992: 63-70.

———. *Discrimination and the Law in Canada*. Toronto: Richard De Boo, 1982.

Tarnopolsky, Walter S. and Gerald A. Beaudoin. *The Canadian Charter of Rights and Freedoms: Commentary*. Toronto: Carswell, 1982.

Tatalovich, Raymond. *Abortion in the United States and Canada: A Comparative Study*. Armonk, NY: M.E. Sharpe, 1997.

Tribe, Laurence. *American Constitutional Law*. 2nd ed. Mineola, NY: Foundation Press, 1988.

Trudeau, Pierre. *Federalism and the French Canadians*. Toronto: Macmillan, 1968.

Tully, James. "Diversity's Gambit Declined." *Constitutional Predicament: Canada After the Referendum of 1992.* Ed. Curtis Cook. Montreal/Kingston: McGill-Queen's University Press, 1994. 149-98.

Turpel, Mary Ellen. "Aboriginal Peoples' Struggle for Fundamental Political Change." McRoberts and Monahan.

Tushnet, J. Mark. "Critical Legal Studies: A Political History." 100 *Yale Law Review* 115 (1991).

Uhr, John. *Deliberative Democracy in Australia: The Changing Place of Parliament.* Cambridge: Cambridge University Press, 1998.

Vengroff, Richard, and F.L. Morton. "Regional Perspectives on Canada's Charter of Rights: A Reexamination of Democratic Elitism." *Canadian Journal of Political Science* (forthcoming).

Walker, Jack L. "Interest Groups, Iron Triangles, and Representative Institutions in American National Government." *British Journal of Political Science* 14 (1984): 161-85.

——. *Mobilizing Interest Groups in America: Patrons, Professions and Social Movements.* Ann Arbor: University of Michigan Press, 1991.

——. "The Origins and Maintenance of Interest Groups in America." *American Political Science Review* 77:2 (1983): 390-406.

Walker, Lenore. *The Battered Woman.* New York: Harper Collins, 1979.

——. "Psychology and Violence Against Women." *American Psychologist* (April 1989).

Wasby, Stephen. *Race Relations Litigation in an Age of Complexity.* Charlottesville, VA: University Press of Virginia, 1995.

Watson, Bradley C.S. "The Language of Rights and the Crisis of the Liberal Imagination." Peacock 88-91.

Weiler, Paul. *In the Last Resort: A Critical Study of the Supreme Court of Canada.* Toronto: Carswell/Methuen, 1974.

Weinrib, Lorraine. "The Activist Constitution." *Policy Options* (April 1999): 27-30.

Weiss, Michael and Cathy Young, "Feminist Jurisprudence or Neo-Paternalism?" Cato Policy Analysis No. 256 (June 19, 1996).

Welch, J. "No Room at the Top: Interest Group Intervenors and Charter Litigation in the Supreme Court of Canada." *University of Toronto Law Journal* 43 (1985): 204-31.

West, James V. "Public Interest Groups and the Judicial Process in Canada: The Need for a More Realistic Jurisprudence." *Occasional Paper No. 5.* Ottawa: Carleton University: Department of Political Studies, 1979.

Wilson, Bertha. "We Didn't Volunteer." *Policy Options* (April 1999): 8-11.

Wilson, James Q. *The Moral Sense.* Toronto: Macmillan, 1993.

Wolfe, Christopher. *The Rise of Modern Judicial Review: From Constitutional Interpretation to Judge-Made Law.* New York: Basic Books, 1986.

Women's Legal Education and Action Fund. *Equality and the Charter: Ten Years of Feminist Advocacy Before the Supreme Court of Canada.* Toronto: Edmond Montgomery, 1996.

Zemans, Frederick, "Legal Aid and Advice in Canada" *Osgoode Hall Law Journal* 16 (1978): 663-93.

Ziegel, Jacob. "Merit Selection and Democratization of Appointments to the Supreme Court." *Choices* 5:2 (1999).

INDEX